GET LAID
OR
DIE TRYING

GET LAID
OR
DIE TRYING

THE FIELD REPORTS

JEFF ALLEN
REAL SOCIAL DYNAMICS

GALLERY BOOKS

NEW YORK   LONDON   TORONTO   SYDNEY

G

Gallery Books
A Division of Simon & Schuster, Inc.
1230 Avenue of the Americas
New York, NY 10020

First Gallery Books hardcover edition March 2011

GALLERY BOOKS and colophon are trademarks of Simon & Schuster, Inc.

For information about special discounts for bulk purchases, please contact Simon & Schuster Special Sales at 1-866-506-1949 or business@simonandschuster.com

The Simon & Schuster Speakers Bureau can bring authors to your live event. For more information or to book an event contact the Simon & Schuster Speakers Bureau at 1-866-248-3049 or visit our website at www.simonspeakers.com.

Designed by Davina Mock-Maniscalco

Manufactured in the United States of America

1   2   3   4   5   6   7   8   9   10

Library of Congress Cataloging-in-Publication Data

Allen, Jeff
Get laid or die trying / Jeff Allen.
p.   cm.
1. Allen, Jeff, 1976–   2. Single men—Sexual behavior—United States—Biography.   3. Man-woman relationships—United States.   I. Title.
HQ28.A45A3 2011
306.81'52092—dc22
[B]   2010046739

ISBN 978-1-4516-2090-0
ISBN 978-1-4516-2091-7 (ebook)

In writing this book, I have stayed as close to the truth as I remember it. Most of the "field reports" were written within a day of the actual events and only edited later for errors and readability. Names of most principal players have been changed. I had literally thousands of interactions with people during the time frame of the story; I have obviously omitted many, and condensed some. No doubt my memory has occasionally simplified the line between cause and effect. I am confident, however, that my memory has not distorted the essential truths.

for my family

"But for some players, luck itself is an art."

—MARTIN SCORSESE, *THE COLOR OF MONEY*

FOREWORD

What you're holding in your hands is a detailed and highly instructional manifesto on how a dude from Northern California went from being a lonely, angst-ridden maniac to screwing the shit out of nearly two hundred women. Is Jeffy the coolest guy ever—one of the iciest, most badass motherfuckers that ever did it? Or is he an immature self-pitying idiot, who indulges in a half decade sex rampage at the expense of all other areas of his life? The truths of life are rarely as black-and-white as most people wish them to be.

Being that this book records a period before 2009, some of the external pickup techniques would be considered old-school compared to what's out there today. The ideas in the pickup community are constantly evolving, and so it's obvious that the methods popular six or seven years ago have been updated and improved (for example, he uses scripted routines, whereas these days Real Social Dynamics, or RSD, recommends starting conversations by saying "Hi . . ." with confidence and physical leading).

You're about to read a story, a graphic account and manifesto, by one of the most lethally effective players to ever "pick up a chick" (yeah, I just said that). A dude who at times is so good at what he does it's scary, and not in any figurative sense of the word. It's going to teach you how to walk like a pimp and talk like a mack, rock the karaoke mic like a belligerent Japanese tourist, kick ass like Van Damme and take names like a two-dollar MySpace whore—and after it's all said and done, maybe even to find what you're looking for.

Interpret it, judge it, label it however you want. Just don't deny that Jeffy spits wisdom and his own truth in these pages, because you'll miss what's being offered to you.

Owen "Tyler Durden" Cook
Real Social Dynamics
November 2010

XMAS EVE 2000 A.D.

Tonight, while shopping for vermouth, I was punched in the face by a homeless person selling *Street Sheets* on the southwest corner of Fourth and Mission in downtown San Francisco.

I walked out of the Jack in the Box already drunk, singing "Winter Wonderland" à la Elvis Presley, slurring the words only somewhat intentionally.

Standing at the corner waiting for the light to change, I belched, loudly and unapologetically. The bum, standing in my immediate vicinity, took umbrage. Towering next to me, he barked, "Ey mayeng . . . don' be belchin' in mah face like dat!"

"Shut the fuck up, bitch." My unthinking and immediate response. *WHAM.*

When he hit me, I was actually surprised. I laughed and mocked him as I went for my brass knuckles. "You think a homeless BITCH can hurt me?!"

Truth is, I was stunned. My arms loaded with paper bags, bottles clinking, he'd just sucker-punched me, a straight jab to the mouth. My pockets were stuffed with jalapeno poppers; I didn't have that instant access to my weapon, and he saw me going for it.

"Pull dat shit out and see what happen," he crowed, agitated as fuck now. Walking off quickly as a crowd began to form, he darted into the alley, joining the indistinct figures of other homeless milling about in the shadows.

I'm shaken up. I duck into a nearby restaurant and enter the bathroom. Looking in the mirror, I discover a large bruise already forming on my mouth. Trembling, vacillating between rage and tears, I reach up and gingerly touch the spot.

It isn't a bruise. It's just dirt from his grimy-ass hand. I wipe it off.

I place my palms facedown on the counter and hang my head with a sigh. Diana, my girlfriend of four years, is leaving me, moving to Los Angeles in ten days, ostensibly to pursue her "music career."

Merry Fucking Christmas.

DEMO TAPE

Someone is sleeping next to me, and I struggle to determine who it is. It appears to be an unattractive woman with an extraordinarily bad haircut. I'm not sure, but I think it's my sister's friend. I vaguely remember having sex with her at some point. Her mouth is open, and she's snoring loudly. I need to get the fuck out of here as quickly as possible.

I manage to stand and begin to look for my clothing. I find my tracksuit on the floor next to the bed. It is covered in chunky vomit, the source of the stench. Flashes of dinner at the sushi bar. I don't want to wear these clothes, but it looks like I have no choice. I shake the chunks off and pull on the pants, slip into my shoes and tiptoe out of the apartment.

I find my car and drive back to my mother's house. I enter the house as quietly as possible and strip off the putrid tracksuit. I'm in the garage throwing it into the washing machine when my sister walks in, in her pajamas. It takes her a second to realize what I am doing, and why, and then she starts laughing. "Hahahaha what the fuck, dude?! You nasty."

"Yes, I banged your friend and puked on my tracksuit. In fact I may have puked on your friend while wearing the tracksuit and banging her. I'm not sure." I close the lid and start the wash cycle.

"Duuuuuude. You were fucked up last night, bro."

"No shit. What happened?"

"We went out to dinner and then we went to the bar. Some ex-girlfriend of yours came down from L.A. to see you. You met her out in the parking lot and sat in her car for like an hour and then she left, and you started crying and rolling around on the ground out front of the bar. They were gonna call the cops, dude. We went back to Gretchen's house, and, uh . . . you stayed there."

Ugh. It's coming back to me now. I was already wasted by the time Diana got there. In her car, I basically begged her to come back, proclaiming my love for her, etc. She just sort of brushed it off. She didn't even reject me . . . she just ignored me. The last thing I remember is sitting in the passenger seat and crying while she made me listen to her "demo tape." Then she was gone. Again.

Bridget breaks the silence. "So what's up with this trip? Why'd you come down here?"

I snap, "What, you don't want me here?"

"Of course we want you here. But it would be nice if you came down more than once every eight years!" She looks sad. "I miss you, dude. Remember when we used to be tight? I just want my brother back."

I can't say anything in response. The truth is, I don't even know if the person she's talking about exists anymore.

What I do know is this: something has to change.

Before last night's debacle, I had slept with only two women in my lifetime. In both instances, I had given myself 100 percent to the relationship, heart and soul, expecting the same in return. Both times, that intensity was reciprocated for a while, but it did not last. It couldn't. Suddenly, it becomes clear that I've been trying to operate within a framework that's inherently flawed. Right here, in this freezing garage at seven o'clock in the morning, I arrive at a decision:

I am going to become a "player."

I chuckle to myself at how ridiculous it sounds. It's a concept that up until this very moment I would not have regarded as anything but a fantasy. A fictional lifestyle from a Too $hort rap. But the more I think about it, the more I warm to the idea. Divorce all emotion from my sexual relationships. Go on a hedonistic fuck-spree and rail a shit-ton of hot bitches; a sort of "salvation through sin." Abandon the ridiculous notion of true love and all of its attendant bullshit. I just don't care anymore. No more feelings. This is war: *Date. Fuck. Win.*

GRENADE PIN

I've begun fucking one of the neighbors. Her name is Helen, and she has a square ass. In any case, she is serving as a suitable rebound girl. I don't feel angry about what happened with Diana anymore, nor depressed. Just numb.

Helen is nice enough, and happens to live five doors down. We met after Jackass had dragged me along to check out their housewarming one night. Jackass is quite the ladies' man himself: a tall, clean-cut American kid with good looks, ripped abs, and a penchant for extreme sports. He's banging Helen's roommate. It's convenient for everyone involved.

We're holding Jackass's birthday party at the house tonight. The theme is "high school." A week ago, I came across a mint-condition Givenchy tuxedo at the Salvation Army that fit me near perfectly, and tonight I am wearing it with a red cashmere scarf and a lapel pin that reads "SEX" in rhinestones.

I clip on my bow tie and walk downstairs to get the party started. Not many people yet. I step through the back door into the yard, only to be confronted by ten girls. Giggling ensues. I am informed by one of the ladies that I have a "girl's ass." Later, Jackass throws me down the stairs in a drunken fit; I counter as he jumps down after me, grabbing him by the collar and dragging him down the remaining flight, shattering a framed *Star Wars* poster. Gathering myself up, I commandeer the entertainment center and force the women to watch pornography. Again.

Staggering around the place, bellowing, I notice a tall blonde eighteen-year-old dressed like Britney Spears in the living room. She's gyrating up on the coffee table, wearing a short plaid skirt and squealing with joy. Six feet of glory with big tits. Who invited this . . . creature? I feel something profound come alive inside of me.

Without thinking, I instantly leap upon the table and start dancing with her, throwing my scarf over her neck and sneering. "Do you read *Teen People*?" I ask. "I've got a real cool article about Britney upstairs."

Her name is Chippy. Upstairs in my bedroom, I dig out the magazine and throw it at her. As soon as she begins reading the article, I literally rip my pants off and jump on her. We make out. She sucks viciously at my nipple rings, partially tearing the left one out. I am too fucked up to care. Over the next couple days, it will swell up to roughly the size of a grape, taking on a nasty purple color. Right now, however, I continue to make out with her and just let it bleed.

As hot as all this is, we don't have sex. As it turns out, she's a good Catholic girl and a virgin. I have a good time, regardless. Finally, she goes to leave with her friends, and I corner her in the hallway.

"I want to take you to lunch," I drool. "I want to eat your lunch . . ." I'm giving her the most intense eye contact I can muster. This tall beauty before me is the most lovely creature on the planet. Helen, whom I haven't noticed standing a mere two feet to the left, glares. I fall down.

Lying there dazed, I black out, only to wake up the next day on the floor in Berkeley, without a clue as to how I got there.

LAKESIDE BLUES

Tonight, I'm out enjoying some fine cuisine with Chippy. I've been seeing her for a few months now. After an extended courtship consisting of several expensive dinner dates and culminating in a romantic trip to Lake Tahoe, we finally had sex.

I guess she's my de facto girlfriend now. I know I've made a critical error. I've set this up to be another long-term relationship, but I know that's the *last* thing I want right now. It's just a knee-jerk reaction to the situation. I need to keep my eye on the ball here.

Do I love her? Sure. Whatever.

Am I going to be monogamous? FUCK NO.

After dinner, we meet Jackass at the karaoke bar. Karaoke has become a hobby of sorts. I enjoy it because it allows me to drink heavily and scream at strangers. All the fun of being in a band, without the "practicing" or "carrying stuff." I also enjoy it because it allows me, for three minutes at a time, to pretend like I have emotions. I've consumed a lot of wine at dinner and on the way, I resolve to start in on the scotch and beer.

Chippy is denied entry to the bar, on account of the fact that she is underage. She goes home. I become enraged and obnoxious, guzzling scotch. I brutally butcher "The Greatest Love of All" by Whitney Houston, then rip through Christina Aguilera's "Genie in a Bottle" like a buzz saw, falling off the stage. Later, I crawl back up and steal the mic from Jackass. As the crowd tries to wave me off, I announce, "I'LL FIGHT ANY OF YOU OUTSIDE!"

I go for a smoke out front and crudely proposition a conventioneer. She asks me what school I went to.

"SFSU," I reply.

"What did you study?"

"Cunnilingus. Hey . . . where are you going? No, seriously, hey come back . . ."

I pace back and forth outside, yelling, "WHO WANTS TO FIGHT!!" as people leave. Nobody does.

A bar worker says, "Come inside young man." The place closes and one of the workers gives us a ride home.

Rather than sleep it off, I smash bottles out front then decide to break into the neighbor's house at 3 A.M. in order to inform her that I have a girlfriend. Not Helen's house, of course, as by this point, she is no longer speaking to me. I'm talking about the lovely Shannon Lake: a lumbering, asthmatic psychopath and prescription pill addict, roughly six foot four, a behemoth weighing in at three hundred fifty pounds. Each of her tits is larger than my head. She has pretty eyes. A typical night might find me crawling through an unlocked window into her living room, eating her food, drinking her liquor, and then entering her room while she is asleep, in order to hump her.

Yes. I have fucked her. Several times, in fact, and I may continue to do so. I'm usually coked up and the smell is vile. I want to experience the nastiest sex possible. One evening not long ago, I decided I would wear a rubber glove whilst making sweet love to her, but a search of her kitchen only turned up a pot holder, which was covered in glittery silver sequins. I returned to her room and started fucking with the sequined pot holder on my left hand, then flipped her over and went doggy. Right before nutting, I pulled out, grabbed a set of "rolls" on her upper back, and FUCKED THE FAT ROLL until I came. She didn't appear to notice.

So tonight, same deal. I go in through the back door, find some vodka in the freezer and drink it, then head up the stairs. She is asleep. I want to fuck anyway.

Door swings open, Jeffy standing there in silhouette.

"WAKE UP! I HAVE SOMETHING TO TELL YOU. I HAVE A GIRLFRIEND, BITCH!! What do you think of that, BITCH?!!"

"Uhh . . ." She looks up, squinting against the light. "I knew it . . ."

"TIME TA FUCK!!" As my clothes fly off I try to mount, drool on her tits, then roll over, off the bed, wasted, out.

THUG LIFE

A few months later, I walk in the door and see my roommate Noah sitting cross-legged in front of the television, engrossed in a video game. Without looking up, he casually announces, "Oh hey dude. Thugs came by to kick your ass. They said they'd be back." He continues mashing the buttons on his controller as I stand there blinking.

I know immediately who it had to have been. I cut it off with my gargantuan neighbor Shannon Lake a long time ago, but apparently she didn't get the memo. I've been ignoring her calls and hiding when she comes by the house. For the past few weeks, she's been threatening to have her brother fuck me up, "as soon as he gets out of jail." I've met him before; he's bigger than Shannon herself, and ghetto as fuck. Looks like he's been released. Fantastic. This is the last thing I need right now. I drop my briefcase and collapse onto the couch. I fall asleep within minutes.

I'm not sure how much time has passed when my phone rings, waking me up. I fish it out of my pocket and look at it. It's John, this dude I know that works as a bartender. I answer it. "Hey, man, what's up? What's going on?"

"Not much. Going out for some drinks with the little woman. You want to come along? Meet us at Annabelle's; we're headed out right now."

Fuck it, I don't have anything better to do, and given the fact that there is a posse of thugs looking for me, getting away tonight sounds like a good idea. "All right, dude, I'll meet you there. Gimme twenty minutes."

I roll into the bar and there's John, sitting at a table with his girlfriend Janie. Looks like they've had a few already. I'm going to have to catch up. I get the bartender's attention. "Hey, can I get a scotch and a beer?"

He looks at me, takes a breath and says, "What kind?"

"The shittiest kind you have. I deserve the worst."

He raises an eyebrow, then says, "All right," as he reaches under the bar and comes up with something labeled "MacGlennan." "How do you want it?"

"Neat." He pours a large glass of it, then he cracks a Bud Lite and shoves them both at me.

I hand him the money and immediately down the glass. It takes two swallows and tastes like paint thinner. I convulse for a second, then exhale sharply, slam the glass down and bring the beer to my lips. A warmth pools in my stomach and begins to spread, that wonderful pang of the first shot of the day being absorbed into the stomach lining. Here we go. I sit down with John and his girl.

Several hours pass and it's getting late. "Hey man, let's get out of here," suggests John.

"All right, where do you want to go?"

Janie pipes up. "John, we could all go back to our place and drink there . . ." She starts rubbing him on the arm.

John considers this for a second, then agrees. "Yeah, that sounds cool." He turns to me. "We've got some very rare tequila back at the house, man. You gotta try this stuff." Sounds good to me.

We walk over to their place. It's a dingy loft on the worst part of Market Street, sketchy as hell. We go up. I look at their book collection and we sit there, talking and doing shots of the tequila. I've just slammed my third when Janie starts pulling her skirt up. I ogle her shamelessly, drunk off my ass. She's not bad-looking. "Look at this," she says, "I was bitten by a brown recluse."

"HOLY SHIT!" I jump back as she reveals a large abscess on her leg. It looks like a fucking gunshot wound. I reach for the tequila and take another drink. "Don't ever show me that again."

She says, "Yeah, how do you think I feel?" There is an awkward moment where we're sort of just looking at each other and then she puts her hand on my arm for no apparent reason. While maintaining eye contact with me, she says, "John, let's break out that E we've been saving."

"Sure. Why not," says John as he gets up and takes a small box out of the cupboard. He opens it up and pulls out a handful of small pills. "Pure MDMA, man. This is some seriously good shit right here." He puts one in my hand. It is blue and has three diamonds on it. I swallow it without thinking.

Cut to an hour and a half later. I'm perched up in the loft looking down at the following scene: John is facing the window on his knees with his clothes off. Janie stands behind him with a cat o' nine tails, and she's flogging him. "YES MISTRESS!" he yells, with every blow. "YESSSS!" I'm vaguely amused by this. My eyes start wiggling. He was right, this is some good shit. I don't know what the fuck is going on and I'm not certain that I care. Hahahaha. Janie opens a trunk on the floor and brings out what appears to be some sort of cat toy, a thin plastic stick, and begins whipping his back with it. It whistles through the air; with every strike, it leaves a red line . . . it's actually *cutting* him. He remains on his knees, shaking and babbling as the assault continues.

Finally, she relents and stops the beating. She rubs him on the head and says, "Good boy . . . now go to your corner." He shuffles into the corner on his knees and remains there. She turns to me, tapping the cat toy in her hand. "Your turn," she coos.

I'm coherent enough to know that I do not want to end up like that guy. "AW HELLS NO," I say. "I'll tell you what, you can spank my ass a little, whatever, but keep that shit the fuck away from me."

"Okay, whatever you're comfortable with." I get the idea that she's done this before. She climbs up into the loft. I sort of get over her lap and she slaps at my ass for a little bit, then she asks, "So . . . do you want to fuck me?"

"Sure, I guess."

I take my clothes off and start fucking her in the missionary position, straight up. I'm pumping away, trying not to think about the spider bite on her leg, when all of a sudden John yells out from the corner, "Yeah Janie, show Jeff what a slut you are!" I can't believe I'm hearing this, but I continue to rail. Then he actually addresses me. "That's right, Jeff . . . FUCK MY GIRLFRIEND! FUCK HER!"

Okay, don't mind if I do, John!

I finish up and roll away, sweating profusely. I take a couple of minutes to recover. When I open my eyes and sit up, John is standing at the end of the bed, stroking his dick and grinning. Okay, now I'm officially disturbed. He says, "Hey, do you want me to suck your dick?"

"No." That's all I say as I get up and get my shit together. I start putting my shoes on. "Look man, it's been awesome, but I gotta go. I gotta do . . . something." I walk to the door.

Janie says, "You sure, sweetie? It's late, you don't have to go."

"Nah, it's fine, I gotta take care of this . . . thing. Thanks for everything guys." I exit and close the door behind me, walking quickly down the dingy corridor and jabbing at the elevator button. Thankfully, the doors open immediately and I get in and descend to the ground floor.

What the hell just happened? I got laid, okay. But all things considered, I'd almost rather have stayed home and gotten my ass kicked by thugs.

FUCKING & PUNCHING

Late spring: a Sunday around three o'clock in the morning. I'm just finishing up an intense shift at work. I've been covering for the night manager, who's on vacation. I unlock the door to my office, throw a stack of papers onto the desk and plop down in my chair. A young girl barges into the office unannounced. It's Olivia, one of my employees. An underage prescription pill addict, a dirty little bitch with a smart mouth. Somewhat hot, though. She's always pouting, complaining about some bullshit. She just loves talking shit to the boss, always poking at me, fucking with me. I honestly don't know whether I want to fuck her or fire her.

She's chewing on gum, in direct violation of company policy, and she smacks on it loudly. The shift closing. "Here, BOSS," she says. "Check my work so I can go home and listen to my dad yell at me some more for being a slut." This chick is unbelievable.

"Where's your name tag?"

"I forgot it." Chewing the gum.

I clench my jaw, weighing my options. It doesn't matter. It's almost three in the morning, and we're the only ones here. If I catch her without it tomorrow, however, I'm writing her up. "All right, whatever. Let's do this." I put my pen down and begin checking her work. She sits on the arm of my chair, peering over my shoulder.

"Why do you wear those boots? They look like moon boots. What are you, an astronaut? You're lame."

I continue reviewing her work. "Yes, I'm lame. That's great."

She leans over and says, "Do you like my tits? Do you think they're big enough?"

I stop counting and glance to the right. Her rack fills my entire field of vision as her gum smacking reverberates through the tiny office. I look up at the monitor as it cycles through the security cameras. Nobody on drive. The garage is a ghost town. I turn back to her. She's staring at me with this smirk that makes me want to slap her. "Fuck it," I say. I kiss her on the mouth, hard. She kisses back. It's *on*. I fuck her on the floor, no condom, she gets rug burns on her knees.

Postcoitus, we're sitting there in the afterglow, and out of nowhere she says, "Well guess what, I have something to tell you . . . I have herpes! Congratulations, dick!"

I sit there, mouth agape.

She yells, "I know you want to fuck me up! Go on! Punch me in the face!" She sticks her jaw out, presenting it for me to hit.

Again, just . . . unbelievable. "Uh, I'm not going to do that." It's all I can say. I get up, straighten my tie, put on my coat, and escort her out of the office and leave for the day.

I'm beginning to think that this "player" lifestyle might be bullshit after all. I mean, this isn't exactly what I had in mind. I've been getting "lucky" (if you can call it that) in seemingly random intervals, and in each case the women have basically chosen *me*; I've had no say in the matter.

Is this what it's all about? Banging skanks and whores? Vomiting on obese maniacs? Fucking psychotic dominatrixes while their cuckold boy-friends bleed and shake in the corner? Too $hort would most certainly *not* approve. This is bullshit. What do I have to do to bang girls that I actually WANT?

I haven't the slightest idea.

And what about Chippy, my loving girlfriend? I've been going out with her for almost a year now, and it's a nice enough relationship, but something's missing. The underlying problem here has still not been ad-dressed. She's a hot nineteen-year-old, sure, but I had to court her for over four months before we had sex. That's not exactly the awesome "game" that I'd envisioned when I made my declaration that morning in my mother's garage. If Chippy were to leave me, I don't think that I'd be able to get a girl of her caliber again. I feel as though I just got lucky. I'm stay-ing with her out of fear.

I don't want to just keep jumping from the safety of one relationship to the next, waiting for things to come my way through work or my social circle. Unfortunately, though, it looks as though I don't have a choice. I just don't know how to go about this, or where to even begin for that matter. As much as I want to believe otherwise, I guess this is just how things are.

BLAUHAUS

I was sitting up in my room racking my brain trying to figure out where I was going wrong in my quest to become a boss player, when suddenly I remembered something that I'd read years ago about a man who claimed he could get any woman into bed using tactics adapted from hypnosis. At the time, I'd dismissed it as a joke, especially considering the hefty price tag he had attached to his "home study course," but at this point, I'm willing to try anything. *It might be worth another look,* I thought.

I went downstairs to the living room. It's set up as a common area, and one of the roommates has put a computer in there for everyone to use. I haven't had regular internet access in years, so to me it's a bit of a luxury. I sat down in front of the machine and entered the words "pickup lines" into the search field. It returned a link to the hypnosis guy's site, along with a host of others like it. As I browsed through them, I found one that was of particular interest: an actual FORUM where guys were discussing "pickup methods" in extreme detail. The site was overflowing with all kinds of information, and best of all, it was free. I felt like I had stumbled onto a secret chamber filled with golden treasure. *This is it. This is what I've been looking for.*

In the weeks since my discovery, I've been lurking in the forum daily, taking in as much as I can and studying the "Player Guide," a sort of FAQ filled with elaborately scripted pickup lines, strategies and arcane jargon and acronyms like *kino* (physical touch), *AFC* (average frustrated chump), *LJBF* (let's just be friends) and *patterning* (subliminal sugges-tion). This stuff is genius. I knew that there had to be a methodical way of going about this, and now I've found it. The information is revelatory, and I am beginning to see exactly where I've been going wrong. It's clear that success is going to require a complete shift in my beliefs and ways of thinking. There are so many things that I've been wrong about, but I'm starting to see the light. For example:

Our culture promotes misconceptions about sex and relationships because it isn't in society's best interest for every guy to be good with women. The media promotes guys buying drinks and having money, looks and power, while being a "nice guy gentleman." In fact, these things have no correlation to attraction. They *can* work, obviously, but they im-mediately slot you into the "regular guy" category, which women habitu-ally ignore and blow off. I want consistency, not statistical roulette.

Women aren't attracted to a doormat or a supplicating fool, even if he's rich or good-looking. Looks, height, and money do not matter as much as confidence, charisma and strength of personality.

Most importantly, to get women, you first have to MEET them. In order to improve my skill set, I am going to have to practice on a lot of girls. That means getting out of the house, which is what I am going to do tonight. I will approach random women and attempt to pick them up. I will likely be rejected. I am nervous as hell.

I head out to a bar with an AFC buddy and one of my female room-mates for "social proof" (you can't be a loser if you have male and, espe-cially, female friends with you). We get drinks and I start looking around. I see a cutie with her UG (Ugly Girlfriend) and get the EC (Eye Contact) going, then approach and say, "Hi. Let me ask you a question. I'm really fucking bored here. Why don't you entertain me?"

The cute one replies, "We're not performers." I sit down and begin chatting them up. After a while, she asks me, "Do you have a name?" I tell her my full name, first and last. I start asking them questions, but then I falter. I can't think of anything to say, and I can't keep smiling. Some dude, a friend of theirs apparently, comes by to say hello, and I'm sort of blocked out. I eject, but I see her checking me out periodically.

I compose myself and approach another girl. "Hi. Will you buy me a drink?"

She's taken aback and simply says, "No!" She walks off and whispers to her friend. They continue to give me weird looks until I leave the bar about ten minutes later.

I walk up the street to Casanova. I'm kicking myself for not having been more persistent with the first set of girls, even though it looked like I wasn't getting a great response. The fact that she looked longingly after me should have told me this. The dode guy was a nonentity. Oh well. I enter the second bar.

I instantly spot two chicks that I like. One of them is a freakishly tall beauty standing with a group of four chodes in polo shirts, guarding her. I get good EC, so I ask my buddies to help me infiltrate the group. My AFC friend says something stupid to one of the guys and is blown out, but my social proof girl manages to get me in. I engage my target, get her into semi-isolation and go to work.

She's visiting from Canada. I ask her about Vancouver and see an opportunity to use a tactic from the forum, "weasel words." I'm a weasel, sounds perfect. This is where you say one thing but secretly plant another thought entirely into her subconscious.

I tell her, "Some people here in the States talk badly about Canada, but I think that kind of stuff is BLOW ME. NOW. WITH ME, I just appreciate everything the world has to offer. Like, I wake up in the morning, and look at the sky and think to myself, wow . . . the sky is so beautiful . . . THIS GUY IS SO BEAUTIFUL." I point to myself while I say this, then touch her on the arm to anchor the "kino" when she laughs. I lean in toward her and then I recite a hypnotic "pattern" about her eyes. She is totally attracted. It's working! I decide to go for the close, and ask her if she would like to meet for coffee later in the week.

She replies, "Yeah, totally, but I'm only here until Tuesday and don't think I'm going to have time. It's too bad."

I do a "takeaway" and go out to have a smoke and collect my thoughts. I decide to go back in and go for the kiss or the "number close" (i.e., get her phone number to set up a date later on). When I go back, however, I don't do anything. I see her at the end of the bar; she's back with the polo shirt guys. I puss out and decide to leave.

Overall, I am pleased with the results of my first night out. I should have been more persistent and aggressive, but I know that I will only improve with time. There's no going back now.

OAKTOWN MACK

I look up at the computer screen. The post I was reading is an announcement for a meeting in the East Bay of something called the "Lair." Apparently, this is a group of local guys from the forum that get together once a month and discuss the latest pickup tactics. A bunch of badass players together in the same room, talking shop? It sounds awesome. It also happens to be taking place on my day off. That settles it . . . I'm going. I jot down the information and send an email to the organizer to let him know I'm coming.

The day of the Lair meeting arrives and I drive over to Oakland. I am wearing a full, two-piece black leather suit, giant rocker boots and various bondage cuffs. My hair is sprayed into a tall pompadour, and I'm wearing oversized gold Versace sunglasses. It's at least 85 degrees in Oakland. I briefly regret wearing the leather, but dismiss this thought almost as soon as it arises. I park the car, double-check the address, get out and walk up the driveway, gravel crunching under my feet.

A short, yuppie-looking black man opens the door when I knock. He regards me with a look of concern. For a second, I think I have the wrong place. "Uh . . . is this the Lair meeting?"

He brightens up and says, "Oh, yeah! How's it going? I'm William!"

I shake his hand. "I'm J-L-A-I-X." I say each letter separately, the name I chose when I registered on the forum.

He nods. "Ah, I think I've read your posts. You've got Eminem in your signature, right?"

"That's me!"

"Yeah," he says, "I've seen you on there. How do you pronounce that handle?"

"I don't know . . . it's my initials. Jeffrey Lewis Allen the Ninth."

William looks like he isn't sure how to take this, but he laughs anyway and invites me in. "Well come on in brother, we're just about to get started! You want a soda?"

As I walk in and look around, it becomes immediately apparent that I am the coolest person in the room. Which isn't saying much. An assortment of scrawny fellows wearing turquoise and silver pendants, obese men with neck beards and senior citizens in flashy shirts mill about, waiting for the meeting to get under way. I take a seat next to a fat guy and introduce myself. He says nothing.

William calls everyone to attention. For the next hour, he leads the group as we discuss neurolinguistic programming, various ways to trick a woman into kissing you and different "openers." Almost as soon as he begins, an unpleasant scent reaches my nostrils. It's coming from the fat guy next to me. At first, I just assume that he farted and wait for it to dissipate, but it continues to grow in intensity until I am forced to pull my T-shirt over my nose in order to breathe. It smells as though he literally shit his pants. I scoot as far away from him as I can and attempt to focus on the presentation.

Finally, William announces a special treat. One of the Lair members recently attended a pickup seminar down in Los Angeles, and he has agreed to share what he learned with the group. There is a tepid round of applause as he walks to the front of the room. He's balding and is wearing a loud shirt tucked into corduroy slacks, high on his waist. He looks extremely nervous. "Uh . . ." he starts, "ahh . . . I'm going to show you guys how to do a new pattern called the Four Dimensional Mind." I notice his slight lisp. "Here goes," he says. He thrusts his arm out in front of him and begins reciting the pattern to an imaginary woman. "I want you to think about your perfect attraction. How do you feel when YOU ARE TOTALLY ATTRACTED. NOW, imagine it on a movie screen. What does it look like?" As he goes through it, he's shaking and sweating profusely. "Now make it bigger. Now move it here," he says, pointing at an area in front of his chest. "Look at the color and notice how it feels when you are really attracted. Now, move it . . . RIGHT HERE." He takes his finger and places it on his lips, then drags it down his chin and rests it on his sternum. He says nothing for several seconds.

I look around to see if anyone else is finding this as utterly bizarre as I am. But no, most of them are sitting at attention, scribbling furious notes. Shit-pants finally acknowledges me, turning and whispering, "This is awesome stuff, huh?" with a grin on his face.

I give him a tight-lipped smile and nod. These are my new friends, the "badass players" whom I was so excited to meet. These are the guys who are going to help me become a deadly efficient pickup artist. So be it. I take a sip of my soda, wishing I'd brought a flask.

MAGIC TRICK

Jackass invited me to a party tonight, an annual event hosted by some of his brother's friends. Each year, they select a theme and go full bore with it, transforming their house elaborately. I'm looking forward to this, as it should be an excellent opportunity for me to practice my pickup skills.

When we arrive at the house, I walk through the door and am immediately impressed; the entire place has been decked out in a Mardi Gras theme. They really pulled out all the stops here; it's amazing. The music is great and everybody's having a good time. I get myself a drink, throw some beads around my neck and walk around, greeting the various people I know. There are a lot of girls here, but not many that capture my imagination, and the ones that do all seem to be paired off with their boyfriends. I go out into the backyard and it is every bit as extravagantly decorated as the house itself is. I continue to jump from group to group, mingling.

I walk back inside, and that's when I see her. The girl that I want. She's sitting on a table with a cup in her hand, amiably chatting with the other people in the room. I'm not paying attention to them, however, as I'm transfixed by the girl. She's short and fit, with long, curly red hair and a cute face. I sort of settle in with the group and listen to their conversation. They're talking about travel when the girl mentions that she just got back from Italy.

Suddenly, a tactic from the pickup forum leaps into my head, unbidden. Framing a sexual comment in the context of a quotation to absolve yourself of responsibility for having said it. Without thinking, I blurt out, "Oh Italy, huh? That's awesome. I heard that the guys there are really forward, though."

All eyes in the room are on me now. The girl takes note of me for the first time and says, "Um. Forward? What do you mean?"

My heart is pounding in my chest. I can't believe I'm going to say this shit. *Just say it. Go.*

I look her directly in the eyes and say, "Well, I heard that they'll come right up to you and say shit like IMAGINE US HAVING SEX RIGHT NOW, AND ME EATING YOUR PUSSY ALL NIGHT LONG, AND FLICKING THE BEAN WITH MY TONGUE, AND FUCKING AND HAVING ORGASM AFTER ORGASM ALL NIGHT LONG. AND TRY NOT TO THINK ABOUT THAT, ALL NIGHT LONG."

The room is silent. The girl actually blushes. She's stunned. The other people in the room look at each other as if to say, "What the fuck is up with this guy?"

I continue. "Do they really say that stuff? I mean, that sounds crazy, I don't think that would actually work."

There is a pause that seems to last for several minutes.

Finally, she says, "Well, I don't speak Italian . . . so I don't know what they were saying!" Everyone laughs and the tension breaks.

I go up to her and introduce myself. "I'm Jeff."

"I'm Roxy," she says, offering her hand. I take it and bring it to my mouth, then turn it over at the last second and kiss my own hand. Another trick from the forum. She laughs. It's on. I can feel it.

We talk for about thirty minutes, standing close to each other, and then we go upstairs together to get another drink. There's a little nook in the kitchen with a curtain hung in front of it. I push aside the curtain and discover a small mattress inside. The hosts have apparently provided a makeout niche . . . how thoughtful of them. I pull her in there and we start making out. It gets intense quickly. People are walking in and out of the kitchen, oblivious to the fact that I'm fingering this girl behind the flimsy curtain.

After a while, I cut it off and we emerge from the nook looking a little disheveled. Some guy wearing a cowboy hat sees us and gives a thumbs-up. "All right, man!" I ignore him and walk her back outside. This is so obviously on it's not even funny, but I'm not sure how to get her back to my place so we can have sex. I'm sort of pussyfooting around and don't know what to do.

She does, however. "We should hang out! What are you doing Monday?"

"Nothing."

"Cool! Give me your number and let's go out then!" We exchange numbers. I hang out with her and some of our mutual friends for the rest of the night, and kiss her again before I go home. She makes some comment about how she's going to have to "go home and masturbate."

Funny, I was thinking the same thing.

Monday rolls around. I have decided to meet her at a bar called the El Rio. I've been there once before with the new roommates. It's nothing special but it's near my house and I figure that should make the "extraction" easier. I call her up as I'm leaving work and tell her to meet me there at seven.

I get to the bar and find out that Monday is Dollar Drink Night at the El Rio. Good to know. I order a vodka tonic, give the girl behind the bar two dollars and settle in. I bring the drink to my lips and take my first sip, then immediately choke. Calling it "strong" would be an understatement. I decide I like this place very much.

Roxy walks in and we hug. She looks good. We start drinking and part of me gets the feeling that this is just a formality. Nonetheless, I am concerned with how I'm coming off. I'm monitoring my tone, trying to maintain "higher value" and avoid "supplication." These are key concepts I've learned from the forum. I don't want to appear needy, but at the same time, I want to move things forward, and I'm struggling a bit as I try to walk that line. We have a few drinks as the place starts to slowly fill up with a strange mix of thugs, lesbians and college students, apparently all brought together by the lure of cheap, strong booze.

Eventually Roxy gets up. "I'm bored," she says. "I think I'm gonna go home."

I say, "Wow. That sounds really interesting and I think I should check it out." As we walk out together, I notice a long line has formed out front, filled with hot young girls. I make a mental note to come back here next Monday.

Cut to her crib. She shows me her room and we lay on the bed. I'm extremely nervous and I'm not sure how to escalate the situation. We talk for a while and I can sense she's getting impatient. Finally, I decide that I've got to do *something* and just kiss her. We make out for a while and then I decide to go against my better instincts and start to take her clothes off. There is no resistance. I take mine off, put on a condom and pound her until we both orgasm, simultaneously. I lie there with her for a while, then get up and leave. She kisses me at the door and says, "You have a magic cock."

I actually did it. My first successful pickup! I can hardly believe it, but I pulled it off. It feels like I've been granted supernatural powers. I picked a girl that I wanted, a stranger, approached her and through sheer *skill* persuaded her to have sex with me. I was beginning to believe that it wasn't really possible, but here I am, driving home giggling and elated. I actually pump my fist in the air and shout, "YES!" Thanks, internet!

For the first time in years, I'm actually excited about something. I'm overwhelmed with a sense of expanding possibilities, like Dorothy stepping out of her house after she's landed in Oz to be greeted by an army of colorful munchkins singing her praises. Whatever challenges await me in this new realm, I'm ready to face them head-on. It's time to hit the yellow brick road, bitches. Let's do this.

JOURNEY

I'm dyeing my hair black when I get a "911" page from work. I ring them up. "What the fuck is it now? Did somebody get their dick stuck in a tailpipe again?"

Turns out that one of my employees scored me a pair of tickets to this private Journey/Cheap Trick concert down at the convention center. There's free food and booze. Not to mention the fact that I am possibly the biggest Journey fan in the whole wide world. I throw on a black Hawaiian shirt, my boots and my Giant Iced-Out Pinky Ring.

I pick up Che and we discuss strategy on the way there. He tells me that the attendees are likely going to be square as fuck, since it's a convention for database administrators. Sure enough, they are all geeks. The women are a little older, but it's cool. We begin to get smashed on liquor. For a while I can't get started, making only halfhearted attempts at conversation with people. I keep needling Che to approach, but I'm not doing shit myself. I realize this and decide to step up. I see two chicks standing there drinking and stroll right up and grab one of them by the arm. "Hey! What's UP?! How've you been?"

She's perplexed. "Hi! Uhh . . . Do I know you?"

"Yeah, from summer camp! Kate, right?" She laughs. "So, do you ladies wanna party backstage with Journey?"

This makes both of them perk up a bit. "Do you have passes?"

I lie. "We're in a band, we usually open for Journey but not tonight, cause it's a special event. Have you heard of Pure Death?"

They're both smiling now, they can't tell if I'm serious or not, but either way they are finding it amusing. I blather on and poke at them. Meanwhile, Che is becoming increasingly manic off to the side, randomly throwing food about, shrieking. One of the women notices this. "What's wrong with your friend?"

"Oh . . . he's just the singer . . . you know what I mean."

They leave.

A bit later, we're standing there watching the show when this chick walks by and kind of spills beer on my foot. I whirl on her and with a smirk, begin shouting, "What the fuck?! Holy shit, what the fuck are you doing?!!!"

She stops short. "Oh my God, I'm so sorry!"

I reply, "Shit, I'll tell you what, it's okay, but now you have to kiss me." Without hesitation, she kisses me square on the mouth. I wrap my arm around her waist and pull her in. She gazes at me and says, "Mmmmm . . . you look really great tonight. You look like a really pretty lesbian."

Now it's my turn to be perplexed. "Like, uh . . . k. d. lang?"

She goes, "Yeah, but way better," and abruptly walks off, leaving me standing there scratching my head.

The show ends. We're outside gaming this sour-looking married hottie. It's an extremely odd situation, because we get right up on her, straight rubbing her crotch, and she is not into it, yet at the same time, she doesn't freak out and tell us to get the fuck away, as one might expect. She just keeps saying things like, "I am not happy with this. I do not like you guys," while appearing bored and making no effort to actually stop us from doing it. Disturbed, *we* actually walk away.

Finally, we decide to call it a night and I drive Che home. I barge in and crawl into bed with his roommate Dummy, a fairly hot eighteen-year-old girl with a speech impediment. We "cuddle" and I slobber things in her ear. Then I go across the hall, fling open the other roommate's door, announce that it is "time to eat pussy" and start ramming my head between her legs as she giggles and says, "Heee heee noo! No Jeff! Hee heeee!" This continues for approximately five minutes, then I go home.

This was a breakthrough night for me. My approaches were fearless. It was total over-the-top ridiculousness. I've been inspired recently by the posts of a guy on the forum who goes by "TylerDurden." Basically, his philosophy is centered around the idea that "attitude determines what you can get away with." This is, in my opinion, *dead on.* I was blown away by one of his recent field reports wherein he approached every girl in a club. Even if they were there with their boyfriends. Every time he felt hesitation, he would repeat the following to himself: "It doesn't matter, and I don't care."

This "I don't care" mentality is, I think, crucial to becoming success-ful with women. The main reason being that, in order to get good, you need to do literally thousands of cold walk-ups on strangers, and yes, you are going to crash and burn *hundreds* of times. It is the fear of this that keeps you stuck on that first plateau in the transformative process.

I feel as though I've stepped up to the next level in my recovery to-night. It was an experience where something just clicked in my head, it was like, *fuck this, I don't care, I'd rather go down in flames than stand on the wall looking like an asshole (albeit a very decked-out asshole).* I did the most approaches that I've ever done in one night. I didn't have too much success, but it didn't matter, I felt great about it. My fear of approach was GONE. I still fucked up a lot, I'll admit it, but I am learning and improv-ing with each outing.

"I don't care" is my new mantra. Additionally, I am going to start throwing myself into "difficult" social situations just for the challenge. As someone on the forum once said, "The first few thousand approaches don't count."

RAGE FUCK

"When using this product: do not use more than directed; excitability may occur, especially in children; avoid alcoholic drinks; be careful operating a motor vehicle or operating machinery; Alcohol, sedatives, and tranquilizers may increase drowsiness."

I look from the bottle of cold medication that I'm holding in my right hand down to the coffee table, where my forty-ounce of Mickey's is sitting, half finished. I consider this for a moment, then unscrew the bottle and take a healthy slug of the meds. I've been sick all week. All I want right now is for the pain to stop, so "drowsiness" actually sounds pretty good. I start in on the forty again. I've been posted up all day in the living room watching television and I haven't showered since Tuesday. I'm aware that I'm beginning to smell, but this is inconsequential. *Survivor* is on.

Halfway through the program, I decide that I want to fuck Beth, a dancer I once left an embarrassing voicemail for, which she never returned. I call her. She answers. We had always had a certain rapport, but back then I had been too chode to capitalize on it. I haven't seen or spoken to her in over six months, but it doesn't matter; I tell her I need to come over.

She asks, "Why?"

"I just do."

She pauses for a second, then says, "Well, I moved."

Immediately, I respond, "What's the address?"

"Six-eighteen Castro Street." I hang up, put my shoes on and walk out the door. I drive straight to her house.

I drag myself up the stairs and ring the bell. She opens the door and I enter the house. I am drunk and sick, coughing. I look and smell like shit. It doesn't matter. I fluff talk her for two minutes, then ask to see her bedroom. She shows me the room. I get in her bed and remove my pants. No warning, no prelude; I simply get in her bed and I take off my pants. I tell her to do the same.

"Why?" she asks.

"So I can eat your pussy."

Her mouth opens. "What?!"

"Shut up, do it."

"But don't you have a girlfriend?"

"Irrelevant. Time to fuck . . ."

She seems uncertain. She stammers, "But . . . but . . . what?!"

I go, "Cut the shit and take your fucking pants off . . ."

This goes on for roughly five minutes. She brings up some objection, and I dismiss it by saying, "irrelevant," "time to fuck," "cut the shit," or some permutation of the three. In my mind, this is going down right the fuck now; it is a foregone conclusion and I'm conveying this with every particle of my being. I just keep blasting away, and what do you know? She sort of shrugs and lies down. The pants come off. I eat her out for like twenty minutes until she comes, then just go in for the kill. It's a good ride, a hot useless fuck. I sink all of my aggression into it.

Bottom line: new addition to the rotating harem. I now have my Primary and three good solid babes I can fuck on any given night. Taking care of business. A life I once thought impossible is slowly becoming reality.

A VERY JLAIX HALLOWEEN

Halloween is fucking huge in San Francisco. It's the unofficial city holiday; every year three hundred thousand freaks go out in costume to the Castro District and party their asses off. This year is no different.

I'm going out dressed as a preacher. I have a little baby doll tied to my belt on a fishing line, so that it looks like it's following me around, humping my leg. We hit up a pre-party at the home of Buzzard, this crazy-ass Satanic dude I know from work. He throws the best Halloween parties.

I'm in the kitchen telling some story to a mixed group. All of a sudden, one of the chicks looks at me and says, "You're an ASSHOLE." Deadly serious. Everyone stops and looks at me expectantly. *Oh man, what's he gonna say?*

I kind of chuckle and say, "Yeah, cool . . . so what is it about assholes that turns you on so much?"

She twitches and gives a startled, sour face. Then she walks over and gets all up in my grill, starts smiling and puts her arm around me, and gets a dazed, faraway look in her eyes. Like she expects me to kiss her. She is a 6, so I just play it off. I'm pleased, though, as that "asshole" comment would have DESTROYED me six months ago. Basic congruence test passing here.

Walking around, I notice this chick who is obviously some kind of stripper . . . you can just tell by the body, not to mention her getup, which consists of practically nothing. I just make strong sexual eye contact at first. It works . . . she comes up and starts talking to me; the eye contact is being reciprocated. I swear, I think the priest shit is turning her on. A little later, I see her sitting with another hot-ass chick, and they're all alone, so I sit down and start fluff conversation. I use the "guys are crude" bit where I say "imagine me eating your pussy all night," etc. There's a strange aura around these girls; it's like people are afraid to talk to these hot chicks. Awesome. Anyway, Buzzard rallies everybody and we hit the streets.

I'm standing on the corner of Eighteenth and Castro, it's fuckin' *mobbed*, I'm ripping pages out of the Bible and yelling, flinging the pages out into the street. Some dude comes up and starts touching me, jabbering something like, "You're cool . . ."

I respond, "Yo, do not fucking touch me," and brush him off. Laughing, he does it again, and I punch his face. His expression is priceless as he reels away, then he starts to come at me. Buzzard, who is six foot three, bald, covered in Satanic tattoos and tonight is dressed as some kind of demonic warlord complete with leathery bat wings and a battle axe, gives the guy a hearty shove and he disappears, enveloped by the crowd.

"The unholy shall be punished!" I shout.

Shortly after this, I find myself walking alongside the stripper. Out of the blue, she starts tonguing me down! Hell yeah! I'm totally getting into it, grabbing her ass and everything; it goes on for a little while, full makeout deluxe.

After that, Buzzard comes up to me and says, "You wanna fuck that bitch?" Turns out he is sort of "with" her. I'm apologetic, but he guffaws, "I don't give a fuck." He turns to her and gestures, saying, "Hey, you hear that? This guy wants to fuck you!" Ridiculous.

We go to Lucky 13. We're standing there in the bar and the stripper asks me to buy her a drink. I say, "I don't buy bitches drinks. Why don't you get one of these striped-shirt chodes to buy us *both* drinks?"

She laughs, then does exactly that. Within five minutes, she returns with two glasses of whiskey, courtesy of some douchebag at the other end of the bar. That settles it; I'm never buying drinks again. After this, her friends arrive, and they're obviously strippers as well, fucking hot. She says, "This is my friend. Isn't she hot?"

I look her over and kind of shrug and say, "Sure. Yeah." Very nonchalant. She introduces me and I say, "Hi, I'm Jeff . . . wait, don't you know who the fuck I am?"

She "thinks" for a second then asks, "You have the ecstasy?" Silly stripper. The first girl starts talking about how cool her new man, Buzzard, is. "Girl you gotta see this guy he's *soooo* punk rock. Hey Jeff, go in the bar and get him."

I'm like, "You're fucking trippin'. You go get him." She laughs.

The bar closes, and we head back up the hill to Buzzard's. I'm wasted now, wandering in the street. Earlier, I was going up to any chick dressed like a Catholic schoolgirl (there have been plenty), and saying, "You're a bad girl, huh? You need a spanking?" At this point, however, all subtlety is gone. I just charge up, start slapping their asses and yelling, "You's a bad bitch!"

I do this to one woman and she becomes very distraught. Some guy that she's with gets really angry as well, he comes up and bellows, "What the fuck are you doing?!"

I immediately sock him in the face.

This makes him extremely upset. Fortunately, Buzzard and his hellions throw him into the street, amused by my dementia. "Now now, Jeff," says Buzzard, waving his finger at me, "no more of that."

Back at Buzzard's pad, we're doing more shots, and I'm still trying to get with the stripper. Buzzard turns to me and says, "Were you kissing this bitch earlier?" Uh oh.

Hesitantly, I'm like, "Yeah?"

He says, "Damn, she's gotta suck my dick with that mouth later . . . HAHAHAHA!!!" He throws his arm around her and pulls her in. Glorious . . . a master at work.

I do a few ice-cold Jäger shots with them and then take off. I learned two things about strippers tonight:

1. Everything they say is bullshit.
2. They love fucking DRUGS. All night these bitches were on and on about drugs. I thought it was funny how when the chick introduced me to her friends, they just assumed I was a dealer.

I want to explore this stripper thing further. I wonder: is there something in the body of knowledge about a "textbook stripper pickup"? Very interesting.

BRAINWASH

I watch the clothes in the dryer go round and round as I wait for the bartender to bring my beer. I've come to a place called the Brain/Wash, a combination of bar and laundromat, in order to see my roommate's band. The bar girl is hot, I start talking to her, smiling and animated.

She seems into it. I ask her to tell me a joke, and she does. I don't laugh because it's so bad. My turn. "Breaking news: Energizer Bunny arrested, charged with battery." She actually walks away from me without saying a word. Shit, I've had some groans from that one but never a straight-up walkaway.

My other roommate, "Me Too" Greg, is reading a paper at a table. He indicates some article to me. For some reason I don't like what it says, so I spit beer all over the page. Greg says, "Asshole! This isn't my paper! It belongs to that woman over there!" He points out an older MILF.

I go over and say, "Hey I spit on your paper, I'm so sorry." She's kind of interested and kind of annoyed. I start to work on her, sit down right next to her on the couch and start my routine. I'm getting drunk here and I don't know exactly what I'm saying, but I go for the "extraction" too soon. I say, "Why don't you come back to my place and check out my cat collection?"

"I don't think so."

I keep persisting, "C'mon, it's cool!" Over and over and over. Very light touching going on. She's still not down, so I go for the number. "Gimme your number then." Again I meet resistance, I say, "Why not, what do you have to lose?" I'm actually getting pissed that this thirty-five-year-old is refusing to give me her number. I say, "You don't seem like the kind of person who would let opportunities pass her by."

She's like, "I'm in a bad spot right now; transition, you know?"

Fuck that shit. I retort, "Listen, if you're not with it, just tell me to get the fuck out of here . . . say it! Say, 'Leave now, jerk!' And I'll go!" She laughs. Finally I try once more, I say, "Listen, I'm just so sick of this transitory world, we meet people once and never see them again. I don't want you to be another one of those people that drifts away into the night . . ." I start to tear up a little as I look down.

She says, "Oh my God, you look so sad!"

I'm like, "Please, let's not let this moment go," or some such shit. Anyway, it still doesn't work, so I eject.

I become totally wasted and end up at some stranger's house wearing a Catholic schoolgirl's uniform and my stained green trench coat, clutching a cheap bottle of chardonnay, standing in the living room yelling at a group of hippies. None of the chicks are hot. Does one *ever* see hot hippies?

It looks like my problems are still the same. I see a pattern here. Need to work in more routines. I don't escalate physically, and I don't do enough to get them to sexual state before I attempt to close. I think I'm afraid something bad will happen if I touch them, like they'll slap me or something. But hell, half the things I say to them *verbally* could get me slapped, so what the fuck am I afraid of?

DOLLAR DRINKS

One thing is becoming clear: in order to learn this skill set, I need to go out a *lot*. Only through massive repetition of social interaction will I be able to cultivate a noticeably improved level of social intelligence. Morality, ideals, fears—these must all be set aside. First get the knowledge, then develop it through practice and repetition. This is the only way to project an abundance mentality.

I've been reading a lot, but only going out sporadically, at best. On the forum, TylerDurden equates this to those ab crunch machines you see on television: if you buy it and it just sits in the closet, you're still going to be fat. You have to actually put in the work.

To that end, I have decided to go out as many nights as possible. Today is Monday, Dollar Drink Night at the El Rio. I've been hitting it up for the past several weeks, and it's really the perfect venue: cheap drinks, close to the house, packed to the gills with cute girls.

We roll into the place a little early: Brian my wing, Angel my "social proof" girl, and me, jlaix. I'm wearing a fucking raggedy-ass tuxedo, open at the shirt with the bow tie hanging loose, covered in blood and wine stains. The usual assortment of jewelry: roughly fifteen pounds of sickening, obviously fake "bling." I've decided it is high time to get a little "in yer face" with these hipsters at the fuckin' Rio. It appears as though I am coming from some glamorous, debauched formal event, and I tell anyone who inquires that tonight was my "GED prom." One chick asks where the prom was held. I say, "It's here, this is it. All these people are getting their GED."

I head out to the back patio, light up my Cohiba and start puffin' it up with the giant iced-out pinky ring, ashes falling in my cummerbund. Some girl, a 5, comes up and starts touching me, "You're so beautiful!"

I'm like, "AWAY."

I see this other girl who frequents the place as she walks through the door with her warpig friend. I've talked to her before and she's a real ball-buster. I saunter on up and say, "What's up?"

She looks at me and says, "Oh my God it's you!"

I reply, "You betcha."

She turns to her friend and says, "Look, he's getting worse every week!"

It's true, my appearance has been getting more extreme by the week. I'm wearing Oliver Peoples nonprescription wire frames, and my hair is like Elvis in the final days. We fluff for a minute, then I remember what happened the other night at Brain/Wash and that I need to run my routines and escalate. So I start touching her.

Next thing I know, she's touching me back! Woo-hoo! She shows me a tattoo on her belly and I finger it slowly, rubbing, then poking and rubbing her hips and waist. I can sense her getting horny; she playfully slaps my hands away as I feel at her pants . . . mind you while this is happening, we are just having a run-of-the-mill conversation about stupid shit. She starts touching my face and saying how cute my nose is and how she wants to nibble it off.

I'm like, "Yeah."

I start running shit. She makes some random point and I say, "Yeah, it's so hard. Believe me, it's soooo HARD. You just need to let that thought PENTRATE DEEP INSIDE YOU. And we can argue about this all night, but the fact remains: I AM GOING TO MAKE YOU COME OVER AND OVER AGAIN to the same conclusion, which is that I am RIGHT. NOW, WITH ME, I'm always saying things like . . ."

I grab her ass and face. I lean in and Eskimo-kiss her, rubbing my nose back and forth across hers, then isolate her to a dark corner and tongue her down, move to a bench and it's on. I'm essentially sexing her up in the bar, with clothes on. She's like, "I've always thought you were so cute when I've seen you here."

Then my pathetic friends have the gall to come up and cockblock me, demanding I give them a ride back to their house. "We gotta go."

I say to her, "Goodbye my sweet, I will see you next Monday."

She quietly replies, "Bye," all wistfully.

FUCK. I could've fucked her, I'm sure. I could feel her getting hot in her pants but my lame-ass "buddies" cockblocked me and pulled me away. I didn't even bother to get her number because she's there every week. It'll happen, but next time I'll leave the chodes at home.

On the bright side, I intended to escalate and conscientiously run more material after the other night's debacle, and I did it tonight with great results. This was a breakthrough night for me in some respects, I learned a lot. The main lesson: ESCALATION IS KING. Start slow, and crank it up. You can feel it making them horny as you touch them. They want it. They need it. It won't make them slap you.

And even if it does, who the fuck cares?

CHRISTMASTIME AT THE EL RIO

I had to fire some guy earlier today over his involvement in a minor accident. It sucked because I personally liked the guy, and it's close to Christmas. He said, "Oh, this is the worst time for this to happen!"

I replied, "Hey, man, think of it like this . . . at least you'll have plenty of time to spend with your friends and family during this magical holiday season." He glared at me.

After that, I perused the ads for the Latino she-males in the back of the *Weekly*, then for my amusement had another worker call up the "best" one to harangue "her" with inquiries about the availability of parking ("But the PARKING! Tell me about the PARKING!").

All in all, another day another dollar.

Now, however, these stresses are but a distant memory as I nurse my drink out back at the old El Rio with Che. I stayed sober all day, took a nap before I left, and I am totally alert and rested. I decide to limit myself to ONE drink. I'm dressed down: plain jeans, boots, black T-shirt, leather coat. As always, my hair looks incredible.

The effects of not drinking are immediately evident: I feel like a pickup ninja. In my interactions I can flip, throw verbal shuriken and vanish in a puff of smoke. It is very interesting. I like it.

I start doing throwaways. I hit up the line for the ladies' restroom. This is funny because they are a captive audience; you can bust them *hard* and they can't leave. "Okay, ladies, on a scale of one to ten, how bad do you have to go? Uh huh. Next question, how white are my teeth?" Che stands to the side, laughing his ass off.

Two girls are into it. Unfortunately, they are not attractive. In order to get them away, I say, "Hey! Wanna see my cigarette burns?" I take off my coat and show them. The one on the right is unimpressed; she just turns her arm over and shows me hers.

I scan the room and see the girl I snogged last week here, Julia Redhair. She is pleased to see me and we hit it off, boom. I almost immediately get her in the corner and we are kissing. I start dropping the most absurd lines I can think of.

"Special, special Julia, I will buy you a boat."

"Your teeth are perfect. Small, straight and white. Just like my cock."

These are delivered with a straight face, and it's actually working. Next thing you know, her friend Autumn walks up. She reminds me of the man-pig guards from *Return of the Jedi*. I chat her for a bit, remembering the importance of winning over the peer group. Somehow the topic gets to kissing and she says, "I'm a good kisser."

"Hmm. Well, when I kissed you, it wasn't that great." I say it with an unfortunate, almost solicitous look on my face. She starts trying to remember if she really did kiss me, then becomes hyperpissed. Steam-coming-out-of-the-ears pissed. I try to mitigate the situation, at Redhair's insistence, by renouncing the statement. "No, really it was fine! I got wood and everything!"

Redhair says, "See? He got wood." This calms her and she lumbers off, eventually finding some foreign bozo to kiss on.

I resume making out with Julia, and at one point I say to her, "*You* actually are a great kisser. See?" and place her hand on my now very-much-wood-having cock.

Closing time approaches, and I am wondering how to isolate. I start talking about the supercute new kitten we got at my house: it's so cute and wouldn't she like to see that supercute baby kitty? She's intrigued but it doesn't seem like she's going to come back to my place. Autumn reappears. She's taking the foreigner home to bang. She addresses me: "You have to come home with Julia, because I'm bringing this guy home."

I'm like, "Oh okay." She gives me the address.

I show up after giving Che a ride back to his place. Autumn answers the door, "Oh it's you." She then grabs me by the shirt, drags me into the house, drags me down a hall, opens a door, then shoves me into the room so hard that I fall down. I look up as the door is slammed behind me and see my girl in her pajamas, looking surprised.

She says, "Are you okay?"

"Yes, I think so." She takes my coat off and instructs me to get in bed with her. I do so.

Neck nibbling, kissing, shirt off, rubbing. "Remove your pants," I say; "it's time for me to lick it." She refuses. I backtrack ("wash-rinse-repeat"); again no cigar. I try this like five times before I get bored/tired/annoyed then just decide to pass out. We fall asleep holding each other. Awwww, isn't failure cute?

I wake up at 8 A.M. to the terrifying heft of Autumn barging into the room, bellowing. "Fuck! That guy wouldn't even fuck! I have blue balls! The little pecker wouldn't fuck last week, now he's saying I should get tested for STDs before we do!! SHIT, motherfucker, this was supposed to be a ONE-NIGHT STAND!!! AARRGGHH!" As I'm laughing my ass off, she asks, "Did you guys fuck at least?"

"No, we . . . got tired."

I leave quickly. It's really only a matter of time before Redhair is mine. Tonight I'll bang Chippy. Another fuck buddy called me out of the blue yesterday to fuck; gonna hook that up later in the week. Life is good.

TRADING SPACES WITH THE BACHELOR

Went to Vancouver, British Columbia, for a week on vacation. During this time, I didn't approach a single woman. The girlfriend was with me. I wanted it to be a restful "down-time" from pickup, to return to the States recharged and ready for action. The way I envisioned it, I'd just be relaxing: smoking weed in the cafes, snowboarding at Whistler, fucking the shit out of the Primary.

What actually happened was this: I spent my twenty-seventh birthday alternately telling her I was going to throw her off the balcony and threatening to urinate on her, until she began crying. I then yelled, "I'm an old man! I'll be dead soon!" Then I got drunk.

I am dead inside. This, then, is the end result of my nightmarish Hollywood-plot background: I feel nothing. Beth described me as "emotionally cauterized." I believe that this is somehow holding me back in my quest for mastery. I can't exactly articulate *how* it actually hinders my game, I just suspect that it is, and probably seriously.

I don't know.

I won't lie: I do feel a degree of guilt with regard to how I treat Chippy. On a logical level, at least. The girl doesn't deserve this. And frankly, I don't deserve her. But I don't know what to do. Although I had already decided to become a player at the time we met, I hadn't yet discovered the pickup forum, and so I spent months courting her in the only way I knew how: THE CHODE WAY. I dropped the L-bomb early in order to bang her. I suppose I was being truthful enough in my own way. It is different for her, however. I'm her *first*. I see in her eyes the same look that I had when I was with Amy in my dorm room back at university.

For better or worse, this is the way it worked out. We spend a great deal of time together. I've let her believe that we are exclusive, when in fact I am seeing other women. She does not know this. She is very devoted to me and will believe absolutely anything I say. I've installed emotional switches in her head and infected her psyche.

After learning a bit of proper game, I decided the right thing to do would be to tell her the truth. But I just don't have the balls to do it. It would crush her. As much as the guilt bothers me, I can't hurt her like that. So the charade continues, and "jlaix" remains a secret identity. For now.

The closest I've come to revealing the truth is telling her, "I don't want a relationship where if we don't see each other every day there is some huge problem. I have many other friends and you can't monopolize all my attention."

She's not stupid, though. Occasionally she'll make a random comment during conversation that suggests she has *some* idea what's going on, like, "Is that a line you use when you pick up chicks?" It's like she knows, but she doesn't know. If she ever were to ask me point blank, "Are you banging other girls?" I would either simply not answer or immediately change the subject. When I go out, I think, "How am I gonna tell my girlfriend that I'm going out tonight without arousing suspicion?" Even worse, I worry what's gonna happen if the chick I pull asks if I have a girlfriend or finds out or something. This is a small city.

Guilt is insidious and difficult to eliminate. It plays tricks on you. My guilt over "cheating" up until now has generally been assuaged in large part by repetition of the act. The more I do it, the less I care. But sometimes, I'll be just sitting there and BOOM! Guilt feelings seep back in. I usually just quash them when they arise and they go away, but I find more and more that this guilt is the main thing holding me back from becoming an Ultra Super Awesome Badass Player. I now believe that this needs to be definitively resolved if I am to get to the next level. I know I could explode onto the scene here like a motherfucker if I didn't have to worry about this shit. If I could just go all out.

Tonight, Chippy wants me to sit at her house with her girlfriends and watch something called *Trading Spaces* and *The Bachelor* on television, while consuming an alcoholic beverage for chicks called "Arbor Mist." Worse, she is attempting to enlist me to buy it for her, as she is under twenty-one. We went to the movies and now, in the car, she proposes this.

"Hahaha! No fucking way am I buying that shit."

Confused, she asks, "Why not!?"

"There is no way I am gonna walk into a store, look some guy in the eye and purchase Arbor Mist. What's next, tampons?"

She sits in the passenger seat and pouts.

"Furthermore, I'm not sitting around with your friends watching those programs, as basically anyone within one hundred feet of that house will be transformed into a gay. No thanks."

Trying a different tack, she grabs at my junk and coos, "Come on, I just want to beeeee with yoooou!"

I shrug and impassively say, "Nah."

Now she's getting pissed. "Why are you being such an asshole!?"

I sigh. "Tell you what, I will buy you forties of malt liquor, how about that? I'll get you whiskey. Hell, I'd even buy you a fucking Boone's Strawberry Hill. I'll buy you virtually any alcoholic drink EXCEPT Arbor Mist. How's that?"

Her lower lip is protruding. She finally says, "No . . . just forget it."

I drop her off at her place and go in briefly, tongue her down for like five minutes. Then I leave. She cries out after me, "Drive safe! Call me tomorrow, okay?"

Eleven P.M. She calls me up; now she wants to come over. I say, "Sure, if you want."

She asks, "Do you want me to?"

"If you want."

She asks again, "But . . . do you want me to?"

I yawn. "Well, I'm just going to sleep, but if you want to, okay."

Pause.

She says, "Okay, I'm going to come over, okay?"

"Okay." Hahahahahahahahahaha . . .

She arrives while I'm chopping it up in the kitchen with my room-mates, and heads immediately upstairs. Remembering the state of my room, I run up past her. Printed-out pickup routines from the internet are lying all over the floor. I kick them under the bed like we're in a bad sitcom. The bed stand is littered with women's phone numbers written on assorted pieces of paper. Chippy picks one up. "Who's Maya?"

I instantly launch into an elaborate story about a customer at work who filed a ridiculous complaint. "That's her number." Fortunately, the note is written on stationery from my office.

We have sex. I go to the bathroom and when I come back, she's already asleep. I stand over her and regard her, expressionless. She looks just like a little angel. I shake my head. *What am I doing?* It seems I have little respect for anything or anyone, including myself.

The other day on the pickup forum, a woman posted her opinion of what motivates someone to become a pickup artist:

> You are angry, you are trapped between the conflicting
> feelings of wanting women and hating them because they
> have frustrated and rejected you in the past. You will "show
> them"! You will become an expert pickup artist; you will use
> and discard them after you satisfy your carnal desires; you
> will leave them heartbroken and wanting you in vain, just like
> they left you heartbroken and wanting them in the past. Isn't
> THAT the source of your hostility?

I saw that and laughed. Fact is, I don't even think about that kind of crap. I wanna fuck dirty-ass bitches, not indulge in grandiloquent vengeance fantasies. I'm not doing this because I hate women. In fact, I don't feel anything toward them. The only reason I'm doing this is because my dick told me to.

As for the source of my hostility, well, I was seething with hatred and rage long before I found pickup. It's probably a combination of genetics and upbringing. I don't know. If anything, I've undertaken this quest as a way to keep my hostility under *control*. I've seen firsthand what can happen when you put your faith in somebody else. My father did that, and when my mother betrayed him, it was too much for him to bear. He lost his shit, and in the process ended up destroying his own life as well as those of the people closest to him. I can never allow that to happen. Ultimately, "love" is a dangerous extravagance. It is a luxury that I don't want and couldn't afford if I did.

WORST NIGHT EVER

There is no longer any fear of approach. I run a standard fifteen-minute routine, and 90 percent of the time I get a phone number.

Seventy-five percent of those are total flakes.

I've been feeling isolated and depressed recently, after weeks of seemingly fruitless "clubbing." I've been fucking girls, but I still haven't had the *club* success I want. My lays have mostly been from working the social circle game (I railed Dummy one evening at Che's, hit up some others through friends of friends) but I've also had a few from number closes at the club, where I ended up fucking them on "Day 2." To be fair, my flakes have been going down, but not by much. And I still haven't done a same-night pull from a club.

I look at my watch. I am about halfway through what has thus far been a horrible evening. I came to the El Rio for Dollar Drink Night, planning to try out TylerDurden's new structure, which advocates hardcore ballbusting and flipping the script on the girl. I have on black leather pants, a black T-shirt, a black punk bracelet, a silver bracelet and a rosary necklace with an upside-down cross. *Fuck it,* I thought, *this is my reality and if they aren't down, then fuck 'em.* Since arriving, however, I've discovered that the cross thing is taking it over the line, essentially bringing religion into the picture, a major no-no. Several chicks have been straight-up *offended*, pointing and yelling, "WHAT IS THAT?!!" In hindsight, that shit is not good. I need to tone my look down to be less offensive.

The cocky attitude has also gone over horribly. I open three girls by asking them to quit shrieking, addressing the ugliest one, indicating that my wing and I are attempting to conduct "A-crowd business." She's annoyed, but the two cute ones seem mildly interested. I tell them, "Hey, you guys are cute . . . any one of you would make a nice new girlfriend."

They look at me like I'm crazy.

Then I say, "Can you guys cook?" No. "Hmm. Well, are any of you rich? 'Cause I need a sugar momma to support me."

The uggster says, "Good luck with that." I turn away. They do not attempt to continue the interaction, and I don't want to be a supplicator, so that's pretty much that. I pass by one of the cute ones later and stick my tongue at her, which causes her to laugh and smile at me. Big fucking deal.

I do the same thing on about five different girls, with varying success. Nothing to the degree where they "actively try to gain rapport" with me as TylerDurden insisted they would. What the hell am I doing wrong here? I think the combination of the extreme cockiness and the "evil" look is too much.

Things start to get demoralizing. I hit up the bathroom line for Brian's amusement. One chick looks at me like I just raped a baby, and calls me a mean name. I say, "That's so neat!"

Her friend says, "You were here last week, and you said the same thing. Do you do this every week?"

I say, "Yeah, I even plan to meet little Powerpuff Girls, too."

"I think I told you to fuck off last time. So . . . fuck off."

I say, "Wow! That's so interesting! Cool!" and walk away. OUCH.

I look in the corner and see some asshole ugly fat guy chatting up a hot chick who flaked on me after a recent pickup. I had a pretty good exchange with her and got her number on the pretense of giving her a "private reading" after having told her I was a "Psychic Ass Model." I sent her an email a couple of days later:

Date: Wed Feb 5 09:07:43 2003 (PST)
Subject: Psychic Undercover Cotton-Breeding Ass Model
From El Rio

Hey, what's up! Great meeting you the other night at El Rio.
I hope you are having a good time here in SF, our little town
must seem awfully bucolic to a cosmopolitan Australian like
yourself. I would have gotten back to you sooner, but I had to

fly to Milan for an ass modeling gig . . . you know how those things are. ;)

Anyways, I still want to speak to you about that private reading. I've been having some very strange premonitions recently, and you need to hear about them . . . this is vital stuff here.

—jeff

That was a few weeks ago. She never responded.

She looks up and sees me, pretends she didn't and resumes talking with the fat chode. I am suddenly struck by how shockingly lame my email was. More demoralizing. I get drunk. Soon I am yelling out on the deck for no reason; it is horrible. I grab my friend and we leave.

We go to the Phone Booth. It seems to be filled with ugly women and severe hipsters. We approach a pair of lesbians. One actually permits me to sniff her ear and rub her thighs, until her girlfriend gets territorial. She says, "Hey BRO, I like how your ass matches your face!"

"Oh yeah, you like that huh? Yeah, I don't know, I guess I just got lucky, they both look great. I'm actually an ass model. Don't get any ideas, though . . . you're not my type."

She replies, "I'm sorry. I thought you were a cocksucker, but I was right."

"Don't be sorry, it's cool. But there's no way I'm sucking your cock." I am working the Ultimate Frame. As a real, live pickup artist, I must learn to deal with whatever they throw at me. If she's being a bitch, why the fuck should *I* leave? I'm going to make *her* leave. I am going to stick to my guns until she LOSES. Still, this exchange fails to elevate my mood.

Out of nowhere, a freaky-looking chick, a 6 in a loud dress, comes up and starts talking to me. I tell her that I am forty-five years old and an undercover cop, and that the television show *21 Jump Street* was "loosely based on my life." I tell her I'm on mescaline. This goes on for a bit.

She exclaims, "You're funny! I like you!"

I'm like, "Yeah, I love karaoke, we should go." Rather than pull, however, I set up some hella sketchy "date" for later on in the week. Choded out. I go home.

This shit was awful. The kind of night that makes me think, *Fuck this shit, I suck at this, I'm never going to improve, why am I doing this? Getting told to fuck off, getting no response whatsoever from the HOT chicks, only lame-ass 6s.* I started this so I could bang girls who are hotter than me, not LESS attractive. I am a 7. This means that to consistently hook up with girls hotter than me, I need to exert a 10 effort.

I start to think about what a "10 effort" really means and get even more depressed. It means I will have to go completely balls-out and likely get told to *fuck off* much more. I know that I'm just supposed to "let go" of my ego and not take it personally, but after tonight, I feel like a complete loser. Sitting alone in my room, which I had meticulously prepared for the pull, clean as a hotel room, looking around and thinking *this isn't me,* honestly too fucked up to even cry.

I can't really see the lesson here. I need some help to put this shit into perspective and get back on the right track. I think something is wrong, or I'm reaching some new plateau in my game. I was having a decent run there, something like a lay a week last month, and now I feel flat. I haven't bagged a new girl in almost three weeks. It is getting so bad that last night I actually had to fuck my girlfriend.

Jesus.

I often find myself walking down the street and trying to think of a pickup tactic to use, some opener that will stop any beauty dead in her tracks, but at this point I've read so much material that I can't think of specifics anymore. I guess it's permeating my subconscious or something, but now I'm kinda at a plateau, a fork in the road. I don't know what to do next except persevere. Fortunately, that's something I'm good at.

TAKE ME TO THE RIVER

Chilling at the Rio with Angel, my female "pivot." Everyone should have a girl like her. Even if she's not actively running game, she is still great social proof and way better than any male wing at disarming obstacles. I just need to make it evident that I'm not "with" her.

It's been a bad night starting off thus far. I've gone out six nights in a row, really putting in time because it's been a couple of months since I posted an actual LAY. Going out so much can really take a lot out of a guy. I'm tired and in a low state, but my extreme horniness seems to be compensating for this somewhat.

There are a lot of dykes at El Rio tonight. I spend twenty minutes talking to a girl only to discover she is a lesbian. I don't eject immediately. I continue to befriend her. All of this going out in the eight months I've been studying this stuff has had an interesting side effect: I have met a *lot* of people, so I'll be out at the bar, talking to some chick, and people will constantly interrupt, "Hey what's up Jeffy!" Or I'll be waving to people across the room. Strangely enough, even those who consider me a creepy asshole say hello.

I have begun to view the club experience not in terms of interacting with individual groups, but more as one giant "100-set." I go to this place every week, so I also need to factor in the fourth dimension of time; playing it like chess, thinking several moves ahead. Really thinking about how the entire El Rio ecosystem functions.

I'm standing out back throwing out some major laser eyes mojo trying to get a little approach invitation. Very few bite, and the ones that do are in groups that I am too tired to feel confident I can break with technical game. I decide this is gonna be a pure caveman night, and begin to put myself into sexual state as the bitches walk by, looking at dat ass, feeling the lust awaken in my heart. It's like a cold, breathless tingling similar to fear or an adrenaline rush. I can almost feel my pupils dilate; my dick gets wood.

I see good ol' Julia Redhair and her friend. I invited her to a party not long ago and she didn't show up. She asks me how it went. I say, "Oh, it was great. Somebody got thrown through the front window. And the Chupacabra showed up."

She says, "The goatsucker?"

"Yeah, the mythical creature from Mexico that may or may not exist, just like your BOREFRIEND."

She's like, "What?! He exists, he just doesn't come to El Rio with me!"

I tell her, "Yeah, it's cool, my girlfriend isn't allowed to come here either. This is MY time." She appears startled, then tries to keep me around as I eject. Later!

I notice two girls pointing at me and kind of snickering-laughing to each other, whispering. I run up and yell, "YO, what the FUCK are you laughing about?!"

One of them says, "Oh! You were at the Arrow Bar last week and you walked into the women's restroom while we were in there and peed in front of us!" They start giggling.

I remember these girls now. I did in fact saunter into the ladies' room and urinate in front of them, busting on them hard. Shocked, one of them had asked me, "Are you at least gonna close the door of the stall?"

I replied, "NOPE," and continued to piss. I finished up, then said, "What the fuck are you girls doing in here? Are you doing coke?" They looked up in silence, with a guilty look on the face. "Well, hurry the fuck up, there are other people out there waiting to do coke as well, don't be so selfish, creeps!" I grabbed the bottle of vodka they were drinking out of the hot one's hands, took a slug, handed it back to her and walked out.

Now she introduces herself as "Michelle" and asks me, "Who are you?"

I say, "Jeffy, baby. What, you seriously don't know me?" Then some guy they are with tries to touch my hair . . . bad move. I grab his wrist and twist his arm down. "DON'T TOUCH THE HAIR, DUDE." Everybody freaks out for a couple of seconds. I apologize to the guy: "Sorry, dude, I'm just really . . . serious . . . about my hair."

The chick says, "When we were laughing, it wasn't like, anything bad." More fluff, then they hit the ladies' room and I don't see them again. Too tired to care. I leave with Angel at midnight and blow some bomb, then we walk across the street to this other bar where it is rumored they have karaoke and chicks shooting bottle rockets out of their asses.

We get there and I order "a glass of the crappiest scotch you have and a Bud Lite." I slam down the scotch and walk up to the karaoke host near the stage to put my first song in. As I approach, I see a girl onstage singing "Careless Whisper" by George Michael. She is sort of chubby, but whatever, I like a thick-ass bitch sometimes. I look her in the eyes as she sings, she looks into mine, the message I send her is, "I am going to fuck you tonight like the little slut you are, you chubby whore, I'm the fucking MAN." I see she receives the message. She's a little taken aback, but interested. I return to the end of the bar and wait. More eye contact as I talk with Angel.

My turn: I go up and sing "Eye of the Tiger" and knock it out of the fucking park, crazed antics. Insane value projection, people are literally stupefied. As I walk back to my seat, she gives me an awed look. I high-five her and kind of hold the contact for a little.

After a while, I walk to the restroom and stop by her, lean in incredibly close and ask her, "So, are you, like, a professional singer?" I'm in *major* sexual state, giving the hardcore bedroom eyes. Turns out she is a bartender at another karaoke bar across town that I have never been to. This totally captures my interest and ups her to a 7.5 in my book. It's clear that she feels my sex vibe and she starts to lightly touch me; we are standing very close. I go to the pisser for a takeaway.

When I come back, I just sit down next to her and her friend and continue. The conversation is straight neutral fluff about singing karaoke, performing and the like. I use the "me too!" tactic a lot here. She keeps telling me to come to the bar on Tuesday.

I'm thinking, *FUCK THAT, we are going to fuck TONIGHT.*

No technical game, save for the occasional comment to spice it up. No conscious "routines." I just find them flowing out of my mouth naturally. Angel leaves after saying to her, "Oh, Jeff is such a great guy. He is so smart and cute and kind and loving."

Oh my God.

The girl says to me, "You ARE cute."

I shrug it off, and escalate to the next level by telling her I am a "cotton breeder" and examine the "textiles" of her clothing by rubbing her tits and inner thighs. "Oh yeah," I say, "this is a combed cotton; that means the short fibers have been removed." More fluff for thirty minutes, escalating, my face is almost touching hers, I stare at her eyes, then her lips, then her eyes. My arm is around her waist. I feel her ass and she gets "upset."

"Hey don't grab my ass!"

I turn away. "Hey, I don't apologize for my desires as a man."

She says, "Well, I don't apologize for my desires as a woman," and grabs me. She talks about how she is "the most virginal person she knows."

Ha! Whatever!

At precisely the right moment, I throw in some world-weary compliment about how "special" she is, and I see then and there that it's GAME OVER. I have won, or should I say *we* have won. A "calming" occurs between us; we are both in sexual state, and we both know it's eventually gonna happen . . . so why not now?

I sing another song. More value. Somehow the conversation gets to the topic of not wearing underwear. I say I prefer to wear it because otherwise, it's cold and my junk hangs low. I need support.

She asks, "It hangs low?"

I say, "Yeah, see?" and put her hand on my erect cock. She gets kinda "mad" but I play it off. At this point I am totally embracing her from behind, rubbing my dick in her ass. Her friend leaves.

I kiss her lightly and she says, "I don't make out in bars."

Oh well, guess we'll have to leave then, huh? I tell her, "If you buy me a drink, you might get lucky."

"Well, I would but I only have enough money for a cab ride home."

I tell her, "Shit, I'll give you a ride."

"Oh okay!" She buys me a drink. I consume it. We leave.

In the car she talks continually about how she never does this. I tell her that I hate one-night stands, and how it makes me feel weird so I don't do it anymore. Then I bust out the classic: "Listen, beauty is common, but great energy and outlook are rare. You seem like you have something inside that makes me want to get to know you." Pffffft!

At her house, I make idle conversation about her garden and demonstrate my extensive horticultural knowledge. Once inside, we immediately start necking on the couch. I say, "Let's move to your bed."

She says, "No, the couch is fine."

I say, "Listen . . . this couch is NOT ergonomic." I crack myself up sometimes. Well, hell, all the time.

But anyway, I drag her to the bed, start gettin' it on, take off the panties and say, "I wanna lick it." And do so. After like fifteen minutes of this, I go in for the stab. She says no. What to do? *Wash-rinse-repeat!* So I back up and go in for lunch again. This time I employ the "Alphabet Technique," spelling out the alphabet with my tongue on and in her snatch. This does the trick, and after another ten minutes she is hollering. I go up and slide in.

She whispers, "We shouldn't be doing this!"

I say, "You are right, we shouldn't be doing this," and just carry on.

She goes, "Ohh but you feel so good inside me!" Nonetheless, she keeps intermittently saying we should stop. So we fuck for like twenty minutes. then she stops me for real, only because I don't have a condom and she's scared I will nut in her.

I wake up the next morning hungover. I eat her out then fuck her again without nutting. I give her my fucking *pager number* then leave. I'll probably stop by the bar tonight to say hi, and get her phone number.

Sexual state and escalation are the fundamentals upon which all technical game rests. I used many techniques here, but only to pepper the interaction, add a little flavor to it and lead it where I wanted it to go. But it was clearly my sexual state projection and persistence that closed the deal here. Without that, you ain't shit.

Finally, a same-night lay. This was pretty much a textbook caveman pull and it was like poetry. I've found that one good win like this is worth a hundred "crash and burns" in terms of learning experience and keeping the drive going. This is my new style. Onward and upward.

WARPIG SURPRISE

Morning. I awaken to a CRIPPLING hangover. As I turn to the side, I notice there is a warpig in bed with me: AIEEEE!!!

Oh no. I quickly check my cock and fortunately I am clothed; I did not fuck it. So I stumble about and get dressed for work, then fling open the curtains and poke the pig, attempting to wake it. No dice. I take all my valuables, lock them in the closet and stagger off to work. How the fuck did this happen? As I drive, I struggle to piece together the events that led up to this:

I arrived at El Rio later than usual last night. Unfortunately, I also had to skip dinner. There was a long line out front when I got there, so I queued up and began to wake up as it crept toward the door. Got inside, discovered my wings were not there. I was solo. So I posted up at the bar and began ordering vodka tonics two at a time. Soon I was very hammered.

A young honey sat next to me at the bar. I turned to her and said nonchalantly, "Hey. Do you know the dirty little secret of El Rio's Dollar Drink Night?"

She said, "No, what's that?"

I told her, "Well you see, they use military surplus liquor. Yes, this is what our boys in the Gulf are drinking right now. God bless those brave men and women, and God bless America."

She found this amusing, so we continued talking. At some point she asked my name, and I really warmed up to her. I told her my friends ditched me, and she replied, "I have friends; come on and meet them, they will like you!' Okay. We went out back to meet her friends . . . and discovered her friends were Julia Redhair and her obnoxious roommate

Autumn. I have given up on fucking Julia and now just use her for social proof. "This is Jeff, guys!"

I couldn't believe it. "Oh boy, THESE are your friends?"

Autumn snarled, "This guy attacked you, didn't he?"

The girl said, "No! He's cool!" or some such shit. Anyway, I continued to work on her, but halfheartedly.

I told some guy they were with that he was "French" and kept busting the guy for being French and not supporting our military forces. All he could do was keep saying, "I'm not French! Really!"

I told them I was going to karaoke and asked if they were coming with me. The honey went, "Oooh! You are performing there?"

I was like, "Yeah, I have a little tickle in the throat, but I'll give it a shot. Why, do you sing?" A bit more talking and it was all set: we were gonna meet up across the street at the karaoke bar.

Here's where I fucked up: instead of *dragging* them over there, I just walked ahead so I could go to the ATM first. Predictably, the moment I left their field of vision, they apparently forget all about our little plan and never showed up at the place. Fuck! Gotta keep the game tight; never let the target out of your sight.

Once at the karaoke bar, I began drinking in earnest. I got onstage and did a horrible version of Chris de Burgh's "Lady in Red." Some guy walked by the stage and mumbled something along the lines of, "You suck." I actually jumped offstage, still singing, and punched him in the neck. He said, "HEY!" and just continued walking to the bathroom. Pussy. As punishment for this, the owner of the bar made me sing "Country Roads" by John Denver.

I continued to slam booze until I became totally embalmed and apparently this was enough to make me believe that the repugnant battle hog giving me eyes at the end of the bar was in fact a lovely, vixeny temptress of desire. What happened next is a blur, but I remember singing some horrid duet with her ("Endless Love") and fucking it up, falling off the stage and spitting.

Then I took her to my house (oh, the humanity!) and tried to pawn her off on my chode roommate while I hid downstairs. He found me and insisted, "Jeff, go take care of your MESS!"

I trudged upstairs to appease the warpig. Fortunately, I became ill and violently regurgitated the ten or so drinks I had consumed on an empty stomach into the can. Then I passed out.

When I arrive home after work, the woman is gone and it appears that nothing has been stolen, thank God. Looks like I very nearly broke my New Year's Resolution of NO MORE FAT CHICKS. After ensuring that none of my valuables are missing, I go downstairs to find some of the roommates having dinner. I relate the tale to them. Sara, who has by now heard more than enough of my stories to render her completely appalled by my lifestyle, simply says, "Dude, you are, like, womankind's worst nightmare, aren't you?" I'm not sure if I should be flattered or offended.

RIOT GAME

This week there have been riots in downtown San Francisco stemming from a massive antiwar protest. Yesterday near the hotel, there were masked "black blocs" stopping traffic, smashing windows, pulling people from cars and fighting, people running over the rioters with cars and bikes, cops shooting tear gas, the whole bit. What better opportunity to run some game? I took a break and waded into the riot for some action.

I met some nice girls from "Boobs not Bombs," got a few pics with them and threw a bottle at the police.

Okay, I dropped a plastic bottle kind of near where the police were.

I don't really give a flying fuck about the war, pro or con, but I sure love to pick up girls and I love mayhem; this was so much fun that I can't begin to describe it. At one point somebody grabbed my shoulder from behind and yelled, "HEY! NO SUITS IN THE MARCH!" I whirled to strike him, knucks out, but it was just some guy I know from El Rio. Good times.

I heard it was only going to get worse as the week progresses, so tomorrow I'm going to wake up bright and early, throw on my "Oakland Cannabis Buyers' Cooperative" T-shirt ("the compassion angle") and take the bus downtown for more fun. My intention is to get pictures of me with girls, with cops beating people in the background.

I arrive late in the morning, and the cops have already arrested a lot of people, so there's just peaceful hippies walking down the sidewalk, no anarchy. The big shit is probably gonna go down at rush hour, like last night when they shut down the Bay Bridge. But fuck that, I've got a date with some chick at seven.

I'm walking along with my roommate Alexandra in the march, and we're pissed because it's lame and pussy. I have brought along a bullhorn and I keep shouting, "SHUT 'EM DOWN! SHUT 'EM SHUT 'EM DOWN!" The bullhorn also plays songs, so I keep blasting the "Marine Corps Hymn" and "The Star-Spangled Banner." The whole thing is really peaceful and douche-like.

We cross the street, and when I look back Alexandra is gone. Even though she's carrying a giant African drum, I can't find her, she's disappeared. As I look around, I notice a small girl in a conservative business suit with glasses walking amid the protesters. *She looks cute,* I think. To my surprise, she approaches me. "Uh excuse me," she says. "Do you know where Folsom Street is?"

"Yeah, what, you don't know where Folsom is? OH MY GOD." Laughing at her.

She replies, "No, I'm not from around here."

I smile. "Okay, where are you going?"

She has to get over to some hotel on Folsom. I agree to show her where it is and we start across the street. Now, this hotel is about four city blocks away, so I know I'll have like seven minutes with this girl, perfect for a well-run pickup. I launch into it:

"So, you're staying at this hotel, are you?"

She says, "No, I'm just here for a conference."

I'm clued in to all the conferences taking place in the city, so I go, "Oh, the dermatology conference."

She brightens up a little and says, "Yes!"

I say, "Cool, so what are the latest advancements in dermatology? I mean, is Botox right for me?"

She looks puzzled for a second, and says, "Botox! What, do you have bad wrinkles? You're too young for Botox!" She giggles.

I take off my sunglasses, look her in the eyes and project SEX at her. "I don't know, have a look." She says I look fine. "Awesome. So you're, like, a doctor?"

"No, I'm in marketing," she replies.

"Oh, Jesus. Marketing. I can see that. You marketing chicks are crazy. Every time I go up to the marketing department, it's all dark and dim, and you guys are always drinking out of some mystery mug that I suspect may contain an alcoholic beverage of some sort."

She laughs and says, "Wow, you're really hard to read!"

She starts asking me questions: my name, what I do, etc. We shake and I hold contact sensually. I find out she's late for her meeting and I bust on her for being a "bad little marketing girl" and suggest that she is late because she was getting hammered last night. I start to think about setting up a date. Tonight I have that other thing with the girl I met yesterday, so that's no good.

I ask her, "The conference is here for three more days, huh? So when you get off tomorrow, we can meet up for a drink. I work in the area."

She nods. "Yeah, that's cool."

We continue to walk along, and I make a comment about how far the hotel is. Then I say, "Damn, you're like, 'Jeez, I've had to talk to this guy for like ten minutes! WHEN is it going to END?!'"

She quickly says, "No, no! I like talking to you!" I bust out a few routines as we continue to walk, keeping her entertained.

We arrive at the hotel. "Cool, well here it is!"

I walk ahead of her slightly and go up to the valet guy. He knows who the fuck I am and so he greets me. I slap five and chat for a while, ask him where the dermatology thing is and say, "She's late for it, she got too loaded last night." The guy whips out the info. I grab a pen and paper from behind the podium and turn back to her.

"Well, my little suit nerd, we're gonna meet up tomorrow for that drink, so here, be creative." She thinks about it for a second, then writes down her number.

The End.

I think there were two things I could have done better: One, tried to make her just forget about the damn meeting and fucked her this afternoon. Two, more aggressive escalation. I didn't even hug her when we parted. At any rate, it seems fairly solid and the meet is on.

HAYE IS FOR HORSES

I'm at home having a nap when I am woken by a call from "Papa," a guy who frequents the same online seduction forum as I do. I've read a lot of his reports and have been impressed; he seems solid. It looks as though he's paired up with another luminary and favorite poster of mine, TylerDurden, and the two of them have been traveling around the world meeting the most interesting characters from the scene in each city they visit.

Apparently, I qualify as one of the "San Francisco All-Stars." Not long ago, Papa sent me an email asking if he could crash at my place when he rolls through the city. I told him I'd be honored, and we exchanged numbers. Now he's calling me up to confirm for next week. I assure him that the couch will be waiting . . . all systems go.

As soon as I get off the phone, I run to meet this babe I picked up last week. I'm running late as it is, and parking causes me to saunter into the bar twenty-five minutes late. I'm sure she's bounced by now.

Not so. She's there, sitting at the bar alone with a beer. She says, "I thought you weren't gonna show." I tell her I was parking. She exclaims, "Oh my God, you PARKED?! In THIS neighborhood?" and it's all good.

We have a couple of drinks. I get some good kino going. I can tell it's on as soon as there's an opportunity for isolation, so I keep it very neutral and fluffy, peppered with a lot of "ME TOO!" action, building commonalities. She asks me about my cigarette burns and I tell her all about my performance art. She's intrigued and asks if I have any other scars. I say she'll have to find out.

She says, "Hey listen, my sister is gonna show up in a minute. I'm really sorry, but we're going to a family wedding tomorrow and she needs to stay at my place tonight."

I'm like, "Great!" All smiley. Turns out the sister is gonna show right after she gets out of her court-appointed rehab meeting.

We continue to talk and I find out her last name is "Haye." "Like, for horses," she adds.

"That's cool," I say, " 'cause I'm hung like one." *Oh snap!*

Little Rehab Sister shows up a while later. We're introduced and I ask her, "So, do you want a drink?" *DICK.*

I smirk and the target kind of laughs, "You're a dick." We have some fun chat; I am being a fun guy. Turns out they had dinner plans at Ebisu and wouldn't you know, I am welcome to join them! I don't really want to blow a hundred dollars on sushi, but I decide to go along because I'm hungry and the place is quite good.

We eat. I make sure to sit next to her at the table and get physical, leg to leg, etc. Over dinner I talk about her favorite foods and how I will maybe cook for her one day. At the end, I go to pull out cash and she says, "No, put that away." She fucking buys me dinner. Things are looking up!

We walk a short distance to her home and the sister goes in, leaving Haye and I outside. She stands there expectantly. I move in and do a few seconds of triangular gazing, then embrace and kiss her. She seems kind of freaked out by it, so I back off.

I look at her and say, "You're an OKAY kisser. I think you can do better."

We kiss again, and this time it gets real, passionate. I start biting her neck, all that good stuff, ramming my erect prick into her. This goes on for like ten minutes before she says, "My sister . . ."

I capitulate, "All right." I kiss her again, briefly this time.

She then says this: "You're perfect."

Now it's my turn to be kind of freaked out. Yet amused. I blast her with laser love in my eyes, and say, "Yeah, baby, see you real soon." I bounce.

I immediately drive over to my girlfriend's house and fuck her.

GFF

"*B*EEEEEP BEEEEEP BEEEEEP BEEEEEP BEEEEEP" I wake up at 8:45 P.M., and my pager is blowing the fuck up. I'm supposed to meet up with Papa tonight, and here I have three chicks vying for my attention; the previous week's hard work is apparently paying off. All you have to do is get out there in the field and DO IT and the pussy will start to flow like a clear mountain stream. Or something like that.

Anyways, one of the chicks is my Chippy. I call her and tell her I'm going out with a friend from out of town and I'll see her tomorrow. Another is an old fuck buddy that I haven't seen in months but recently started calling. I decide to blow that one off. The final choice is Haye. She seems the most solid, and hey, *she bought me sushi.* I call her up, but she doesn't answer her phone. I hang up and call Papa to figure out where we're gonna meet.

As I'm heading out the door, Haye pages my shit again. I call from a pay phone and say, "Hey hey, Haye, it's Jeff, looks like we're playing the phone tag here. So, I'm meeting my friend for dinner, but I'd really like to see you, so page me up and I'll call you back. Maybe this time, you'll answer your phone . . . DORK!!"

I meet up with Papa, who introduces me to his friend Christophe, a fellow pickup artist. Christophe is this little French dude who recently moved to San Francisco. He barely speaks English, but Papa assures me that his game is sick. He was born and raised in Paris, and when I ask him what it's like there, he says, "Eet sucks. Fuck zees plaize." When Papa tells me he played guitar in an internationally renowned French rock band, he just shrugs and says, "Yah, whadavair. Eet wahs cool." A few years ago, he helped write a popular piece of media player software, and when it was sold he cashed in big-time. Now he's basically retired and just plays music and picks up girls. Yeah. I like this guy.

While we're eating, Haye buzzes me again. I wait until we are done with dinner, then call her back. It's about 11:30 P.M. This time she answers. There's loud music in the background, and she's yelling unintelligibly into the phone.

I ask her, "Are you fuckin' drunk? What the hell is this?"

I determine that she's at a club called Badlands in the Castro, a neighborhood with a predominantly gay demographic. So, she's at a fucking gay bar and wants me to meet her there. I say, "Damn, Haye, you ARE a dork."

She goes, "Jeff, you don't know the half of it."

I reply, "Well, I'm gonna find out tonight."

The guys start cracking on me about how I will likely have to fend off male advances and how I may have to face her Gay Fighting Friends. I mentally prepare and disembark.

I drive out to the Castro. As I drive by the place, I notice it is literally crawling with flamboyant men in various states of undress. It is slightly after midnight, and I am sober, since I took a nap and have been drinking nothing but water all night. I roll up and she's standing outside talking to some obviously gay dude. As soon as she notices me, I go up, grab her by the arm, spin her around and kiss her, using Papa's "100% Spin Kiss Maneuver." Her companion, whom she introduces as Larry, seems impressed. I chat them up and make some jokes, then we enter the club.

Inside, the place is fucking ridiculous beyond belief; a total fucking West Hollywood industrial-chic Jetsons deal. The crowd is full twink deluxe, gyrating on the floor to Britney Spears. I need booze. I tell Haye, "Buy me a drink and you might get lucky."

She asks me, "Are you any good? Will it be worth it?"

"Bitch please!" She buys the damn drink.

We hit the dance floor and it's, like, a hundred gay guys writhing around to Christina Aguilera and TLC, with Haye and myself stuck right smack dab in the middle. I'm dancing it up with the girl, grinding as though I'm oblivious to where I am. I alternately do this and talk to Larry. I say, "You guys are SOOO MUCH FUN!! YOU GUYS ROCK!!" This goes over well. After a while, however, she starts to ignore me and grind on Larry, as he is a better dancer. This leaves me looking like a chump; I realize I need to do something fast, or get freaked on by *men*.

Suddenly, I see somebody I know. I can't believe it . . . it's Neil, my old college roommate. Apparently he's come out of the closet, as he is now sporting an expensive haircut and a muscular build. I say, "DUDE! What's up!?"

It takes a second for him to recognize me. "Oh my God . . . Jeff? Hey bro! What the fuck are you doing in a GAY BAR?" I give him a big hug (with manly backslap thrown in, of course) and explain what's going on. Sweet. Now, I'm proofed and also have something to do while the target plays with her little friend. I talk with Neil for a while, then go off to take a piss.

The restroom is absurd. It is literally right next to the dance floor, with no doors, so dudes are standing right there pissing in full view. As I step in, some guy is standing in front of the urinal as his boyfriend helps him take his cock out.

This is going to make for a very unusual field report.

Back on the floor. While I was gone, Neil's been talking me up to the target. Good. He pulls out these purple star-shaped stickers that say, "I'm A Star!" and gives some to me, puts one on my lapel. He says, "Man, these stickers are great for the bar, dude. There's a lot of fag hags here; you give 'em these stickers and they will fuck. I've seen it happen."

I consider this for a moment, then take some and place them on Haye's nipples and start spanking her. I yell over the music, "If I follow you home, will you keep me?"

She replies, "WHAT? No! I'm not gonna PEE ON YOU! Gross!"

It's getting late and I'm thinking, *FUCK THIS SHIT TIME TO FUCK*. I put myself into sexual state and basically slam her up against the wall and start feeling her up. Some wack Madonna song is playing and every dude in the place is singing along. I kiss her.

Closing time. We go out front, where there are roughly twenty men milling about. This is where the competition starts. It's obvious that her friend Larry doesn't want me to go home with her, and there are a bunch of other gays trying to hit on me ("You arre so bootiful. Where are de drrugs?"). I tell them I'm a k. d. lang impersonator and this cracks them up. Larry attempts to kiss me. I just say, "NO."

I look over and these other dudes are trying to mack my girl. "You weel come parrty weeth us, you are the preencess." She's kinda just standing there drunk. Neil runs interference with these guys for a while, giving me time to get her out of there, but I keep getting interrupted. Finally he takes me aside and says, "Look Jeff, I can't do this anymore, you gotta do something."

Meanwhile, Larry keeps telling Haye, "*Andiamo*, let's go back to my house."

Fuck. It's now or never.

I get up close to her and say, "Hey, if I follow you home, will you piss on me?"

One of the queers overhears and yells, "OOH! Sassy!"

I turn to him and shout back, "This chick is nuts, she said she's going to urinate on me!" Then I get closer to her and whisper, "Listen, I should drive you home. I'm sober as a mortician. And remember, I'm a professional driver."

She scoffs. "Oh yeah?"

I say, "Yeah, I'll give you a ride."

Drunk, she considers for a moment and then says, "You'll give me a ride? What happens then?"

I say, "I'll give you a ride."

She pulls some shit about how she's afraid if she does that she'll never see me again. I roll out the old "beauty is common, but great energy is rare. You're special, Haye."

Okay!

As I drag her away, I slap five with Larry. He says, "Be nice to my friend." A warning.

I reply, "Hey, bro, I'm very respectful."

Driving home, the chick is going bonkers in the car, crawling into the backseat and shit with her ass all up in the air, her skirt is all hiked up, it's fucking obscene. I start smacking her ass as she pulls shoes, cups and assorted trash out of the backseat. Unreal.

We get to her house. As I pull up she says, "I bet you think you're coming in."

I ignore this, get out the car, quickly walk around the car and fling her door open. "Get the fuck out of the car." I then tell her, "Damn, all this alcohol. Lemme use your bathroom." We go up, being quiet so as to not disturb the roommate.

In her room, I basically rip my pants off and get into bed. I say, "Don't worry, nothing bad is gonna happen." I sprawl out across her bed, angst-ridden, and tell her, "No. No. Don't molest me. Don't do it." We start to kiss, and after twenty-five minutes of this I say, "I wanna lick it." I lick it. This goes on for like fifteen minutes. Then something happens and she just turns into a fucking beast.

All of a sudden, she's rocking my fucking world, it's like she has transformed into a goddamned ANIMAL, holy Christ. She's riding me and fucking holding me down, growling and snarling. Awesome. She puts her hands on my neck, starts choking me out . . . like, really cutting off my airway. I can't breathe.

Oh shit, this bitch is fucking choking me. Damn, what have I gotten myself into, I knew pickup would get me into trouble . . . oh shit, I can't breathe . . . damn, I better stop her, smack her hands away, or something. Hmmm, wait a minute. Fuck it . . . I honestly don't give a fuck . . . what, am I gonna die? Who fucking cares? All right then . . . here we go . . . EROTIC ASPHYXIATION!

We finish off and my vision clears as blood starts flowing to my brain again. She's suddenly all sweet and cuddly, and I decide to stay the night. We fall asleep in each other's arms.

I bang her again in the morning, and have breakfast with her before leaving. I really like this chick, I mean, she's kind of a butterface, but her body is tight as fuck, and after that performance she's definitely a keeper. As Jackass always says, "It's not the face you fuck, but the fuck you face." I think my next choking appointment will be on Sunday.

TWELVE-YEAR-OLD GAY THIEVES; HELD AT GUNPOINT

Monday night means El Rio, and that's where I'm headed right now with my roommate, Brian. I'm meeting the Suit Nerd from the riot there.

She arrives just as we do. As she walks up, I see she is cuter than I remembered, but it soon becomes apparent that she is a complete nerd. She tells me that she lives with two Indian engineers and went to MIT. I'm somewhat turned off by this, and as such keep my distance. As we enter El Rio, she tells me *she has never been to a bar before*. "In that case," I warn her, "I would advise you to stay away from the dollar cocktails, as they are reputed to contain military surplus liquor." We have one drink, then get stamped and leave.

We go across the street to the karaoke bar. I sing. The manager warns me not to slam the mic into my head like that. I start working on Suit Nerd. I ask her about her life and all this, then I notice a fucking RING on her left ring finger. I ask, "What's this, are you married?"

She's engaged. She starts telling me about her fiancé, and all of his flaws. He has all the qualities she thought she wanted in a man, but the reality isn't what she expected. I agree and talk about the "natural woman" that needs to be satisfied, blah blah blah, then I tell her that the fiancé is great and all, but it's not his fault that he can't fulfill her fantasy or whatever. Bored with this, I let Brian occupy her while I blatantly game up this other chick who has approached the bar to order drinks.

As this is happening, I notice a group of people at an adjacent table looking at me and talking, then some dude walks over. He comes up to me and asks, "Hey, you're Jeff Allen, aren't you?"

Not knowing exactly what's going on, but understanding that this guy is attempting in some way to tool me, I grab him by the shirt front and yell "WHO THE FUCK IS ASKING? WHO THE FUCK ARE YOU?!"

The guy's buttons actually rip off. I know he's going to want to kick my ass, but for the moment he is taken by surprise. I capitalize on this by immediately "apologizing" and yukking it up big-time with him. The girl I was talking to at the bar appears worried. I see what's happening now. I must have gamed the girl before with this guy in the set. They're probably together. I say, "That's your girlfriend, huh?"

He goes, "Yeah . . ."

"So," I say, "when are you guys getting married?"

He mumbles, "Four years . . ." and wanders off in a daze. Odd. I look at my watch, it's 10:30 P.M. Fuck this nonsense. It's prime El Rio time. I grab the nerd and we head over.

As expected, there is a huge line outside the club. I march past, making derisive comments about "the line for Space Mountain" and walk through the entrance, slapping the door chick five. The place is fucking packed. Suit Nerd appears terrified. I know a lot of the girls here tonight, and high-five all of them as we walk around. We run into one of our other roommates, Taz, and we all go out back together.

I see a girl I met last week. I had brought Papa to the Rio and he had gamed her up in front of me. I stop her. "HEY!"

Her eyes light up as she recognizes me. She asks about Papa, and I tell her he went home. She says, "Yeah, he's smooth, though . . . he pulled a fast one on me!" I ask her what she means by that and she says, "He did this thing where he spun me around and kissed me."

The 100% Spin Kiss Maneuver. I laugh, I say, "Yeah, that sounds like Papa. He's cool as a motherfucker. I'm really not that smooth though, it's not my style."

"What's your style?"

I say, "CAVEMAN," and kiss her. I back off, and she tells me to do it again. Unfortunately, she's sort of a poor kisser and I'm not turned on at all, which is strange because she's hot. So I'm like, "That's fun, well hey, great to see you!" She walks off.

I'm on a roll now, and I kiss another chick that I vaguely know as she walks by using a similar caveman approach. Meanwhile, poor Suit Nerd is still standing right there, totally bewildered and shocked by the whole El Rio scene; it's like a fucking Hieronymus Bosch painting come to life. Fortunately, Brian and Taz continue to occupy her.

Soon, however, the Nerd says she has to leave. I keep telling her she can stay at our house, it's cool, but she insists on leaving. Whatever, she's a major low self-esteem case. She keeps standing there repeating, "I'm a 4. I'm a 4!" Finally she makes her exit. I hope she gets home alive.

Taz, Brian and I start practicing our alpha caveman roars/grunts until a staff member tells us to shut the fuck up. The vibe at El Rio is getting really strange; the clientele seems to be getting younger and younger, it's almost like an underage joint now. I attribute this to the dollar drink prices. Don't get me wrong, I'm not complaining about teenage girls, but it's certainly interesting.

The crowd parts for a second and I see this girl whom I almost fucked last week. I pulled her from Rio back to her dorm room at USF but was ultimately cockblocked by her roommate. She's there with an entourage of what appear to be twelve-year-old gay boys. I mean, these kids are seriously underage, they are in fact fucking TEENAGERS. As she walks by, I reach out, draw her near and say, "HEY Alice!" She is very pleased to see me, as is Jon, one of the twelve-year-olds. We merge groups and go over to an isolated corner area. I sit next to the girl and initiate heavy physical escalation.

Out of left field, she informs me that she just broke up with her fi-ancé. "See? I just met you last week, and this week I broke up with him. See?"

I'm thinking, *What the fuck is this shit?* I just ignore it and bite her neck. Soon, I convince her and Jon to come back to our place, I tell them we are in a fraternity and we live in a frat house, emphasizing that "it is cool." I figure the one guy will be easily distracted by my roommates.

We start to leave, but as we get about halfway up the block, three people come running up: it's her annoying-ass roommate who kicked me out of their dorm room last week, another gay kid and some random dode she apparently intends to hook up with, judging by the way she's hanging on him. The guy looks strange, like he's on mushrooms or some-thing. The annoying friend asks, "Where are we going? We're coming along."

The kid Jon pulls me aside and says, "NO. I do not want these people to come." I know I should listen to him and prohibit them from com-ing, but I permit them to tag along. I am too drunk to stop myself from committing this tactical error.

We get back to my house and more drinking ensues. Taz keeps hol-lering fucked-up shit at the two kids:

"You look like you're twelve! Oh man, this is a sting!"

"Wow! You guys are the gayest little dudes I've ever seen in my fuck-ing life!"

"You're so SMALL!"

He keeps saying this stuff OVER and OVER and they are getting pissed. I think it's funny, but I do not laugh. Finally, I somehow get them to leave my room, and I'm isolated with Alice. I start the endgame. She says, "This is crazy, I don't even know you!"

"What do you want to know? And why?" This shuts her up, and we continue kissing.

There is a knock on the door. I ignore it. I am sucking on one of the girl's near-perfect tits when her phone rings. She doesn't answer. It seems as though her friend Annoying has finished screwing around on my couch downstairs with the mushroom guy, and has decided that it's time to go and that she *will not leave without Alice.*

Too fucking bad. She's going to have to wait. Alice is enjoying herself. I tell her that "I wanna lick it" and take off her panties.

Yes. This is the moment I live for.

As I'm performing cunnilingus, her phone rings again. This time she answers it. I'm struck by the absurdity of it: *she is talking on the phone as I eat her pussy,* trying not to moan as she says, "No. NO! Ahhh . . . oh . . . no, give me—ah!—fifteen minutes . . . ahhhh no twenty minutes! OH . . ."

This is bad and I know it, so I try to make it quick. I squirt lube on my cock and just as I get the tip inside, my roommate Alexandra starts POUNDING on my door, yelling something about "respect."

Well, that does it, the girl's state is completely broken, and she gets up. I open the door, and Annoying comes in and forces her to get her shit together and go. She says, "Alice, you so owe us for this one."

I say, "Hey Alice, you don't owe her shit."

Annoying says, "Listen, guy, I'm not gonna let my friend just stay here."

"I don't understand what your deal is; nothing is gonna happen that she doesn't want to happen."

"Uh . . . yeah, but . . ." She has no real response to this. Be that as it may, Alice writes her number down and they leave.

Things go sharply downhill from there. I get totally drunk and hit Brian in the shoulder with an aluminum tee-ball bat in a blind rage, yelling, "GET AWAY, COCKBLOCKERS!"

Then we make a ruckus out front hitting cans into the street until the next-door neighbor, who happens to be an officer with the SFPD, comes out in his pajamas with his gun in his hand. He confiscates the bat, says, "Gentlemen, it is three in the morning," and walks back inside.

In the morning, I go next door retrieve the bat. My neighbor just shakes his head and says, "What the hell were you guys doing last night?" I put on a sheepish grin, apologize and take the bat home. Looks like I'm really putting my best foot forward with the neighbors here. To make matters worse, I discover that one of the kids stole my sunglasses. Fuck that shit. I know where they live.

LITTLE MISS TWELVE GAUGE

I stand poised to log my first lay from an online pickup.

I'm calling her "Miss Twelve Gauge." The girl is a solid 8. She is twenty years old and keeps a shotgun under her couch. She lives in the East Bay, about forty minutes away. She initially sent me a message on Friendster because she thought I was "hot." I assume this was based on my photo, a ridiculous black-and-white "glamour" head shot (think Barbizon) and my profile, listing my occupation as Psychic Undercover Ass Model From The Future/Thug. In any case, she sent me a message out of the blue: "Can I make you my bitch?"

I replied, "I don't know . . . CAN YOU?"

From there it was on, some banter back and forth about some "booty call" I was going on. I then sent her a lengthy message saying I had kinda lost faith in girls as a whole, because they were predatory and evil, and how I met this chick at the bar and she had an engagement ring on, and I was totally turned off, but the chick just wanted have her beta loser provider guy and also have this thing on the side with me, an alpha seducer guy, chicks are so fucked up, using me as a sex toy . . . how can I know if she's any different? She sent back a message that was very genuine.

Yesterday she took it to the next level, initiating chat with me. I busted on her for thinking I was serious about being scared of predatory evil women ("Dork!"). Then I told her to come over and clean my house. I told her to come out to the Rio on Monday, indicating that I can get her in despite her being underage, "because I'm in the A-crowd."

She said, "Oh you can buy me drinks!"

I simply replied, "HA HA HA." I suggested she could perhaps get a "striped-shirt fag" to buy her and me drinks throughout the course of the night; after all, she was claiming she would be "the hottest one there." She alluded to having me pick her up, but I squashed that and told her to take the BART. I got her to give me her number without asking for it by saying, "Okay, I'll call you tomorrow."

• • •

call her and it's set up: she's gonna come by my place this afternoon, ostensibly to "clean my house." She arrives in the city, calls me and I go to pick her up at the BART station. I roll up and want to get out and hug her to set the tone early, but she recognizes me as I drive up and jumps in the car. She is fucking hot, hotter than I expected. I am pleased. The mood is light, I'm feeling confident, drinking a Pabst Blue Ribbon. We get back to my place.

We talk about gardening. I show her my yard. Then I MAKE HER CUT MY GRASS. While this is happening, I'm tripping out; I have a hot young chick whom I met on the internet cutting my fucking grass for me. This whole process takes over an hour. Meanwhile, I'm focusing on RAPPORT. I know this is my weak spot, so I keep the cocky crap to a minimum, as I've already completed that stage. I do fractionate back occasionally, however.

After the ordeal with the grass, I am tired, so I lay down on my bed with her. I'm trying to position myself, but the damn cats keep jumping between us. I knock one away, and another jumps up. Finally, I knock them all away and I ask her how good a kisser she is. She says, "An 8." I tell her I don't believe it and kiss her.

Kissing lasts about twenty minutes, then I take her shirt off. Five minutes of this, then the patented "I wanna lick it" as I remove her pants.

She says, "What if I told you my pants don't come off?

I reply, "Hmm, that's weird, it *looks* like they come off!" I remove them swiftly.

More resistance as I try to take the panties off. She says, "I don't sleep with strangers. I have morals."

I just ignore this, say, "Yeah," and take off her panties.

Then something horrible takes place. I kind of slide up on top of her, and I hear her SCREAM! For a split second, I think I did something to upset her, but then a searing sharp FUCKED UP agonizing pain shoots up my chest; something is TERRIBLY WRONG and I realize that my nipple ring has gotten locked up with her belly button piercing and it is yanking our fucking piercings out. I try to remain calm and move so that

I can fix it, all the while she's thrashing around and shit, GOD the pain is so intense it feels like my nipple is ripping off but finally I somehow manage to dislodge it, and I roll off, yelling.

My nipple is bleeding; there is blood coming out the tip of it like I'm fucking lactating. She sees this and says, "Oh my God . . . you're pregnant with Satan." Her navel is bleeding too. This kind of derails things. We lay there bleeding and shit for a while.

After a brief period of recovery, I take up where I left off and it isn't long before I have her saying, "Fuck me from behind." Awesome. I do her twice then drive her home.

At her house, she graciously makes me dinner. I decide to stay over and bang her some more. In the morning, she prepares strawberry pancakes and bacon for breakfast. We wash it down with Budweiser. I think I'm in love.

Upon arriving back at the Blauhaus, I find that she has already messaged me: "You rock." This may be the hottest chick I've ever laid. I'm amazed at how easy it was . . . easier than an ugly chick! It's something that's said a lot on the forum, but it's true: these techniques work *better* on hotter chicks. Banging this girl has shown me that I CAN get hot chicks and it's in fact easier in many respects.

Total time from online meeting to lay: four days. I was skeptical, but now I believe. The internet CAN get you pussy, perhaps at the risk of losing some of your edge in real life, but I'm not complaining. This chick is hot.

Ahh, sometimes life is good.

I've got about three other online leads that seem feasible. Shit is getting out of control. I think I'm spreading myself too thin between my Rio chicks, my fuck buddies and my girlfriend. Now add this internet crap to the mix. I can't keep track anymore. Time to trim down to a manageable stable.

TD AND PAPA AT EL RIO

"**F**ucking bastard, FUCK YOU! You fucking don't return my calls and just fucking call me out of the blue to fuck! Fuck you, bastard, if I ever see you again I'm gonna KICK YOUR ASS!!"

Oh brother. Another threatening phone message. I should be accustomed to these by now, but this one is different. For one, it's coming out of my answering machine *at home*, and this time it's not from an employee. It's from Haye. I fucked her back in March, and in the three months since then I've seen her maybe twice. Looks like she is a bit upset.

This chick knows where I live, and after this I definitely don't want to ever fuck her again, especially in light of the fact she was down with the asphyxiation. Gotta pare down the stable before it spirals out of control. I have no experience with this, with chicks acting crazy. It's odd, because I didn't lie to her. I thought I did an excellent job of spelling out from the beginning that I didn't want a relationship, that I have an *extremely active* social life where I see women. Basically, I let her know what the fuck I am: a player. I mean, Christ, whaddya expect, I picked her up off the street and we were fucking less than a week later. Who the fuck did she think I was . . . Ward Cleaver?

Bitches. Shit.

I erase the message. I have bigger fish to fry. I am awaiting the arrival of TylerDurden.

Papa's coming through SF again, and this time he's bringing Tyler with him. Two of the best guys from the online pickup community, staying at my place. This is going to be awesome. What's even more exciting is that they have started conducting paid "workshops" where they take guys out to the club and do live instruction. There's one scheduled here in San Francisco next week, and in exchange for my hospitality they've invited me to attend the program as their guest.

They arrive at around 8:30. I greet Tyler enthusiastically, like an old friend. He seems standoffish. He explains that he is tired as fuck as a result of his hectic travel schedule. Nonetheless, he begins methodically getting dressed for the club, spraying his hair before throwing on a fishnet shirt and a faux-snakeskin jacket. He puts a pair of sunglasses on as he walks up to me. "Dude," he says, "I'm so exhausted that I'm not in the mood to go *anywhere*. Like, if I was invited to a Puff Daddy party I wouldn't go. But I have to see the famous El Rio."

Finally, we roll up to El Rio at 9:30. Of course, by this time there is a MASSIVE line outside. I am mortified at having to wait in line but TD is a lagger. I blame him entirely. I try to use my clout to get them in but it is a poorly coordinated effort and it just doesn't happen. Chicks are laughing at me. "I never thought I'd see YOU standing in LINE!!! HAHAHA!"

Almost as soon as we walk in, a fat creepy gay guy goes caveman on Tyler, giving him an intense leer and projecting sexual state. Tyler is deeply disturbed. I pull him away and we go out back.

It becomes readily apparent that Tyler cannot STOP talking about game. He talks about it more than I do. The next thing I know, he's forcing me to approach girls . . . groups of chicks much hotter than I am usually accustomed to approaching. "I'm doing this because I can sense your fear," he says, "Go. Go. Go. Go. Go. Go." He starts goosing me in the side until I do it. I run several sets in front of him. To my astonishment, most of the approaches go pretty well. I expected to encounter a higher level of "bitch shield" when approaching hotter girls, but it was really no different than approaching a 7, maybe easier.

After a few of these episodes, Tyler critiques my style. Most of my errors lie in body language. Holding my drink up instead of down at my side. Crossing my arms. Feet not far enough apart. Overgaming, i.e., too much ballbusting when the chick is obviously into me. Very insightful. While this is happening, Papa is spin-kissing a fucking model, unusual because model-caliber chicks are rarely found at the El Rio. She invites him to a party on Wednesday. I am impressed. I am inspired.

I look around and see a girl giving me strong eye contact. I go up and get her to buy me a drink, start running the standard shit. There is chemistry from the second I start talking . . . the chick is so into me it's absurd.

All of a sudden, out of nowhere, Tyler appears and says, "Hey, jlaix, let's go to the karaoke bar."

The chick asks, "Oh, you're leaving?" All frantic. I eject.

I'm not sure why he pulled me out when it was going so well, and I ask him this with a slightly irritated edge to my voice over by the shuffle-board table. "You always want to do a takeaway on a high note," he tells me. *Okay, that makes sense.* We leave the bar.

We go to the taco place first. As we are eating, who walks in but the same chick. "HEY! You weren't at the karaoke bar!" After some talk, I simply throw my phone at her. She says, "What's this for? To give you my number?"

I just give her a disdainful look and say, "Pfft. Be creative." She actually punches TWO numbers into my phone before leaving. Crazy.

We go to the karaoke bar. I am riding high. I walk by the bouncer dude and say, "Yeah, you know who the fuck I am." Inside, it's intense, they have set up this bizarre, giant mechanical hog onstage and a fucking warpig woman is riding on it, all sweaty, singing Bon Jovi. A pig on a hog. This sends me to the ground in paroxysms of laughter.

The bartender, this chick with tattoos all over her arms, starts talking to me. Christophe told me that he was in there last week and she had been asking about me "Where's Jeff? He's the hottest guy in this place." At the time, I thought he was bullshitting me to raise my confidence or something, but when I walk up to the bar now, she shoves a scotch in my face, free of charge. I start gaming her. I sing, and when I get offstage I see she has gone outside.

I follow her out with the boys in tow. She is smoking a cigarette. I grab it out of her hand and drag on it. She says, "You're the best-looking guy in here." I'm not sure how to respond to this. I ask her what days she usually works, then I go for a Spin Kiss. Problem is, I'm fucking wasted, and I fuck it up and actually INJURE myself, possibly incurring the first ever injury sustained from the execution of the Spin Kiss Maneuver. She has on some kind of metal bracelets, and I spin her around really hard, so much so that she spins like 540 degrees, and I notice the metal bracelets have slashed open my finger, there's a flap of skin, and blood running down my wrist as we walk off.

Tyler, Papa and I get back to my pad and we stay up until four debriefing and going over all of the interactions with a fine-toothed comb. What a night. These guys are not only very skilled, but also very cool.

Tyler says, "Cool, man. It's gonna be great having you as a guest instructor on the program. We're going to give you a spot on the seminar panel too."

I look over at Papa. "Guest . . . *instructor?* You didn't say anything about that! I thought I was just going to attend the program for free!"

"It's fine, man," says Tyler. "Don't worry about it. Just get up there and talk for fifteen minutes, you'll be fine." He points the finger guns at me. "After all, you're the famous JAY-LAX. You the man, baby!"

"Well, that's true. But I'm still not sure how I feel about all this."

"As for the field portion, yeah, your skill set needs work but you're still better than most of the guys on the forum." I'm skeptical and get the feeling he's blowing smoke up my ass so I'll agree to help them out. Tyler seems to sense this and says, "Think about it, dude. That girl went out of her way to look for you at the bar, and when she didn't find you there, she searched the vicinity, spotted us in the taco shop, then came in to talk to you. She did it in front of all her friends. Solid game. Don't sell yourself short. You have a LOT of potential, dude. This the kind of thing that's only going to make you stronger."

I reluctantly agree. Knowing he's right doesn't make me any less nervous.

PICKUP WORKSHOP

The workshop begins in the afternoon with a seminar. About twenty-five people are in attendance. When it's my turn to speak, I get up there and reel off an improvised fifteen minutes during which I expose my beer gut to the crowd and declare that it "is named Kuato and he is destined to save Mars from the evil Recall Corporation." Half of the audience is appalled; the other half find it hilarious. Which is encouraging.

Then we split up into groups and hit the field. Since I'm only a "guest instructor," there isn't too much pressure on me to dazzle the students. Still, I resolve to help these guys to the best of my ability, while of course simultaneously trying hide the fact that I really don't know what the fuck I'm doing.

For the fieldwork, Tyler and Papa have chosen a series of high-energy dance clubs. From the beginning, I am out of my comfort zone. I don't work clubs, I do BARS. But as soon as we enter the main part of the club, I know I'm hooked. The women here are all so much . . . *hotter.* This is something that I've been needing to do for a long time.

The place is extremely loud. A rock band is playing and the chicks are getting very drunk, very quickly. Papa's spin-kissing bitches left and right; his face is literally COVERED in lipstick. When we get to the next venue, a hip-hop club, it's also very loud, 50 Cent plays as HOT HOT girls writhe around on podiums. It's obvious that I'm out of my element . . . this certainly isn't El Rio. I try to approach, but it is just too loud. My voice isn't powerful enough to carry over the music. No fucking way the Dental Floss Opener is going to work here. I try it a couple of times regardless: "Hey guys, quick question: do you floss your teeth *before* or *after* you brush?"

They either say, "WHAAAT?" and turn away, or simply ignore me.

I start opening by just rolling up and yelling, "OH MY GOD YOU'RE MY NEW BEST FRIEND!" It doesn't really work at first because I'm not congruent with it, but I slowly begin to get them to stop, at least for a few minutes. Meanwhile, Papa is going fucking nuts; while I am talking to one of the students, he runs up and yells, "We have ten minutes! I need eleven more kisses! AHHHHH!" He is covered in red smears and looks like he's been attacked or something. He grabs the student and runs off to make out with some more girls before we have to leave for the next club. Tyler sees this and is disdainful.

"Flash game," he scoffs. "Mental masturbation. They won't pull."

I say, "I'm in agreement, but hey, they're having fun and we're just standing here." I start to dance. These girls come up to me and start freaking me. They are very drunk and I'm not sure how to react. No matter, time's up; we leave for the next club.

I wake up on Sunday morning, having survived my first pickup workshop. I didn't get laid. I didn't even get a phone number. What I did get from the program was this: valuable knowledge about something I'm not really familiar with, the club scene. I thought that it was going to be similar to the bar scene. I was wrong. It's crazy intense, crazy loud and the girls have crazy bitch shields up. This is the big leagues, and I'm going to learn to play at this level, even if it kills me. The journey of a thousand miles begins with a single step.

It's Tyler and Papa's last night in town. We head to 1015 for some more intense club training, only to find it's closed on Sundays. We settle for a smaller club up the block, the EndUp.

We get to the door and I ask the chick, "Is it cool? I don't want to pay a cover if it's lame." She tries to prevent me from looking in. I tell her, "If it were cool, you'd let me look." She relents, letting me go in while the others wait. I come back out and say, "Two words: homosexual and Asian. There are maybe two 9s in the place."

The door chick looks at me like I'm insane. Tyler laughs and says, "Yeah, we're assholes, eh?" I want to bail, but I also know this is my last chance to game with these guys, so we all go in.

It is totally gay. And Asian. Loud-ass music, dudes with no shirts making out, Asian gangsters, many large steroid chodes with sunglasses on. A very eclectic scene. I'm not sure why Asian gangsters would be here, but hey, welcome to San Francisco. We approach a couple of mixed groups of guys and girls. Papa amazes me by cavemanning a girl up out of her seat and sitting her on his lap, before getting her to give him a back massage. As cool as this may be, the problem remains: there are just not that many good sets here.

I do, however, spy one singular Super Hot Tall Blonde Thing. She's on the dance floor. I ask what to do. "Well," says Tyler, "you wait for them to trickle off." Soon enough, she walks off the dance floor with a sunglasses-wearing alpha male type who just *looks* like he belongs with her.

Tyler says, "Go."

I'm frozen in place. "WHAT?!!"

He looks at me sternly and says, "The dude is gay. GO approach the girl. You have to learn this. Go."

Whoa. I take a deep breath and go. As I approach, yet another huge man with sunglasses joins them. So now it's me, little ol' jlaix, rolling up on a turbo hottie and two alpha males.

I get about five feet away before I balk. I turn around.

Tyler is standing right there, in my face. He shakes his head, and forces me to turn back around and open the group.

I walk up like I'm marching to the gallows and proceed to crash and burn. As I approach for the second time, the chick has now turned away and the first dude has positioned himself between us. "Dental Floss Opener" bombs. I have to yell over the music, the guy makes me repeat myself three times, and looks at me like I'm a total idiot. My brain turns to jello, I can't think of anything to say and I feel like the biggest loser on earth, so I high-five him and say, "Yeah you're cool," or some shit as he cuts me out of the set. I walk back in defeat.

I just got *disintegrated*.

I explain what happened to Tyler. Why did he force me to approach after I turned back? Because he knew it would be a disaster . . . one that would teach me a valuable lesson about proximity. I had too much proximity for too long and this generated negative social proof, in my mind as much as theirs. By lingering in their periphery too long, I basically *ensured* that my approach was going to get snubbed hard. These were fucking serious alpha dudes and a SUPER HOT BABE, so in this instance "too long" was a matter of the SECONDS it took for me to stop short, turn around and go back. Hardcore. I can say this much, though: I will never make that mistake again.

This weekend has been enlightening. I know what my next steps are now. I need to start going to these high-stress club environments if I want to take my game to the next level. I've grown accustomed to small bars where the music isn't superloud and the girls aren't as hot. The club is much different than the bar, and in my opinion, if I can game there, I can game anywhere else with ease. Four nights a week for a month, and I think I'll be good. I must find a way to continue this quest, while at the same time managing my stable of fuck buddies.

THE PRESUMPTION OF RESPECT

I have settled into a fairly regular weekly pickup routine now. Mondays are El Rio night. Tuesdays are for fucking Miss Twelve Gauge. Wednesdays I reserve for Day 2 meets with new candidates for the harem. Thursdays, Fridays and Saturdays are split between girlfriend time and club game. Sundays are a time for quiet reflection.

On Sunday afternoon, I sit in my office and go through a process that I refer to as "checking my traps." This means I ring up all the numbers I got during the previous week and follow up, attempting to arrange meetings. I also take this time to manage fuck buddies, giving them a ring to let them know I am still thinking about them. I'm rapping quietly to myself as I go through my phone directory: "... *checking my traps like a dirty rat, I was born to mack, I'm hookin' hos like crack* ..." The phone rings. Ahem. I answer it. "Thank you for calling Sky High Valet Service, this is Jeff, how may I assist you?"

"Hey Jeff! What's going on? It's me, Olivia!"

She didn't have to tell me. I instantly recognize the voice. Olivia, the supposedly herpes-ridden employee who I fucked in my office over a year ago. Crazy bitch. Worst couple of weeks of my life, waiting for the results.

Thankfully, I lucked out, and in more ways than one: the test came back negative, and she ended up quitting the job a few weeks later, of her own volition.

Of course, being the dumbass that I am, I fucked her without a condom again a couple of months later, and repeated the whole process over again. I swore from then on that I would be more careful.

"Oh yeah. Olivia," I say. "Great!"

She goes, "I know, isn't it? Yeah, I just moved back here, I've been living in Arkansas."

"Oh, wow, well that sounds perfect for you."

She pauses. "Uh yeah. Don't you love me still?"

I laugh, "Oh yes, I love you so much, you are like my disease-ridden little sister! What the fuck?!"

"I know right . . . listen, my tits are bigger! They grew!"

At this point, I just resign myself to the insanity. "Huh? What do you mean? Did you beef up? Were you on a high-protein diet?"

She says, "No, I was on a fat diet."

"Oh, so you're fucking fat now. Even better."

She giggles and says, "No, my tits grew! I'm only eighteen, remember?"

I hear myself say, from far away, "Oh yes, well how magical. Listen, I gotta go . . . give me your number." *WHAT THE FUCK ARE YOU DOING JEFF?* She reels it off and I hang up.

Oh Christ I hope I don't bang this slut again.

I find myself developing a hot-chick dependency. I spend almost all my time around women now. When one is not around, I have started experiencing a strange withdrawal anxiety, like, "Oh my God, how come I have no messages from my girls, how come they aren't calling, I need to see one NOW."

I have become addicted to attention from hot girls. I need them to bust on (literally and figuratively), I need them to bring me tacos and beer, I need them to cut my grass, clean my room, pet me and say nice things. This is getting to be a bona fide problem.

The real issue, however, is that there are NO nonpickup-related sides to my life anymore. Pickup is my fucking life, that's it. I MADE it my life, so I would get good FAST. But really, y'know what? This is fine. I wanted it, now it is reality.

Later, at home, I'm browsing the forum when I come across a post that disturbs me. Specifically, I'm bothered by the following quote:

> If all men on this earth could find their own worth without
> pussy approval from women, then this would be a site for
> women to figure out how to get guys.

I read it twice, trying to comprehend what it is that I am seeing here. What the fuck is this. "Find your worth"? "Pussy approval"? Nonsense. I just wanna fuck hot chicks.

The forum has taken a strangely abstract turn lately. It seems the topic du jour is what they're calling "inner game." A bunch of horseshit about feelings and values and stuff. I used to have those, a long time ago. Even when I first started pickup, I still wanted to feel somehow justified in my behavior.

Now, I've quit fighting it and I let my dick do the talking. What are my "end values" in all of this? Honestly, I haven't even thought about it. If pressed, I would probably say INDULGENCE. I'm just having fun having sex with lots of girls. In the end, I'd probably want someone who shares my interests and who maybe can cook. I haven't cared enough to really think about it yet. The thing is, there is nothing like the experience of getting NEW pussy. You cannot synthesize in any lab that rush you get when taking the panties off for the FIRST TIME. For me, this is about SEX, pure and simple. I refuse to pollute that beautiful purity with "ideas." I will pollute it, if I must, with a nice dinner at an exclusive restaurant. On her dime.

Reading further, the poster goes on to deride the use of systematic tactics and techniques as a betrayal of one's "true self," even going so far as to suggest that their use is in and of itself a form of supplication to women.

I can take this no longer. I crack my knuckles and fire off a response, typing angrily:

Say what you will, but the "tactics/techniques" I've learned merely expedite the process, don't tell me they don't. Let's look at the statistics:

In the twenty-six years of my life prior to finding the forum, I had sex with a total of seven women.

In the TEN MONTHS after that, I've been with twenty-one women, and those women have generally been much hotter than that original seven.

So there you go. And I enjoyed the process of gaming every one, springing my "supplicant tactics" at just the right time for maximum effect, resulting in nasty, sweaty fuckfests which I will treasure for a lifetime.

I hit the "submit post" button, then go out for a burrito. When I get back, I see the original poster has responded, asking, "But where is the humanity in that?"

Mouth full of burrito, I reply once again:

Humanity?!

Who cares?

Sounds like hippie shit to me. You guys can burn patchouli and talk about the age of Aquarius all you like, but I am having sex with hot, young girls using these methods.

I hate you all. See you in Hell!

SEX WITH GIRAFFE

Got another lead from my internet trawling, some manner of tall woman from the looks of her photographs. After the standard message banter I coaxed the number out of her.

I call her after work and tell her to meet me. She doesn't want to go to El Rio. I don't blame her, as that's my place of power. I run a couple of routines as we talk on the phone. Eventually, she says, "Okay, meet me at my house. But you can't come up. Yet."

I reply, "Whoa, you think I'm just gonna go into your house? You probably have some dude with a bat there and you're gonna steal my kidney! Or it could be a cult or some shit!"

She laughs her ass off. "I might not have the energy to deal with you," she says.

"Ha, yeah, I see how you could get that impression . . . listen, I'll just get all stoned first, then I'll be subdued." She laughs again.

I've just gotten a new haircut from my Supercuts bitch, Anita, except this time, instead of using my patented "Stop . . . more sexy" line to coax a better haircut out of her, I said, "Stop . . . more romantic."

She thought for a second, then pulled out these special scissors and said, "More romantic . . . yes, young people like."

So the hair is on point. I'm wearing black jeans, black Zero T-shirt with white skull on it, Top Gun sunglasses, Giant Iced-Out Pinky Ring, bondage cuff, freshly buffed Tiffany bracelet and ancient New Rock Boots. Just before walking out the door, I look at the mirror and say to myself, "You do this ALL THE TIME. This is your FUN. This is WHAT YOU DO. Kill it."

I meet her at a cafe just outside her apartment. As I roll up, I can see that she is very tall, at least six feet two, and she is pretty. Anyone else would call her a 7.5, but I got a thing for the tall white girls. I give her a tentative

8.5, pending her performance later. I sit down and go for a high-five, but she insists on a hug. Okay, after that I make her high-five anyway. We get up to go eat.

As she stands up, it becomes apparent that I am at least half a foot shorter than her . . . in my boots. Kind of strange, usually I don't trip on that kind of shit, but it takes a block or two for me to figure out how to approach the whole thing, from a body language standpoint.

At the burger joint, we sit at a Ms. Pac-Man table and play while we wait for the food to arrive. She orders a burger and fries; I just get a beer. She is very aggressive on the game and kicks my ass. I do mini-cold reads on her. I gently bust on her at times, for example, when she looks at the Giant Iced-Out Pinky Ring, I tell her it is real and it cost eighty thousand dollars. "Oh, I see," she says, her voice dripping with sarcasm.

"What . . . you actually believed this was real?! FREAK!" But for the most part, I just go for rapport. She starts talking about how, judging from my profile, she was scared I was gonna be a cool guy indie rocker dick or something. A random five-year-old comes up and peers at us. She turns to him and says, "He's not a jerk, huh? He's a nice guy."

The kid looks at me.

I go, "Nah, trust me, I'm a jerk. She looks just like a little angel though, huh kid?" and smile. The kid stares at me as though he's just as stoned as I am. He leaves.

I eat all of the girl's fries. She kicks my ass at Ms. Pac-Man a second time. We go to a bar, where I order a glass of the shittiest scotch they have, and a Bud Lite. She gets a beer.

I ask her if she's legal to be in the bar and we do an ID exchange; I tell some little story about it. I ask her if she knows any jokes, we go into a Dirty Joke MC Battle. After she tells a rather distasteful one, I reply, "Well, looks like you're out of luck, because I have the dirtiest joke ever. You ready? Okay, here goes: Energizer Bunny arrested . . . charged with battery." I start saying random shit, like, "I think it's funny how pirates were always running around looking for treasure, but they never realized the real treasure was the magic moments they were creating." I call her a Powerpuff Girl.

I start running some marriage role-play time distortion shit about how we are gonna go to Tahoe for Christmas. I love her so much. We are so in love. It's crazy, we really are a lot alike. There are several moments where we say the same thing simultaneously. We use a lot of the same quirky, idiosyncratic phrases. She belches A LOT, as do I. I say, "This is scary, we are too similar . . . I don't know if this is gonna work out in the long run . . . we'll just argue all the time, then have, like, freaky makeup sex. I don't think I'm ready for one of those volatile relationships right now. Then again, maybe I am. You're making me so confused!"

She finishes her beer and I spring the Kiss Bet: "I usually don't buy girls drinks . . . they buy me drinks." She immediately gets up to buy me a drink. I stop her. "Heheh whoa whoa whoa! Listen, I think we can work something out. Tell you what, I'll buy you a drink after you kiss me . . . if it's any good."

Pause. Another pause. She seems shocked and excited. "Here? In the bar?!"

"Yeah." I lean closer, and BOOM. We proceed to seriously make out for five minutes straight. Awesome. I suggest we go to the karaoke bar.

She says, "No, I'm going to go home and watch this movie I rented. You can come too, if you want."

"Yeah." This is too easy. I run Incredible Connection: "I don't know, it's weird, you know, being here talking to you. It's like I get an intuition, like when you feel this incredible connection . . . you know, when you're around someone you really like." I pause here and subtly point at myself, then continue, "Someone you're really attracted to . . . you just feel that CLICK, and it's like time slows down, and you've known this person forever, and you just feel totally drawn to this person. I think a big part of that is knowing that you can just RELAX with this person and have a good time, y'know?"

She looks like she's in a trance. I kind of stutter and say, "I don't know. Can you kind of feel that's how it is?" I touch her on the arm, acting flustered. "What am I talking about here?"

I deliver it all hesitantly, as though I am "trying to work out my feelings" or some shit. Lately, I've been playing with tactics that fake the characteristics of a chode to bring my value back down if I sense I'm coming off too smooth. Too fucking funny. It goes down perfectly.

We leave. As we walk to her house, I tell her, "I'm cold because criminals stole my coat out of my car," and we walk "à la French Promenade Style." I put my arm around her waist. It's a rather amusing scene, she is hella big. She puts her arm on me. It is like walking with a basketball player.

We go up to her apartment, and I get in her bed as she puts the movie on. I decide from here I'm going pure caveman; the chick is so tall and fit that there is no possible way I am gonna be able to "take advantage of her." I decide to just bring pure Neanderthal aggression, if she doesn't want it, she can just slap me away, "Away little man! Away!"

I start biting her neck. I jump on her and start grinding away. On the television, some character in the movie says the line, "I said I was only gonna go to first base tonight!"

Giraffe Girl blurts out, "That's what I said!"

Fade to black . . .

Afterward, she's like, "You can rest, but you can't stay here." I just laugh at her and go to sleep.

I have a strange dream involving a great white shark, a giant cake in the shape of a pool table and someone's birthday party. It takes place in the chick's apartment. The shark is very frightening, it is out of its tank, thrashing around on the floor, trying to put its gills by the ventilator. I keep telling the girl to put it back in the tank, as it is dying. I wake up. I fuck her again, then go back to sleep.

She buys me a fresh-squeezed orange juice in the morning; I drive her to work. I'll be seeing her again.

So, I've got a new nickname: "Giraffe-Fucker." Brian has been calling me this incessantly since I got back from my little sleepover. Total time from meet to lay: a blistering three and a half hours.

I've been thinking about that dream, though. Something was off about this whole thing, and I think my subconscious was trying to work it out. The dream centered around a birthday party. A party is a celebration, a social event where you meet people. The cake was in the shape of a GAME. I think the shark represented ME, the predatory player. There was something different about this girl. Looking back, she was actually in control the whole time, from the second she told me to meet her at her house to the moment she invited me up. I, the supposed "player," didn't do much of anything but show up and not be a complete pussy. I felt out of my element on some level, like the proverbial "fish out of water."

I think, for some reason, I actually have feelings for this woman. Then again, I basically feel that way EVERY TIME I fuck a girl, at least for a short period, after which it wears off.

But when I ran the connection routine, I genuinely felt it. Of course, the words weren't mine, but when I run that kind of shit, it's straight-up Method acting, so I have to truly experience it on some level. I look for things that support the idea that we have an incredible connection, so I MAKE IT REAL. Every time. Still, this one feels different. Time will tell.

JLAIX ACTUALLY CRIES

I open my inbox this morning to find an email from Giraffe:

Subject: I suck

Message: Hey—I needed to let you know that I crossed a boundary that I set for myself, and I feel uncomfortable about it . . . so I need to step back. I also need to not have contact, but I wish you well. I hope you understand.

What. The. Fuck. *She's* dumping *me*?!

This never happens . . . looks like the shark dream was somewhat prophetic. I actually liked this girl, wanted to make her my new girl-friend. After reading this, I'm pretty heated and write back the following:

Subject: are you fuckin' kidding me?!

Message: I'm like shaking right now, I feel used and that's not cool . . . I mean, I wasn't under the illusion that we were gonna be some like Boyfriend/Girlfriend monogamous cou-ple or anything, but I also didn't expect to get played like this. I was genuinely looking forward to being your friend, which is unusual for me, my friends even commented that I was act-ing unusually excited after meeting you. I think I'm gonna cry or something.

Despite what my little profile or whatever says, YOU are in fact the "total asshole," not me.

I delete her from my friend list. Fuck, I am really bothered by this . . . the player got played. FUCK!!!! Gonna get drunk. Just a second . . .

After taking fifteen Bud Lites to the head, I feel better. I know that my response to Giraffe Girl was not the ideal one. There are two angles I'm considering here: either she is genuinely disturbed at how fast things proceeded, like a movie—in fact, during the pickup she actually said that "she wasn't going to go past first base that night." Now she feels like a ho, and is freaked. That, or she is a player and it's a brush-off. If that's what's going on, I'm pretty much fucked no matter what response I give. As such, I focused on addressing the first scenario, in which case the response I gave will obviously make her feel bad, as I told her off pretty hard.

I decide to call up Jackass and get some counsel; he's probably the best "natural" I know, and I'm sure he's got some insight for me. After I tell him what happened, he thinks for a second, then suggests that I could have responded more like this: "Yeah, I'll be honest, my emotions got the best of me that night, maybe things went too fast, but I liked it and I want to do it again, I mean, let's go out for dinner, if nothing happens, no big deal, I just want to stay in contact."

But due to the slightly acerbic tone of her initial email, specifically the explicit "no contact" provision, I feel the asshole comment was warranted. Under these circumstances, the way things played out, I may consider calling her sometime in the future, at LEAST a week. Play it by ear. May blow her off entirely.

Fuck, I fell for this one. I use a "Method acting" style when I'm delivering rapport material. I proactively try to fall in love with the chick, and get her to feel those same emotions. This creates a genuine feeling "one-itis" in me that usually lasts for about four fuck sessions. After it wears off, I cycle them out of the rotation.

In this case, Giraffe Girl hit me in my most vulnerable state: the postcoital, pre-get-bored-with-her afterglow window; my ONLY EMOTIONAL WEAK SPOT now that I've started playing the game.

I became a player so I would never again have to experience the pain of getting burned by a chick. It's a lot less likely now, after eleven months of study and fieldwork, but it still happens. Fuckin' feelings and shit. Heh.

I think that's why I assumed she was genuine . . . I didn't want to entertain the notion that she could actually be a player, out of pride. That the whole time I thought I was gaming her, she was just GAMING THE FUCK OUTTA ME. If that's the case, then I got outplayed and THAT'S what hurts the most. Funny, the one girl in the past year I can actually envision a long-term relationship with is the one that burns me.

Later, I'm sitting around the pad bitching about it when my roommate's friend Erica says, "It was karma," and tells me, "maybe you should stop playing people and then they won't play you." I download another Bud Lite from the beer bong and belch in her hippie face.

I'll be better tomorrow, but damn, this got through my armor. Understand that this game is like any other game. Sometimes you lose and it hurts a little, for example crashing and burning on a cold approach. Sometimes you get a crushing loss, akin to getting eliminated from the playoffs . . . and that's what this was. There will be another match.

GET BACK GIRAFFE?
DON'T MAKE ME LAUGH

I'm sitting in my room, thinking obsessively about the Giraffe scenario. Impulsively, I call her from my phone, knowing she won't answer. I leave this message: "Giraffe. It's Jeff. Listen. I'm sorry I called you asshole. I'm not mad at you, I don't think you're a bad person. But I was really hurt by your message and I don't think it's fair, to either of us, to end it like that. We're adults, we can talk. Just hear me out for five minutes. I won't contact you again if that's what you want, okay? Five minutes. Call me."

She calls back within ten minutes and I say, basically, "I was really angry and upset when I read that. I thought it was a brush-off, like I sneezed the wrong way and you wanted to get rid of me. But then, I realized that that didn't seem right, I mean, you didn't strike me as that kind of person, it was incongruent with the Giraffe I saw that night."

She interjects something about feeling uncomfortable over having slept with me so soon.

"Yeah, and realized I was having a lot of those same feelings . . . I mean, you must think I'm this promiscuous dude or whatever. I'm not like that at all. I've had those kind of experiences before and they always made me feel hollow and empty. When I went to meet you, I wasn't thinking that was gonna happen AT ALL."

She agrees, "Yeah! Me too!"

"But you know, I felt a real connection, and my emotions got the better of me, maybe things went too far. But I liked it, and I'd like it to happen again, you know, it was a mistake, but it would be a bigger mistake to let an opportunity pass us by and just go on with our lives. Let me take you out to dinner. If nothing happens that night, whatever, no big deal, I don't care. You know, be a little flexible with this and take a chance."

Now I KNOW this is very chode-sounding, but I think that it's the only thing that might feasibly work. Then she throws me a curve. She expresses that she was really bothered by some of the violent stories she somehow elicited from me, and when we got undressed and she noticed the pentagram, she was really freaked out.

Yeaaahhh . . . the pentagram. I'd cut it into my own shoulder years ago, when I was nineteen years old living in a punk rock hovel out in the Sunset, as a sort of do-it-yourself tattoo. Years later, it remains a thick, raised and very permanent scar.

And that's why the Giraffe has reservations about meeting me again. She thinks I'm a fucking psychopath.

This is strange. The scar's never been a PROBLEM before. I usually just tell them that "I fell," and they laugh it off. But I guess it was only a matter of time.

Hmmm. I didn't calibrate this one right. She is a "nice girl." Considering how I was dressed and my stories of violent mania coupled with the self-mutilation, I was pretty dumb not to see this coming. I could tell from the moment I met her that she was more dorky and square. I should have toned it the fuck DOWN. Be more aware of how you are presenting yourself. Lesson learned.

Anyway, I tell her, "Look, I am not a psycho. I'm a nice person, my friends can vouch for this, but whatever, think about it." She says she is leaving for North Carolina tomorrow, and she will call me when she gets back. But she still sounds kind of hesitant. Total time of conversation: five minutes.

After the call, every instinct is telling me to drop it and just let it play out. But I just can't leave it alone. I can't. Several hours later, I sit down and write her another email.

Subject: hey

Message: Yeah. I'm glad we talked earlier and clarified things. And you know, regarding the whole "violent past"

thing, those stories happened a LONG TIME AGO when I
was a kid and didn't know what the hell was going on . . .
you know, I was just a nerdy kid that had a lot of bad things
happen to him, and I was really confused and messed up
by it. But please don't judge me for stuff that I have long
since moved on from. I'm not proud of those things, but I'm
not ashamed either. I know it's kind of weird, but hey, I am
a unique and beautiful snowflake lol. I have a lot of love and
generosity I want to share, and I want you to be a part of
that. Anyways, I'm not gonna sit here and qualify myself all
night, call me when you get back from NC, we WILL go out,
you WILL NOT be sorry. Dork.

I send it. Almost as soon as I do, I know it was a mistake. I read it
again and see that it's painfully idiotic. But what's done is done. That's it.
The matter is closed as far as I'm concerned; I can now proceed with a
clear head. I did my shitty best.

AIR SUPPLY

Rio times are at hand. I've arranged a meet with yet AN-
OTHER girl I met online, Texas. She's only twenty,
so I know I'm going to have to smuggle her into the bar; fortunately, I
purchased a fake ID from the Odeon bar last week. I was in there getting
drunk and noticed they had a sign that said "Fake ID For Sale" with some
bitch's ID taped to it. I guess they had confiscated it from her and now
they had put it up as a joke. Long story short, I bought it; they wanted

twenty bucks, but I talked them down to five. I called Texas on the phone and she agreed to meet me at the taco shop at 9 P.M.

I roll to El Rio to get my hand stamped with two wings: my roommates. One is a new guy, freshly moved in this past week. We enter and I do a throwaway as these three Irish chicks walk by, using Tyler-style "Moving Target Stopper Body Language," meaning I open them, continue talking and stand my ground, not chasing them or even moving my feet as they pass, just rotating my torso. I open with "Dental Floss," a flawless execution. I sense they are not opened properly after it's run, so I stack another opener, "Jealous Girlfriend," after lobbing out a false time constraint: "Look, lemme ask you something else. I gotta bounce pretty quick, but check it out . . . so my boy has been going out with this girl for a couple of months and they actually just moved in together. So the other day, she's going through the closets and finds his shoebox of old photos and letters, and a lot of them are from his ex girlfriend. Long story short, she freaks out and DEMANDS he get rid of them. What would you do in this situation?"

This unlocks them, I start in hardcore, face them, call them Powerpuff and assign them names (Pepper, Chippy and Butters). Being Irish, they think these are the actual names of the Powerpuff Girls. I run "A-Crowd" with my Walgreen's aviator shades. I bust on them. I do a TOTALLY MORONIC palm reading on my target. It is so stupid it hurts ("See this line? That indicates a fiery aggression"), but they eat it up.

They totally start qualifying themselves to me. I isolate my target under the pretense of "learning a jig." I perform a little jig for her, then start in with the "we're getting married" crap ("We'll have Christmas in Tahoe with our insect children"), and next thing you know, I pull her in for tonguedown. I look at her watch, it's 9:03 . . . oh shit! Texas is waiting for me at the other place! I excuse myself and bail.

I walk over to the taco shop. Texas is NOT HERE! Oh man, the jlaix getting stood up? Unheard of. I eat a taco and go to the karaoke bar.

In the bar, I meet up with my wings again. I start in on the bartender, this woman who doesn't like me very much. I really game her ass hard, using all the standard tactics. She's freaked out by it. In fact, she calls me "gross."

I ask her, "Yeah . . . so what is it about gross dudes that you like so much?" and continue.

I go to the bathroom. My turn arrives to sing. I go up and belt out a new song, "All Out of Love" by Air Supply. It goes far better than I ever expected it to. I literally hit every note perfectly. Unbelievable. As I walk offstage, the bartender chick looks at me with a new respect and says, "That was awesome."

Brian later tells me that she said to him, "I like Jeffy, he is so cool!" Dumb fuckin' bitch. Haha, perhaps she will see precisely how cool I can be when my wee-wee is in her anus. As I forge ahead in this pickup jihad of mine, I find myself more and more having sex with girls whom I just DON'T LIKE, and who DON'T LIKE ME. But it's cool, 'cause hey, then there's no risk of emotional attachment. Maybe I'll get a taste for her in a couple of months. Call her up, show up at her house and take my pants off. Works for me. I do sometimes feel bad, though, when I fuck a nice girl and know that I have no intention of calling her again . . . EVER. I just ignore it, because maybe I'll get a taste for her a few months down the road. Usually she will act "upset" that I didn't call her but that is IRRELEVANT because she NEEDS the cock. And I will be more than happy to furnish that experience for her.

Players fill a need.

We leave and return to El Rio, mocking the giant line outside as we walk past. I scream, "EL RIO IS FOR LOOOOOOOOSERRRRS!!!!!" Once in, shit is packed, the bar is four deep. We go out back. I circle once, and I've got chicks all over my ass; one is this psycho DJ bitch I deigned to hang out with a few weeks ago. I kiss her for the hell of it, and pinch her cheek, then slap her ass and hug her. Ugh . . . drunk! More girls that know me clamp on. It's peculiar. I continue to stagger around the club, deranged.

Suddenly, lo and behold, I see Texas! She's there with her friends; somehow she managed to get in despite being underage. I bump into her and bellow, "HEY WHAT THE FUCK BITCH!??" She's startled, then she realizes it's me. We hug and stuff. It turns out she went to the wrong taco shop, but she's here now, and that's all that matters. After a few minutes, her friends take off; they literally leave the bar and go home. Cool.

We go out back and start talking. I am running the customary game: "You look just like a little angel!" etc., cranking up the physical escalation quickly. But crazy DJ Bitch pops up behind her, causing trouble, getting in my face, vying for attention. Another girl comes up as well, and it's awkward as hell. My target is standing there, confused.

The DJ chick reaches in my pocket, grabs my Sharpie and runs off. She comes back shortly and returns it to me and says, "I wrote 'Jeffy is an asshole' in the bathroom." I actually find this amusing. She leaves.

I continue to spit game at my girl, then some guy she knows walks by and he starts talking to her. He's some bald squid with a leather jacket and a turtleneck. I start rubbing his head derisively, fucking with him aggressively. He's got a solid frame, though, and looks completely unconcerned. It's as though I'm not even in his reality. I say, "Isn't it funny how this guy is just completely ignoring everything I say? That's cute, he's just totally focused on you. It reminds me of this special I saw on TV about the serial killer and rapist Ted Bundy. He would get totally focused on his rape and murder victims just like that—in fact his facial expression even looks identical! Dude, don't rape this chick man!" Texas looks disgusted. Just then, I inadvertently knock a drink out of some girl's hand. She starts yelling, I throw a dollar at her and immediately drag Texas out of the bar. I just grab her and say, "Let's go, let's go," over and over, although I'm so drunk the noises coming out of my mouth are something more like, "Sko, sko, sko, sko . . ."

We go back over to the karaoke place. Dallas, a young guy with a long, flowing ponytail and a natty mustache who looks like he should be working a vaudeville circuit, is sitting on a stool right outside the door. He knows who I am. I introduce him to the girl: "Dallas? Texas. Texas, Dallas. Huhuhuh." He cards her. Fortunately, I have given her the fake ID. It's important to note here that *Dallas is the guy I bought it from last week*. He looks at it and it takes a couple of seconds for him to recognize what it is. He looks up at me with a raised eyebrow.

I smile, then look away, whistling.

A few more seconds pass . . . finally, he smiles, says, "Dude. Hahaha," and punches me in the arm, HARD. He waves us both in.

I sing "Eye of the Tiger." I run the Kiss Bet, but she doesn't go for it. I turn up the physical escalation even more, rubbing her thighs now, etc. I run Incredible Connection. Some chick that I know is there and comes up and starts gushing about what a great performer I am, how I kick so much ass. Nice. I sing "Against All Odds" by Phil Collins and I decide it's time for a DRAG CLOSE. I drag her out of the bar and we walk to my house.

Once there, my hot roommate Alexandra proofs me even further ("Oh, Jeffy is so cool!"), and next thing you know, I am in bed with my girl. She is reluctant to lie down at first, but I tell her, "Whoa, don't get ahead of yourself, we're not having sex tonight, I don't have sex on the first date." I really mean it; after the thing with the Giraffe, I don't want her to get buyer's remorse. Plus, I'm so drunk I doubt I could really do a good job anyway.

That said, I start heavy tonguedown. I'm on top of her, dry humping and so on. Next thing you know, "I wanna lick it." She resists, she won't let me take the pants off, I kind of snuffle and lick at her pants. She starts writhing around and moaning and stuff, I wash-rinse-repeat a number of times to no avail, finally I give up and go to sleep (or pass out) embracing her.

I wake up alone; apparently she left at some point. Or maybe she's hiding in my closet. I don't know. I should probably call her. Anyway, my cat is on the bed, so at least I woke up with pussy.

I just now got a call from a fuck buddy. I'm gonna go over and rail her after I write up last night's report on the forum. Tonight I plan on fucking Miss Twelve Gauge out in the East Bay; it's Taco Tuesday with fifty-cent drinks out in Concord. Can't beat that.

IRC CHODE FUCKS UP
THE PROGRAM

I get an email from Miss Twelve Gauge, right after I finish up with my other girl and as I'm about to head out to the East Bay to meet her:

Subject: heffy

Message: An interesting thing happened today. One of the regulars in the friendster irc channel on efnet asked me if I knew you because this girl that he likes said she went out with you. Friendster is evil.

I know I really have no place to get jealous or hurt by this, but she's definitely hotter and more talented than me which indefinitely invokes some amount of jealousy.

I generally don't allow myself to have feelings about people for this reason. I know we have no obligation to each other. I like to keep it that way to prevent getting people's feelings hurt.

I can't deny that over the last few months I've developed some feelings for you (no matter how masochistic that may seem). Believe me, I try as hard as I can to not involve emotional attachment with "fuck buddies."

But for some unknown reason, I like you. I adore the fact that you're totally nuts and how you just don't give a fuck. My mother would hate you. That's hot.

I find it difficult to take you seriously, which makes it hard to understand you. On the surface you appear to have no real emotion. I admire that because I'd like to be that way (teach me sometime?).

But . . .

I wish nothing could hurt me or make me angry. I wish
everything in life was peaches and fucking honey. But no
matter how hard I try, I can't avoid my human reflex to feel
adverse emotions. Which also makes it hard to believe that
you really don't feel anything except for the effects of mari-
juana and alcohol. Correct me if I'm wrong.

Heavy.

There's no denying that over the past few months, Miss Twelve Gauge
and I have grown pretty close. I see her with a fair amount of regularity,
and we have our little inside jokes and cutesy names for each other, all
that. She even took me on a romantic date to get me a shotgun, after
seeing how much I enjoyed playing with hers; we made a day of it, going to the Castro Valley Gun Shop and afterward having a picnic in the
cemetery. I do care for her, in my own way.

But that's the thing. "My own way" is completely fucked.

I mean, I should love this girl. She's beautiful, hot, funny, smart and
understands me more than most people do. But I don't want to be understood. I don't want anything. I don't give a fuck. I just don't fucking care.

•

Anyway, I go ahead and meet her at the bar. She doesn't bring it up,
and I know I shouldn't either, but I am curious about who this chick
was. So I ask her . . . and guess what? It turns out to be GIRAFFE.

She asks me point blank, "Did you fuck her?"

"Yeah. Just once."

BOOM. That's it. She starts crying in the bar; it is horrible. I tell her,
"Hey, we didn't have any exclusive relationship, what the fuck! And who
the fuck is this guy?!"

She tells me who it was. The guy just asked her because he is really
into Giraffe and wanted to get information about me; apparently Giraffe
used me as an excuse to not date him ("After Jeffy I can't date anyone
anymore!").

That's when she lays it on me: the ultimatum of exclusivity. I simply walk out. And that's it: I just lost Twelve Gauge. Now I'm really pissed at this chode asshole, fucking up my life. I've already determined exactly who he is, and am pondering my next move. I'm not sure what the correct course of action is here. Should I expose his behaviors to Giraffe? Should I just slash his tires? I don't know.

PEACE TRAIN

All right. I have decided to go ahead and send the chode who blew up my spot a quasi-threatening message.

Within the hour, he replies with a threat of his own: to report me to the NCIC and have me charged with "threatening to inflict bodily harm." Note to self: don't threaten people over internet. Do it verbally, in real life.

I reconsider, and send him a well-reasoned retraction:

Subject: re: threat

Message: All right, man, I don't even know you, I usually don't go around threatening people, and I want to retract those statements right now. It was wrong of me to imply that and I apologize. For all I know you're a cool guy, but look at it from my perspective: you said something to one of my girlfriends about a past relationship of mine that really ended up hurting her. She cried and cried last night because she's gotten so jealous. I was starting to like her, but you know, it was just too early in our relationship and it's probably over now. So listen, it's cool and all, but just do me a favor and in the future, think before you repeat gossip about other people because you never know what effect it's going to have. Peace.

His response:

Subject: re: threat

Message: Retraction Accepted. Dude, here's the deal. Essentially, I went out with this chick that I met a few weeks ago. Maybe it was the end of June. Date one went really well and we were going to go out again. Something strange happened after that—she met some guy that totally creeped her out. I don't know specifics except that it was some guy named "Jeff." She didn't even want to tell me, but I was curious so I interrogated her . . . I was interested in her and wanted to find out what he (you) might have done to creep her out so I could avoid doing it myself.

So essentially, this girl went from being gung ho about dating to wanting just a "friends" relationship. We went out a second time, then she started to get really weird. Drama ensued and we're not in communication. I was concerned about her well-being and she didn't like being asked if she was okay. Yadda yadda yadda. I didn't care that she fucked someone else, cause we had just met but I was concerned that she would have such a rapid change in her sentiment.

The other day . . .

Twelve Gauge was online talking about how she was pissed off about men (I have no idea) and I bitched about how I met this hot chick on Friendster who got weirded out by some Jeff guy. I didn't realize that Twelve Gauge was in fact your girl. So she pumped me for information, and before I realized it, I had told her what I had heard. I didn't see the connection until your message to me when I looked at your page and saw a whole bunch of comments from her, and then it dawned on me.

So it was totally accidental. I know what you are going through though. My woman and I split up in March due to some similar drama after being together for five years and having a wedding planned and everything. I totally was not trying to fuck shit up for you. I've got enough bad karma as it is.

I'm going to stay out of this one. If there's anything I can do to mend things between you two, let me know.

Jesus. I can't even be pissed at the guy. I actually add him to my friend list. Go figure.

FOOL'S MATE EIGHT

Monday afternoon. I am at work when Chippy calls and begins taunting me about El Rio, goading me about how I'm gonna pick up chicks there, or "meet my other girlfriend there."

"Which one? I have thirty," I reply, yawning.

I go home, read awhile and take off for El Rio with my roommates Ben and George at approximately 9 P.M.

Get in, run an assessment. It's too early yet for the hotties to be there. I decide this is gonna be primarily a "get drunk" night, and a "pickup" night second. I double-fist one-dollar vodka tonics and make idle conversation with my friends.

Looking about, I spy a familiar person across the yard, in a hut area. Could it be? No.

Yes.

It's Chippy, there with some dode I know and a dumb-looking chick. I am not concerned about the dode; he's a harmless Star Wars dork. I'm upset because she's fucking with me by being here when it has been made expressly clear that Mondays at El Rio are my private time. I finish my drinks and leave without acknowledging her.

Outside, I call her and say, "Yeah, hey. I just wanted to say you crossed a boundary. Don't call me, don't contact me. It's over." I hang up, ignoring her subsequent calls. We get a taco and go to the karaoke bar, where there are no targets but plenty of glasses of scotch, which I drink.

After an hour or so at the karaoke joint, we decide to return to El Rio. Chippy is gone, nowhere to be seen. I start drunk gaming, hard. I do a few approaches, short set method, trying to feel which set is gonna get me the lay. I get good vibes from one or two of them, but there are more targets that I want to hit up before I put my eggs in any one basket.

Suddenly, something unusual happens. I'm at the bar trying to get another drink while simultaneously keeping an eye on some targets, when this chick, a young girl, like an 8, opens me by grabbing my arm. "You're hot," she says, leaning into me. "Buy me a drink."

"I don't buy chicks drinks. They buy me drinks. Hmm. I tell you what. I'll buy you a drink after you kiss me, if it's any goo—"

Before I can finish the line, she starts aggressively making out with me. Awesome. After a while of this, we stop. I say, "It's time to smoke!" She pulls out cigarettes. I say, "NO, it's time to SMOKE!!" and make the universal "toking" gesture for the chronic. She understands I am pulling her, and we walk out and head back to the Blauhaus.

On the way home, I calibrate and realize this chick is pure party girl and this is textbook FOOL'S MATE (the quickest possible win in chess). As we walk, I give her some basic cocky attraction stuff to keep her in state, some light marriage role play, by no means am I doing any Deep Connection–type shit with this broad. God, she's hot, but demented; she seems really wild and drunk. Her phone rings while we're in a liquor store buying cigarettes and candy. She answers and proclaims, "I'm with this REALLY hot guy. Yeah. Yeah. Bye." Awesome. Great self-esteem boost.

We get back to my place, go upstairs and commence making out on my bed. "I wanna lick it," says jlaix. The chick says she is on her period. I say, "I don't give a fuck! I'm a nasty mother*fucker* GURL . . ." and take off her pants. I am so loaded that I really don't care. Yet, to my great pleasure and surprise, she isn't bloody at all. I lick it for a while. I am pretty drunk, there is a mild whiskey dick effect, but she's so hot that it negates the alcohol.

She asks, "Do you have a condom?" I'm moving to retrieve one when she says, "Well I do!" She holds up four different kinds; I grab one and start to rail.

We finish, then she talks about how badly she wants to do crystal meth. I veto this, and then suggest she play with my shotgun. She likes the idea, and prances about wearing nothing but a black garter belt with the shotgun. I am in heaven. My roommate arrives home and knocks on my door; the chick answers it. His jaw drops to the fucking floor. I chuckle.

We go down to the garage; she's now wearing my blue silk kimono, just hanging open. I have no shirt on, with the gun strapped to my back. As we storm through the house, the roommates are astounded at the scene. They're having some kind of dinner party in the kitchen, and all of a sudden they're faced with this nonsense. A thin patchouli man who looks like a vegan summons the temerity to ask me, "Why do you have a gun on your back?"

"Dude, it's the hip new accessory for fall."

Down in the garage, Fool's Mate and I take turns beating the heavy bag hanging from the ceiling. I start thrashing it with the gun and actually break the wooden stock. This stokes the chick into a weird erotic frenzy and I tongue her down while she sits on the clothes dryer. We go back upstairs and I fuck her again; the girl gets totally fuckin' buck wild on top of me. Really good sex. As I climax, I bellow loudly in a manner that my roommate, who lives two floors below me, characterizes as sounding like "Chewbacca getting a cold thermometer shoved up his ass."

After that, we chill for a while, and then she gets up and she writes her number down in a childish scrawl. She leaves. I try to call her a cab, but she insists on walking. As I watch her walk away, I get the feeling it might just be a one-night stand, but you never know.

This was just the thing I needed right now, a gimme lay from an 8 to boost my confidence, almost a year to the day after I discovered the whole "pickup community." Who knows why this girl approached me. I remember being kind of irritated that this was being dropped in my lap at the Rio at that particular time, because I wanted to "game" more, but I wasn't about to let such an obvious lay with a quality hottie slip through my fingers. A year ago, I probably would have blown this one by not recognizing it for what it was. I would have spent time trying to "run game" on her instead of realizing she was ready to fuck and just pulling her.

I call Chippy the following day. She apologizes profusely and takes me to dinner at Boulevard. I have the foie gras and the filet, then the strawberry tiramisu with a fifty-dollar port. Over dessert I ask her, my girlfriend of two years, if she would still love me if I were to all of a sudden rip off an elaborate costume and reveal that I was actually a bald Latino she-male with a fully functioning cock.

"Yes," she answers. Pause. "Would you still love me?"

Silence.

She looks down and says, "Haha . . . what am I saying, 'still'? You never *did* love me, huh?"

I say, "You know I can't feel that." She actually starts getting tears in her eyes. It's awful, but shit, I don't want to lie to her.

Again, I know that this emotional disconnect is somehow holding me back. But I still have yet to identify the exact mechanism by which it's doing so.

I just don't know.

What I *do* know is this: I am not the same person I was a year ago. I'm starting to get a handle on this stuff. Looking back, the turnaround points were:

First, changing my beliefs (not putting value on any one woman; I am the prize).

Second, changing my lifestyle (from a monogamous dating frame to that of the player ready to run game at ANY MOMENT).

Third, meeting other COMPETENT guys and doing fieldwork with them.

Mostly, it is the cumulative field experience that has brought me this far. There is no substitute; it is the only way to develop that intuition of how to react in any given scenario. The future for me holds a lot of fieldwork. I think the area I want to focus on now is qualification, giving the woman reasons to believe that I want her for more than her ass. This is the least developed part of my game, and as such I have massive problems with "buyer's remorse" and last-minute resistance from time to time.

So this kicks off my sophomore year in the game. I figure it will take a couple more years at least before I become a master. But of course, this is a journey, not a destination.

HITTING THE SUCCESS BARRIER

I feel like I'm treading on dangerous ground these days. I am at the point now, twelve months after starting this trip, where I am enjoying reasonable success on a fairly consistent basis. I always knew that players existed, but never thought I could be one. Before, I only got laid intermittently and mostly as the result of luck. Now, my problem is that I have *too many* women to handle. Last year, if I were to hear someone complain about such a thing I would have told them, "Shut the fuck up, I wish I had your 'problems.'" This is, however, a very real issue once you start hooking up with a lot of girls; not only do they take up a lot of your time, they can also tire you out physically.

The upshot is that, since you have so many chicks competing for you, the "I am the prize" affirmation is no longer a mere *affirmation* but rather a REALITY. These days, I often find myself thinking, *I cannot believe this is my fucking LIFE.* It's truly awesome.

So, by no means am I complaining here. I think of it more as a warning. DON'T GET COMPLACENT. Consistently work leads one at a time, adding fuck buddies to the list. I just hit chick number 23 using my newfound skills. Who's gonna be number 24?

Again, I am not that good. I have "fair" success on a *relatively* consistent basis. Having said that, why do I succeed?

I think it's just WILL.

"Everyone gets everything they want." That's my philosophy. But when I say want, I mean WANT, at a deep level where it's become almost necessary for survival. I get laid because I really want to. It is up there among the top priorities in my life, so much in fact that it sometimes adversely affects my work life and my health. I try to balance these things; time and experience have revealed that necessity. I mean, I'm constantly thinking about pickup. I used to constantly talk about it too, until I learned that not everyone thinks it's an admirable way to live.

Some will get into this stuff and dick around with it for a while, then quit. Others will go so hard that they quickly burn themselves out. Others will stop at the first plateau they hit, content with remaining at that level. To truly succeed, however, to become *elite,* I know I have to be in this for life. To that end, I must cultivate a deep, enduring love for the game itself.

Gotta have the love, baby! The love for the GAME!!

The other night, I was sitting around the pad. I had about an hour to kill before a first meet with some girl, a 7. I was stoned, just shooting the basketball and thinking about the meet. *Is it gonna go good? What routines am I gonna run? Golly, I hope I don't fuck up!*

All of a sudden, a thought came to me. This date I was about to go on was no different than the activity I was currently involved in: shooting hoops from the top of the key.

I've made this shot thousands of times. I have also missed it thousands of times. The point is, somewhere in my kinesthetic memory lies the knowledge of the exact signals my brain needs to send my body in order to make the ball go in the basket.

I said out loud, "YOU KNOW HOW TO DO THIS."

I shot the ball.

Swish!

I continued: "Furthermore, this is fun for you!"

Swish!

Suddenly it came to me. "Method plus fun equals success."

Swish!

After sinking three perfect shots in a row, all feelings of tension and nervousness just evaporated. *I know how to do this, I have done it many times before and it is what I do for FUN.* Needless to say, I went on the date and killed it in under three hours.

This is the attitude. This is the way.

The only thing that bothered me about this particular lay was just how very formulaic it was. I was "painting by numbers." It was just mechanical. Is this what being a pickup artist is? I don't know. I know there is a certain beauty in mathematics; maybe I need to view it that way.

Again and again, it becomes apparent to me that to excel and continue to excel at this, one must learn to take a certain pleasure in the mundane, the repetitive acts. You gotta have the love. At the same time, however, I must never cease expanding into new, more advanced territory. I mean, banging a 7 is, at this point, a lot like playing a video game I've already beaten. Sure, it's fun and sort of challenging, but I know exactly what to do and when to do it. I need a new video game. I think it's called "9s and 10s."

It's time to step up to the majors, which will likely involve a concomitant period of agonizing crash and burn.

JIMMY SCHWAG

After a fitful three-hour "sleep" (passed-out unconsciousness) following an unusually strenuous night at the karaoke bar, I drag a razor across my face, make a part in my hair and resign myself to what I am about to endure. Wincing at the sun as I step outside, I go to get in my car and find the window smashed out. The driver's seat is covered in tiny cubes of glass.

One of the neighbors is smoking out front and tells me he saw the whole thing. Apparently, some fat "Filipino or Chinese" guy drove up in a silver Toyota at 9 A.M, stopped directly next to my car, got out, smashed my window, got back in his car and sped off. This was in broad daylight on a very busy street.

Enemies are targeting me for destruction. They will not succeed. I have to wonder, however, who is responsible? I don't recognize the guy from the description. Maybe a disgruntled ex-employee I fired? Some pissed-off bitch whom I dumped having her new chode boyfriend exact revenge? A roommate I evicted then jacked for his security deposit? A random asshole who didn't like my Oakland Raiders antenna ball?

Fuckin' FUCKS.

I somehow make it through work. After taking a short disco nap, I'm ready for another Monday dollar-drink saga at the El Rio.

As we roll up, I see a chick sitting on the curb. Well well, if it isn't Crystal, the crazy bitch from the other week, aka the Fool's Mate 8. I walk by her and say, "HEY," and stop a couple of feet away and talk to her over my shoulder. I tell her, "It's good to see that you're alive . . . see ya inside," and continue on.

As we walk past the thirty-minute line, I mock it, as usual. Several people acknowledge me as we pass, I slap five with some dudes and a hot chick even yells out, "Hey Jeffy!" I blow her a kiss and we walk right into the club. At this point everyone in line must be thinking, *Who the fuck is THAT?*

Not many targets. I open a few girls for my roommates' entertainment by asking them if they would "date a guy in a wheelchair." It opens solid all but once. A typical response is, "Well does his dick still work?" Hahaha, fuckin' chicks—only one thing on their mind.

My French wingman Christophe arrives. We start to scope for real. Not many viables in the place. I see Crystal being chatted by a dode, and as I walk by I put my hand on her ass and push her out of the way gently. "Move." Not many targets out back either.

Well, there's always Crystal. Fucked her once before, figure it should be no problem to do it again tonight. I go up and tell her it's great to see her, and that I was really worried she was dead. Some chode walks by and says to her, "Do you need another drink? Okay!" I spit out my drink and laugh out loud at him as he goes off to get her another cocktail.

I say, "Hey it's time to SMOKE. And this time, it's personal." She apologizes, but it's her friends' last night in town before moving and she ditched them LAST time to fuck me. Very well. She asks me for my phone number. She pulls out her phone and I see there is an entry waiting for her to input my number. It says "Jimmy Schwag."

I'm pissed, and yell, "What the fuck is this? JIMMY FUCKING SCHWAG?!!" Apparently this is her nickname for me, due to the fact that the smoke I promised back at the house during our initial encounter never materialized. Still, fuck that.

I decide it's high time girls started buying me drinks. I straight-up command some random chick to buy me a drink. She asks, "Why should I?"

I respond, "Because you're my mommy," in a bizarre, high-pitched voice. She considers this for a second, then buys me the drink. Glorious.

Time passes and we leave. Outside, some fat chick literally begs me to come home with her. I politely decline, having been over there several weeks ago intending to fuck her roommate. I'd arrived at 2 A.M. with a baseball bat and started riding some girl's bicycle around the living room breaking shit, then reconsidered for some reason and left.

The roommate in question happens to be standing there with her boyfriend. This fuckin' guy has been eyeing me all night, so I go up and say, "Hey man, you are so cool! High-five!" He refuses. I grab his wrist and yank his arm up, "Like this!"

He's getting pissed and pulls his hand back, yelling, "I don't do that!"

"Yeah!!! You're cool, champ!"

"My name's not Champ!"

I point my finger at him and bark, "If I say you're Champ, YOU'RE CHAMP!" and walk off laughing.

We go to Phone Booth. The usual coterie of hipsters is there. I see a beautiful hapa girl who approached me earlier at Rio. She exclaims, "It's you! The SNEER guy!"

I say, "What am I, fuckin' Billy Idol?!" I game her good. Some wannabe alpha asks me how I know her.

"I fucked her."

This blows the guy out and she laughs. She pays attention to her friend for a SECOND and I do a takeaway. Who do I see but Annoying, the girl who banged Mushroom Chode on my couch. She gets up in my grill and starts talking some nonsense. "Jon says you said I called him a white supremacist!"

"No, no, no. I said you called *Alice* a white supremacist."

She looks confused for a moment, then goes, "What? But . . . that's not true!"

"Yeah? So?! *I say whatever the fuck I want.*" I wave her away.

Some other chick asks me to buy her a drink. I say, "What? Do you know who the fuck I am? You should buy ME a drink."

She asks, "No, who are you?"

I flatly state it: "Jeffy." I let it hang there for a second. "Okay, tell you what. I'll buy you a drink after you kiss me, if it's any good . . ." She gives me a weak little kiss. I say, "Fuck that. Listen, why don't we do this: you can go get one of these fucking chodes here to buy us BOTH drinks."

When I say this, the chick LIGHTS UP and leans in toward me, and starts whispering, all conspiratorially, "Yes! I do it all the time! Hee hee! I am the master of getting drinks!" She then demonstrates by getting this guy who is standing literally a foot away, and who in fact heard the whole thing, to buy her a drink. Unbelievable.

Last call. I walk out to leave. Out front, the hapa girl is there and says, "You're coming home with us!" She tries to drag me into a cab. I see all these other morons getting in and I decide I want no part of this . . . too many chodes.

I say, "Listen, I'm going home. But first I want to know seven things." She asks what they are. I say, "Numbers." She recites her number.

I start to walk away, and she says, "No wait . . . kiss me first!" I smile, turn back and give her a nice one.

I stop and say, "I'm not some tacky club guy. I'm for real." I kiss her again, then leave, chuckling to myself. I'll call her later tonight to check in.

JEFF AND THE GIANT NAZI

Papa is back in town this week for a one-on-one work-shop with a newbie from India, and once again I've been invited to help out. This is no longer just a hobby for Papa, it's a business; he and Tyler have incorporated under the name "Real Social Dynamics." Over the past several months, I've become more involved with the company; they've even started flying me around to guest instruct from time to time in various cities.

This weekend, however, we're in San Francisco. On the final day of the program, we decide to book a fake bachelor party on the Party Bus. This is just what it sounds like: a large bus, usually filled with like a hundred chicks on bachelorette parties, which drives around to three of the city's most sleazy, uberdrunken slut clubs. My roommate Brian is coming along for the ride. A few other guys from the forum are in town as well, and have decided to join us. I'm stoked to finally meet these guys in real life.

When I get home from work, Brian gives me some bad news: he forgot to book our tickets for the bus, and it's now sold out. I am pissed. We decide to go and meet all the guys for the pre-event dinner regardless. I'm angry about the ticket thing, so I start getting drunk.

I drink a six-pack.

I then drink a half liter of Stoli.

As we walk to the diner, I game up a 9 on the street. It goes okay, but she leaves. Throwaway practice interaction: complete.

I stop off at a liquor store and grab a twenty-four-ounce Budweiser.

Brian says, "Damn, dude, take it easy!"

"Fuck it, these guys expect me to be this drunken maniac, I'm gonna oblige and give them the full jlaix experience!" I pound the beer. A bum asks me for change and tries to shake my hand. I tell him, "I would, but my hand is real dirty." I am getting very drunk. The night air feels pleasant as I stroll in my Journey T-shirt.

We get to the diner. There are some introductions and stuff, it's cool. For shits and giggles, I display my "accidental phone call tactic" for everyone. Here's how it works: you take a girl whom you haven't spoken to in a while, or who flaked, etc., and you dial her number, then just set the phone down on the table and go about your business, chatting friends or what have you. It will appear as though you accidentally "pocket-dialed" her, and she's highly likely to call you back. You answer as though surprised to hear from her, and when she tells you that it was in fact YOU who called HER, you dismiss it as a pocket dial and then proceed to game. I go ahead and do it right here in the diner. Shortly, some flaker chick calls back. I bullshit her for a few minutes, then end it with some vague promise to "hang out . . . totally!"

I go to the store and get another twenty-four ounces of beer.

We go to the venue to register for the tour. I ask the chick if we can still get on without reservations. She's like, "Oh of course Jeffy!" I'm puzzled . . . how does she know me? "What, you don't remember me? I'm Beth's roommate." Ah, Beth . . . the RAGE FUCK dancer. Funny. We pay and we are IN.

Things become hazy as we file onto the bus. There is much chick-shrieking and a lot of movement. I spy a girl that for some reason strikes a chord in my perved-out, alcohol-soaked brain: she is some sort of giant foreigner, a tall, thick-ass bitch: I wanna fuck it. I hear Sir Mix-A-Lot ex-horting me to approach. She appears to be alone, not affiliated with any of the parties. I start talking to her. She is from Germany, visiting here, and decided to go on the tour by herself for fun. She speaks very little English, so my usual material won't work. She just kind of says, "Ja, ja," to everything. I spin-kiss her.

We arrive at the Glas Kat. It's a big hip-hop club, lots of hot girls swarming everywhere. Very loud and intimidating but I am fucking HAMMERED and I'm having a great time just running around spin-kissing chicks and high-fiving. I wing with Papa for a while. He's doing great as well. He isolates a 9 in the corner and I decide to let them be, but first he hands me the bachelor to-do list. Now it's my turn to be the "bachelor." The list just has the phrase "make out with a girl" printed on it like thirty times. I go around kissing chicks for a while using the gim-mick; it's fun. Then these fucking male strippers get up on this stage and start simulating sex acts with random party chicks who they pull onstage. It's fucking crazy, it's getting really weird, and you can sense the chicks in the club getting all worked up.

I randomly see the German chick standing there. I drag her onto the floor and attempt to get her onstage to get fucked by the stripper dudes. She is like, "Nein nein!" and so I just start talking in this weird broken English baby voice to her:

"You like here? I want A-DOPT you, like little sister! I love you we get married! Go to Tahoe." I can't believe what I'm saying, and further-more I can't believe it is actually working. We go to the next club.

As we get off the bus, we're standing outside the club and I just say to her, "This place very bad, very very bad, many sluts drunk here. Come on, let's go, good place . . . Club Jeffy." I take her hand and we walk to my car. I drive to my house wasted, doing ninety on the freeway. We go in, and my roommates are at a loss as they make halfhearted attempts to converse with her. I drag her upstairs, sing a Chicago song on my karaoke machine and pass out.

In the morning I wake up severely hungover, cuddling a Giant Nazi. My cock is extremely hard. I dry-swallow five Advil out of the industrial-size jar next to my bed and start rubbing her pussy. I say, "I wanna lick it," but she does not understand what this means. I attempt to rephrase it, "I put my mouth on it." Still, she seems baffled (I should learn how to say "I wanna lick it" in various languages in case I encounter this problem in the future).

So I just start biting her neck and kissing her while rubbing pussy. Next thing you know, she's on top of me, riding away and making soft little German noises as I unleash a massive sperm load. I was kind of late on the pullout; I hope come May next year there isn't a little spaetzle-eating Jeffy spawn poppin' out the Giant Nazi oven over in Hamburg! Ah well, she probably wouldn't be able to track me down anyway.

I was late for work, but fuck it, I done America proud.

MATH

I hook up with a new fuck buddy whom I picked up at Rosewood a few weeks ago. She happens to be Chinese and is uncharacteristically loud and obnoxious. After we have sex, I get up, cross the room, retrieve a calculator and throw it at her. "Here you go. Do math, Asian! Do some math!" She presses at the buttons in an exaggerated fashion while I unwrap the taco that she has so graciously brought over for me. I watch her do math while I eat, clapping, delighted.

DRUNK AT THE BIZZLE

I wake up at 8 P.M. and pour myself a Jack and Coke. Tonight I am hitting the Rio with a new wing, Celine. He's the night supervisor at work. After months of listening to my pickup anecdotes, he decided to get in on the action himself. We've gone out a couple of times; his game pretty much sucks, but it's not bad enough to be a deal breaker. He arrives at my house and we shoot the proverbial shit. Nine o'clock rolls around and the dude asks, "Hey man, shouldn't we get going?" Historically, on a Monday night at the Rio, you get there before nine or you're waiting in a forty-five-minute line.

"Nah, it's lost its buzz man," I say, pouring another drink. "It ain't like that no more. We got time. The bloom's off the rose, dog!" We leave at around 9:30.

Of course, we approach the Rio and are greeted with a forty-five-minute line out front.

I am shaking as I walk to the front, stoned. I think I'm gonna have a panic attack. I'm so nervous I can't even mock the people in line like I usually do as I walk past them. I get to the door and I'm trippin'. There's a chick that looks EXACTLY LIKE Garcia, the usual door person. But it's not her, and she cards me, and now I'm really freaked out. I smile, showing as much dimple as I can, shrug, and weakly say, "I woke up late," as I give her the two bucks cover. We walk in. I get a Bud Lite and breathe a sigh of relief.

God, I'm so cool.

We go out back. I pass an extremely hot girl, a 9, brief eye contact. I have brought Celine along as my wingman for several reasons. His appearance contrasts with mine: tall, not white, vaguely good-looking. Plus, he doesn't qualify himself too much. Still, I haven't done a great deal of pickup with him before, so I'm not sure what to expect. I see the 9 and her friend, another 9. I exhort Celine to approach. I reel off some opener for him to use, but he simply cannot do it. He is too intimidated, saying shit like, "My girlfriend's coming!"

"Fuck this shit, follow me." I literally must force him to follow me over there. I walk past the two chicks, then open them with super low-key, disinterested body language. "Hey guys. Settle an argument we're having. You guys smoke pot, right?" They start shrieking and giggling. "All right, if you're gonna eat, do you smoke before or after?"

They say, "BOTH!"

And here we go, blah blah blah. I high-five them. "Oh my God, guys, I love you. If I didn't have to leave right now, I'd adopt you as my little sisters." More giggling and shrieking. Christ, I am surprised it's going this well. I mean, these are solid 9s. It really is true: this game is optimized for and geared toward 9s and 10s. I do a takeaway to get another beer. I return to the set by grabbing Celine and saying, "Are you guys being nice to my friend here? He's extremely shy."

One of them compliments my Giant Iced-Out Pinky Ring. I say, "Yeah, cool so, I guess you're ready to get out of here then?" More giggling. I say, "Stop it, you're making me feel weird, like, all emotional, I can't think logically. The next thing I know you're gonna be asking me to go to your house to 'check out your stereo.' These girls are total sexual predators, man!" Yadda yadda yadda.

Okay, then it comes: she asks, "What's your name?" Nice.

I turn to actually face them. "Brad Pitt," I say as I take her hand, bring it up to my lips, flip it over and kiss my own. I say, "You know what? I'm attracted to you guys, but I need TRUST and COMFORT first, you know?"

They're like, "Oh me too!"

I say, "Shit, we wouldn't get along . . . we're too similar." I do a small backturn and she grabs at me. I say, "Nah . . . we'd just argue all the time and then have, like, freaky make-up sex. I'm not ready for one of those volatile relationships right now. Then again . . . maybe I am. I'm so confused!" I tell the target, the girl who is more into me (her friend is at this point hanging back while Celine lamely occupies her), "If I was your boyfriend, I'd fuck you twice a day." She asks what I do. I say I'm in textiles and start rubbing her stomach and her thigh, saying, "What's this, this is a cotton blend, probably combed cotton," and shit. Then I tell her my real job. I'm in comfort-building phase now, and this goes on for a while, then they say, "We have to go get our friend, wait here," and leave.

I turn to Celine and say, "We HAVE to be talking to different girls before they get back. Let's go." And I split off and open another group, sitting down at a table with a dude and a few chicks; 7s at best. I run some stuff. I can tell I'm overqualified for them and my shit is blowing their hair back. It's too much. It's like, "Why is this guy talking to US?"

The dude talks some shit about my clothes. I say, "Oh! Cool! Wow, man, you're like my personal assistant! That's AWESOME, man! Keep the advice coming! 'Cause you KNOW I gotta impress YOU guys!" I slap him on the arm and laugh. The guy looks like Johnny from *The Karate Kid* and I start busting on him for this; it's hilarious. A nearby group of people overhears this, looks at the dude and sees that he does in fact resemble the character, and joins in, yelling, "Hahahaha JOHNNY!" and pointing. This obliterates the poor dode, who after this can no longer look me in the eye.

One of the chicks barks, "Go get me a cigarette!"

I start laughing. "Hahaha do you know who the fuck I am? Bahahahaha!" Then, as punishment for her ridiculous outburst, I grab some old guy with glasses, a hairy beard and a beer gut, and say, "Hey man, these chicks wanted to ask you a question!" and shove him into the group, then immediately walk away. He sits down with them and begins talking in an animated fashion. Ahh, there are few pleasures in this life like foisting a creepy weirdo on a set of rude girls.

I belly up to the bar. I tell the bartender I am gonna start promoting El Rio on college campuses to attract more teen girls. He is visibly disturbed. I look next to me. There's some other girl that I tongued down at some bar a few months ago but who later turned flake when I tried to call her. I say, "Hey, girl. Sorry I never called you, I feel like a total asshole."

She says, "Yes, YOU DID call me. I didn't call you back."

I bust on her for being fake, saying, "Listen, I mean I came at you in a genuine way, and you were just drunk and being fake, that's so cool." This seems to be getting to her. Her friends are now glaring at me. I start in on them, "Wow, you guys are like the mean cool kids from high school. Where's Molly Ringwald?" I look around for her.

She says, "We didn't even have friends in high school!" in a weird plaintive tone, and I walk off.

I see my original target (the 9) talking to some player; he's good-looking and big and he's all touching on her; she seems to like it. I go up and say, "Excuse me. May I cut in?" and then I go to kiss the guy. He freaks out, and she starts laughing her ass off. I say to the guy, "Yeah man, I'm just fuckin' around, seriously though, I'll give you a hundred bucks to take this girl off my hands." She turns her attention to me and the player disappears.

These girls are like little frolicking kittens, hopping around from one stimulus to the next. I tell them this. They're like, "Ohhhhh! Heeheheee we are! Heeeheee!"

I read her palm with some retarded shit, then say to her, "Close your eyes." She does it and I kiss her. She's like "ohh" and I'm just standing there as though I don't give a fuck about nothin', least of all her. I'm just a chill guy being real. I say I have to go, but tell her we should meet up. I ask her, "How could we get a hold of each other?" Going for the number close here.

"I'm here every week!" *Denied.*

I drop it cold for now, just saying, "Cool! Nice! You're totally my new homegirl!" and give her a hip-hop half hug and walk away.

Celine rolls up and yells, "Let's hit up some Phone Bizzle!" So we walk out, but not before this fat chick asks me to take her home. Literally. It's pathetic. I look her dead in the eye and say, "I would, but, you know . . . you're a fucking psychopath." And it's true, she is.

We get to the Phone Booth and Ross is bartending. I ask him what's good. He says, "Well, Jeffy, do you like Jack Daniel's?" I nod, licking my lips, and he pours me a large glass of it, neat. "Three twenty-five." I love this place.

I'm at the bar talking to some random guy and drinking the whiskey when who do I see but the "fake" girl from the other bar. She's standing at the end of the bar with her friends and giving me that look. Like, "I wanna fuck you," type shit. I ignore it, then another chick walks up to me, and she's giving me massive indicators of interest. Turns out I met her last week at this shithole dive bar called "The Mucky Duck" of all places. I mean, come on, the MUCKY DUCK. I had been with Chippy at the time, but spit a bunch of game at her nonetheless. Now here she is, asking me to buy her a drink.

I say, "Whoa whoa! I don't do that shit. Tell you what . . ." Kiss Bet. She grabs my head and we go for it, not just a little peck, but tonguedown for real . . . tacky club shit, my hands on her ass, the whole nine yards. God bless America!

Before I know what's happening, Fake's friends are up in my face, telling me, "Shannon wants to talk to you."

"About what? I don't care."

They literally drag me over to her. She doesn't acknowledge me, so I stand there with my back to her, facing the wall and pretending to look at a large velvet painting of a matador set in a golden frame. My grandparents had this exact same painting in their living room, back in Illinois. In fact, this might very well be the same physical painting, somehow transported to the Bizzle. I stare at it, momentarily lost. This goes on for roughly a full minute. Finally, the girl says, "Are you gonna talk to me?"

I look over my shoulder, say, "Huh? What? What do you want?" Slowly, I turn to face her. I'm so drunk that I don't know exactly what I'm saying, but I get the feeling that I can probably go home with her. The thing is, I don't want to reward flake behavior. Maybe if I see her again I'll give her a chance, but not tonight.

I return to the chick from the Mucky Duck. I tell her I have to leave, because I'm so drunk I just wanna hit the hay, which is the truth. We kiss some more and she punches her number in my phone.

Overall, a good night. Number close and two makeouts. Not many lessons, just reinforcement of the basic tenets: Hit up 9s and 10s in mixed groups, go in low-key, don't appear to be too interested in the outcome, and blow it the fuck up. I put my phone in my pocket as I walk out the door and drag my ass home, avoiding the projects.

TOTAL DUCK MIND-FUCK

I call up the girl from the Mucky Duck on Thursday, and after I run my usual phone rap, she agrees to meet me at the Odeon for Kostume Karaoke. They've got a large assortment of clothing and props set up, and you assemble some form of "costume" when you go up to perform. It's good, clean fun.

At the bar, the game plan is as follows: start with VERY LIGHT routines to reestablish attraction. After that, I have a short list of comfort-building talking points: use her name a lot, use punishment and reward to keep her in a heightened emotional state, withdraw if shit-tested (as opposed to going cocky/funny), connection, triangular gazing. I arrive late and she's already there, looking annoyed. I sit next to her and get a drink. After I settle in, I begin regular fluff conversation, and start layering in the material. She busts my balls a couple of times, and I respond by looking sad and turning away. "I thought we were past all that ballbusting foolishness," I sniffle, "Be nice, okay?"

She agrees and is all "Noooo don't be upset Jeffy!"

Okay. I tell her, "I feel weird, like I'm surprised you actually met me. I thought you were fake, since we made out so soon after meeting in the bar. You know, I've been burned so many times before." I'm trying hard not to laugh here. "I don't like to be that tacky club makeout guy, you know? Of course . . . I can be that guy when the situation calls for it . . . watch." Then I kiss her. Okay. Good.

We talk about writing and she tells me about some story she wrote, I respond by telling her about my screenplay, "The Summer of Ripped Abs." I run So Genuine: "You know, you're so genuine . . . you're just, like, real. I just want to treat you perfect . . . even though you probably don't deserve it. I just want people who I feel that genuine connection with to feel good when they're around me."

She says, "You're either the biggest bullshitter or that's the sweetest thing I've ever heard!"

I laugh and think, *Both.*

We get interrupted by none other than Bambi, a fifty-three-year-old transsexual. She groans, "Ohhhh Jefffffy." Bambi is a regular at this place, one I'm unfortunately all too familiar with. One evening I struck up a conversation with "her," which consisted of me listening to her name-drop continuously in an elitist sneer. "I know David Bowie. I kissed Henry Rollins, darling." I was totally hammered and I sang some bullshit, almost falling off the stage in the process. Some J-girls rushed the stage; I crouched down and touched their hands.

When I returned to the bar I began screaming at the bartender, "Li-Li! I wanna be SICK!! Give me more liquor!! I wanna get SICK!!!" while slamming my hands on the bar. Her name is not "Li-Li." Nevertheless, she brought me big glasses of Cuervo Gold and I told her I wanted to marry her. The next thing I knew, I was singing "Edelweiss" onstage while Bambi simulated fellatio on me with a microphone. The last thing I remember is standing there with my sunglasses on, blinded by the stage lights with Bambi kneeling next to me, as I gently petted her hair. At that moment, I thought I was Jesus.

I snap out of it. I say to Duck, "Yeah, me and this guy sang 'Endless Love.'"

Bambi begins effusing to Duck, "Did Jefffy tell you about our night together? It was fabulous. Ohhh. I deep-throated a mic stand and scratched my esophagus." The girl appears petrified. "You know," she continues, "he's a playah, he won't be there for you. But he is *sooo* cute and has a great ass. Barkeep! Bring me the Bambi Special!!" That's great, thanks a lot Bambi. Fantastic. Get the fuck out of here.

I resume regularly scheduled gaming by easing into Incredible Connection, playing it hard, like I'm struggling to describe what I'm feeling. She says, "Now I know you're not bullshitting me, because you'd have to be way too creative to come up with this stuff!"

I am tempted to say, "Shit girl, you don't know the HALF of it." Instead, I bite my tongue and run a one-two punch: My Cat Got Laid into Evolution Phase Shift. It's basically a quirky story about how I walked in on my cats having sex, which then segues into a physical escalation sequence: "Blah blah blah, my cat got laid. And it's crazy, 'cause when they fuck, you know, it's actually pretty violent, they kick and bite each other on the back of the neck. But it's interesting, because the thing is, that's just how evolution has wired them, and all mammals in fact. Like, see, when I pull your hair like this [I gently grab her hair at the nape of the neck and pull] it feels good huh?" She murmurs her assent. "Another interesting thing is how the most sensitive areas of the skin are the places that bend. Like here, and here," I say as I run my fingers over first the crook of her elbow, then the back of her knee. I point at my neck and say, "Bite me here." She does.

I look her in the eye and say, "Not bad," then smirk and glance down at her lips, then back up to her eyes. We kiss. She suggests we move to a couch. We go over to a dark area, sit on the couch and begin tonguedown in earnest.

While this is going on, another bizarre regular of the establishment known as Autistic Brian is performing onstage. He attempts to sing Devo while standing next to a giant cardboard cutout of a Crispy Chicken Sandwich. He's writhing around in a strobe light and going, "Whii . . . whhiii goo! Ya! Whip! Whiiieeep!" It's totally surreal. This however does not deter me from getting truly egregious with the public makeout session. I am feeling her up and everything. I put my hand between her legs and her pants are totally soaked through with pussy juices. I decide it's time to go, and take her home; more tonguedown on her stoop. I decline to go up to her place, since I have to work early. I go home and go to sleep.

The next night, I call her up again. I dispense with the frills and just tell her, "Hey, come over to my house and we'll watch a movie." She tries to get me to go out on the town with her. I say, "No, I'm staying in tonight, but go ahead, have fun. I'm sure I'll find somebody who will hang out with me."

She quickly says, "No, no! I'll come over." Sure enough, she arrives about twenty minutes later. We watch the movie *Sunset Boulevard*. I give her the tour of the house. We stop at a particularly interesting part of the house: my room. I close the door behind me and we lie on the bed.

So we're lying there, and out of nowhere, she says, "Can I ask you a question? Do you have a girlfriend? Is her name . . . Chippy?"

I say, "Yeah, that's one of my girlfriends," and immediately begin hardcore makeout. I follow the usual script and after twenty minutes, "I wanna lick it." There is resistance. I wash-rinse-repeat. More resistance.

Freeze out time. I suddenly leap up and say, "Cool! Let's play a game."

She's like, "What? Huh? I mean . . . are you mad?"

I reply, "What are you taking about? I'm not mad at all! I understand, you know, a lot of people have these hang-ups and stuff. I mean, a lot of people are repressed and aren't comfortable with their sexuality. Come on, let's play Horse." I start shooting Nerf Hoops. I'm relaxed, just being cool and sweet like there's nothing wrong at all. Shortly, she warms up. I challenge her to a round of Horse and she agrees.

After this, I sing karaoke to her for a while, then initiate kissing once more. We get to a certain point and resistance surfaces again. I go into lockup mode and have my teddy bear do a backturn on her ("Teddy's upset"), then I say, "You're being fake, get the fuck outta here."

She says, "I sense harshness. I'm gonna leave."

You sense harshness? Wow, we got a genius here! She gets up. I immediately slam gears and start acting sad, telling her how I thought she was real, and it turns out she's just playing me. "I'm not ready to be somebody's therapist girlfriend or emotional tampon," I say. "You came over here, you get in my bed, what do you think, we're gonna play Cub Scouts? If you want to spend time with me, sex is part of the deal." She considers this, and then sits back on the bed. "This reminds me of a story." I launch into "100% Perfect Girl":

"Once upon a time, there lived a boy and a girl. They were completely average in every way. But they were unique in that they both believed that somewhere out there, there existed the 100% perfect person for them.

"One day, they were walking down the same street and bumped into each other, and they immediately KNEW. 'Oh my God,' said the boy, 'you are the 100% perfect girl for me!'

"'And you,' said the girl, 'You are the 100% perfect boy for me.'

"They walked to the park and sat down and got to know one another and it only became more apparent that this was true. As the hours passed, however, a small sliver of doubt began to creep in . . . I mean, could such an astronomically improbable thing really happen? If so, it would be a miracle.

"So they devised a test . . . they would go their separate ways, and if they truly were the 100% perfect person for each other, then they would run into each other again, sometime, somewhere. When they did, they would know it was real and get married on the spot. And so they parted and went their separate ways.

"Well, they never should have done this, because they really were in fact the perfect ones for each other. That winter, a fever epidemic came and many people died. They were affected, but they survived . . . However, they lost their memories and had to rehabilitate themselves for many years. Eventually they reintegrated into society. Fourteen years passed.

"Then, one day, they were both walking in opposite directions on the same street where they first met, and bumped into each other again. The faint glimmer of the lost memory came back, like a faint rumbling in the chest, and again, they KNEW:

"She is the 100% perfect girl for me.

"He is the 100% perfect boy for me.

"But the memory was too weak, and faded away. Silently, they passed each other and walked on, disappearing into the crowd. And they never saw each other . . . ever . . . again.

"The end."

The girl seems unhappy as I sit there with a somber look. She says, "I don't like that, it's sad."

I say, "Yeah, you know, sometimes we live our lives according to parameters, and sometimes this makes us miss out on opportunities that are right in front of us (self-point). Well, I'm going to bed, you can stay here, or you can sleep on the couch downstairs." She lies down and I ask her to tell me a bedtime story.

She tells me about a girl who was hurt before and met this awesome, funny, smart, crazy, entertaining, cute guy, and she was totally drawn into his reality and wanted to be with him, and couldn't think about anything but him all week, but then started slipping back into her own reality of hurt past emotions, and got confused.

Okay, whatever, I turn around and hug her. She asks me if I have some pajamas for her. I get up and get some pants out; she gets up and takes her pants off. I start kissing her while we are both standing. Soon she lies down and takes off the panties, I begin licking it, after ten minutes she whispers, "I want you inside me!" and I fuck the shit out of her, raw dog. It was intense, good sex, multiple positions. I blow my fucking wad and yell out, "FUUUCK! Ahh! Shit! DAMN! Christ! Wooo!" and fall off the bed. I get up and go to take a piss.

I get back and she's all upset; her eyes look sad. I ask her, "What's wrong?"

She starts blabbing on. "I wasn't going to do this, I have precautions usually, I never do this . . ." and on and on.

I tell her straight up, "Hmm. You have the buyer's remorse? Interesting. Listen, Duck, you couldn't help it, it wasn't your fault. My game is just too strong, see? It just overpowered your defenses. Also, I just lick pussy too damn good. You couldn't help yourself, so *it doesn't count.*"

She says, between sniffles, "Yeah, you do lick pussy really well."

"I know, I know. You gotta bring soul to it, that's the only way, either you got it or you don't." I just hold her for a while, until she slowly regains a semblance of emotional stability. I start getting horny again, so I resume feeling her up. It's like a switch is flipped: she gets all freaked out, gets up and says, "Dammit!! Things were fine until your lust for pussy reawakened!"

"Lust for pussy?" I can't help myself. I begin convulsing with laughter, and I can't stop. She gets really pissed. She gets up, gets dressed and leaves. I'm still laughing as I get out my scorecard and pencil in the new lay before I go to sleep.

This woman came over with absolutely no intention of hooking up with me, and I just totally mind-fucked her into wanting and having sex, playing her emotions like a fiddle. I almost feel remorseful for having done this; she deployed all her "anti-slut defenses," but I managed to circumvent every one. At this moment, sitting alone in my room after she's left, it hits me that people are basically dumb animals who respond in predictable ways to certain stimuli. Given that, becoming a player is pretty much the only reasonable course of action, if you think about it. I've tasted the fruit of knowledge and there's no going back now.

A key thing that pervaded the whole encounter was my attitude toward her. I was very relaxed, and I assumed rapport as though she was my long-term girlfriend. Even my roommates commented that it was strange how I was fighting with her and talking to her in an extremely familiar way. Alex told me, "You came downstairs and said, 'We're having a fight, I'm not talking to her . . . for five minutes.' You haven't even known her for five days!"

With regard to the whole emotional outburst scenario, I don't think it's beyond repair. Even if it is, that's okay. I was a bit worried about this new chick, worried about who I was going to dump out of the rotation to make room for her. Trial and error has taught me that I can only handle one primary and a maximum of three fuck buddies at a time; even that is a full-time job leaving me little time for fresh gaming, much less for quiet time to myself (necessary for mental well-being). In fact, I prefer to have just two fuck buddies, as it gives me more leeway, but you know, I think with my dick a lot.

Anyway, I left her a message after work: "Hey, it's me, I just wanted to make sure you were okay, you know, not dead in the gutter. Having said that, I gotta say, you are sort of . . . eccentric or something. Call me." She has since called me twice. Unfortunately, I haven't answered, as I must depart soon to attend tonight's Teen Dance Party.

CODEINE, AMNESIA

It's early evening when I finally wake up. I have a soul-crushing hangover, the result of the previous evening's dollar-drink adventure, which had seemed promising at first but ultimately turned out fruitless. I worked on a few flakes, kissed a couple babes, the usual. Christophe and I dragged strangers to my home and I forced everybody to listen to me sing Elvis on my karaoke machine while I played my shotgun like a percussion instrument (*click-KLACK! click-KLACK!*). After this, I proceeded to pass out, not to regain consciousness for sixteen hours. Scratch that . . . I did fade in and out of consciousness several times, but since I was unable to get up and retrieve the Advil, I would just listlessly jack off to relieve the pain, then pass out again. Despite this lengthy recuperation period, I am still feeling like utter shit.

I notice several missed calls on my voicemail. One of them is from Kravitz, the guy who runs the karaoke night at Amnesia. In the message, he extends a personal invitation to karaoke this evening, during which he assures me I will be "hooked up," whatever that means. I drink two beers and pop two codeine pills. Twenty minutes later, I'm feeling well enough to get out of bed and put on my leather pants and Giant Iced-Out Pinky Ring. I put on my black pinstriped blazer, get some hairspray on, grab my aviators and walk out of my bedroom. I go downstairs and the roomies are assembled there, watching some lame flick. I attempt to persuade them to accompany me to the karaoke bar. They refuse for a variety of reasons. I growl, "Well, looks like Jeffy's goin solo tonight! Eh . . . won't be the first time." I walk out the door.

It is extremely dark inside Amnesia. The bartender is a little Asian turbo, and she is delighted to see me. She gives me an unfamiliar licorice-flavored alcoholic beverage. It is disgusting. I am totally fucked up on codeine at this point, barely coherent. Like, I'm turning to people beside me and saying, "What?" and they're all, "Huh? I didn't say anything . . ."

I stagger to the stage and write my name on the list, then stagger back to my seat.

Three chicks walk in and sit next to me. They look a little older than I am accustomed to (read: not fucking TEENAGERS). They're like 7s, and I am wasted on pills and booze. But something in me, habit I guess, makes me open them. I improvise some shit, "Hey guys, lemme ask you a question. Do you still respect Paris Hilton after these shocking sex tape revelations?"

They respond, "We never DID respect her in the first place, but it makes no difference."

I reply, "Oh good. 'Cause I got one coming out soon, and I want to know if my peers will lose respect for me. God, I love it in here . . . the extremely low lighting makes it impossible to see my many, many skin flaws." They're somewhat perplexed, but they laugh.

I stack a couple of openers until they open up for real, then move quickly into Sexual Predators ("You chicks are making me feel weird!! I feel so emotional."). While I'm gaming the two hottest, the third comes over and says, "Are you bothering my friends?"

I say, "What the fuck? These sluts are hitting on me!" They laugh. I run Little Sister. I run Powerpuff. I tell them I'm an "ass model," then rebuff them when they ask to see it, demanding thirty dollars.

They shit-test me: "Why are you here alone? You come to the bar alone and practice hitting on girls, huh?"

I say, "No, I only hit on little POWERPUFF girls." I start talking about Journey with them and they scream how they love that song "Separate Ways." Just then, I am called to the stage, where I sing none other than that very song, and, quite frankly, slam-dunk it. When I return, I downplay how good it was as the bartender gives me a beer. I get the sense that the women have had a talk while I was gone, because now only one of them is focusing on me. She tries to take off my ring, I tickle her. The other girls begin to give each other some kind of eye-code, and I call them on it, demonstrating attunement to their subjective reality and thus building rapport. I run a personality-conveying story about how I get my hair cut at Supercuts. I do Nice New Girlfriend push-pull qualifying: "You know what, I think you'd make a nice new girlfriend. Wait a minute.

Can you cook? Awesome. Are you rich? Because I want to be a stay-at-home husband. Awww damn, okay . . . well, do you at least have cable? 'Cause you KNOW I GOTS to watch my Montel."

I say to her, "Listen. I have a problem, maybe you can help. I think I drink too much, and I'm a total whore."

She squeals, "Ahhh! ME TOO!"

This is actually a pretty standard response to this.

I tell her, "If I was your boyfriend, I'd fuck you once a month and you'd buy me shit all the time." Apparently one of the pills' side effects is telling the truth. I go up to sing my second song, "Glory of Love" by Peter Cetera (from the *Karate Kid, Part II* soundtrack). Again, a remarkable performance, given my drug-addled state. I fall down the stairs as I get offstage. I return to the target, who is looking at me with love in the eyes.

She asks my name. I tell her it's "Brad Pitt." She tells me her name is Rose, and that her dad was a botanist. What a coincidence: I used to be a horticulturalist myself. Time for comfort building, although from the indicators of interest I'm getting, I sense that the need for this is minimal. I run Incredible Connection, then return to normal fluff for a short time, then qualify her with You're So Genuine. After that, it's a simple matter of running My Cat Got Laid into Evolution Phase Shift, and after a bit of triangular gazing, I am making out with her in the bar as her friends watch, astounded.

We start talking sexually. She's touching me and saying shit like, "Do I make you nervous?"

I laugh out loud and say, "What the fuck, do you know who the fuck I am? NO, you are NOT making me nervous." She asks me if my cock is immense. I say, "Nah, it's very average, but my real value comes from the fact that I give expert cunnilingus. Now, as you're probably aware, a lot of guys SAY they like it, but are full of shit. Not me. You gotta bring SOUL to it."

She says, "Will you take me home with you?"

I say, "Okay, but don't put the cart ahead of the horse here sweetie." She assures her friends it's okay and we leave.

Back at the heezy. We go upstairs and I introduce her to Alex, with whom we smoke a blunt. I hustle Alex out of the room, close the door behind her, jump on the bed and begin tonguedown. After the clothes come off, I pause as she lies naked before me. Now, no shit, I literally do a fucking ASIDE TO THE AUDIENCE like Zack Morris in *Saved by the Bell* and say, "I wanna lick it." The rest, as they say, is history. Bang her three times.

She takes me to her house and makes me breakfast the next day. Her roommate is hot. I am going to attempt the three-way; they seem like liberal chicks.

Another textbook lay, two hours from start to finish, I am pleased. Seems like the nights I leave the chodes at home and go it alone are the times I actually get laid. Bear in mind, however, that this chick was, after all, only a 7. Proving, once again, that I have very solid 7 game and a decent 8 game. The 9s, however, continue to elude me. I know it's only a matter of time given my dedication.

HER SHREDDED SOUL

Twelve Gauge reached out to me yesterday. She sent me a text asking me if I was dead yet. I replied, indicating that I was, in fact, alive and well.

"Too bad," she sent back.

Long story short, I met up with her later that evening and had a drink, then we headed back to my place. Things quickly became emotional. It ended with her crying in my bed, saying retarded shit like, "WHY DON'T YOU LOVE ME HEFFY??" and, "Please fuck me!!"

Needless to say, I was totally disgusted by this. I informed her that she was behaving like "a little animal scrabbling for cock." She got pissed. SUPER PISSED. So I kicked her out of my house. Mind you, this chick is an 8; before learning game, I would have supplicated and bowed down, eager to take whatever I could get. But I just didn't wanna fuck. I found her antics highly distasteful. I'm like a chick now. The tables have turned.

Can't take it, bitch? Huh? HUH?!

I decided to make the most of the night, and headed out to a nearby bar. Some weird guy I'd never seen before in my life came up to me and said, "You're the guy who teaches pickup, aren't you?"

I said, "Nah, you got the wrong guy pal."

He was like, "No! It's you . . . I KNOW," and appeared rather smug. The guy intermittently hassled me all night about teaching him pickup. I guess word travels fast in these parts. Whatever.

I've been doing this shit for a year and a half now. Going out and banking hos. Confusion and frustration has been replaced by a fascination bordering on addiction. I know that it's somehow altered me on a fundamental level, yet I feel like I've only seen the tip of the iceberg. I don't know, I feel like something's changing, that things are taking a turn. Whether that turn is for the better or worse remains to be determined.

FAT FUCK

I'm sick with some throat thing that's going around. I lie in bed listening to Tony Robbins subliminal music, ill and feverish, passing in and out of consciousness. I have a nightmare in which literally every woman I know comes to my house at the same time. When I refuse to open the front door, they break it down, file in and begin tearing the place apart, completely laying waste to everything in sight, breaking all the windows, destroying all the furniture, kicking holes in the walls. When they are done and the house and everything I own is in ruins, they start to attack me. They take hold of me by the arms and legs and start to rip me apart.

When I wake up, I don't know what time it is, but it's dark outside. I sit up in bed and look down at my body. I am becoming a fat fuck. This was brought to my attention by one of my fuck buddies last week. While we were having sex, she poked at my belly and bourgeoning man boobs and said, "You're so squishy!" and started laughing. She got ass-fucked for that one. But the fact remains. I have let myself go. I'm twenty-eight. My metabolism has changed. I can no longer eat nothing but burritos and consume three thousand calories of alcohol every night and expect to retain my svelte figure. This is disconcerting. On the other hand, I have game now, which essentially negates the "looks issue," so I really don't feel it's that big of a deal.

Christophe has a friend in town from Montreal, and we're all going out to the Rio tonight. His friend is known on the forum as a real alpha asshole type guy, and I'm rather excited to see him in action. We hit up one set out back with two hipster guys who immediately try to deflate us. He gets their names and asks them for a cool place to go in San Francisco. Then he begins incessantly tooling them. He says, "Hey Chris! Why don't you have a seat?" while offering him a stool covered in rainwater.

The guy looks at it and says, "Uh . . . that's wet, and my name's not Chris."

"Yeah, so? SIT DOWN, CHRIS." The hipsters leave.

I get all loaded and start running sets, experiencing various degrees of blowout with the 7s and occasional 8s there. I see a chick I fucked a while ago, the Duck Girl. Apparently she's come looking for me. I bust her ass for being fake and not calling me. She apologizes and we abscond to a dark area where we lightly kiss.

My phone rings; it's my girlfriend. She says, "Hey, I just dropped my friend off, are you at El Rio?" I tell her to come by, and she says she'll see me soon. I turn back to Duck and resume talking. I figure I have at least ten minutes to get her number again (I deleted it after I fucked her last time). Then, all of a sudden, just as she's punching it into my phone, Chippy is STANDING RIGHT THERE. Literally two minutes, tops, have elapsed since I got off the phone with her. She must have been right outside the place. FUCK. She is standing there in our faces, glaring.

Duck asks, "Who's this?"

Chippy says, "I'M HIS GIRLFRIEND." Duck appears terrified and leaves quickly. I don't blame her. Chippy is intimidating. She's fucking pissed. "I don't think we should see each other anymore," she says in a strained voice.

"What the fuck, because I was getting someone's phone number? That chick is having a party next week and I wanted to go." We leave immediately and go back to my house. I tell Chippy that the chick was "Jackass's friend Joe's girlfriend's friend. You met her at his going away party, remember?" This is actually true.

She sighs. "Why didn't you just say that. I hate how you act with this El Rio thing . . . how I'm not allowed there and I know you get girls' numbers."

I say, "I'm sorry I hurt your feelings." But that's IT. If she's gonna say shit like "We shouldn't see each other," I'm gonna call her fucking bluff. She seems to sense this and as such doesn't bring it up again. She just starts to cry.

I kiss her and hug her for a while, and she seems better and says, "I love you."

"I love you too."

BRINGING THE TRUTH

It is Chippy's birthday. I have just spent several hours with her and her insipid peer group and now we are driving home. I sit in the backseat of her car, miserable, as they chain-smoke cigarettes and sing along to Britney Spears at top volume. I moan, coughing. "If you're going to sing this shit, can you at least hit the notes accurately?"

"Oh, shut up Jeff!" she yells back.

I decide to have the "talk" with her. Tonight. On her birthday. Nobody said that being an asshole was a necessity for pickup, but it does, unfortunately, seem in some respects to be a necessity for being jlaix, and as such I need to find a way to integrate that into everything, including my game. I didn't intend to do this until later, but she's seriously pissing me off. I've been living a fucking lie with this girl, and I know that if I don't do it now, I might never.

As soon as we are alone, I tell her the truth. I tell her that I never should have gotten into a "relationship" with her in the first place. That I didn't want it, but I was on the rebound. I tell her it's not her, it's me. "I don't want to be in a 'relationship' with *anyone*. I *can't* and it's not fair to you for me to pretend that I can. I love you as much as I know how." I tell her I am not attracted to her anymore, and that I am going to see other women. "I'm sorry," I say. "I'll understand if you don't want to fuck with me no more."

When I finish, she sits there in tears. First, she tries to get me to explain why I'm not attracted to her. I tell her she isn't the same. We have both changed and we are both moving on, even though I care about her a lot and I have loved the times we have had together. I explain to her, "Look. Seventy percent of me is better than one hundred percent of some *loser*."

This goes over horribly, as expected. She becomes very angry and says that this is unacceptable and that if I am going to see other girls it's over between us, and we will just be friends.

I reply, "Yeah, I expected you to say that."

She runs to the bathroom and becomes physically ill.

I'm sad, but at least I'm not LYING to her anymore. This has been a big weight on me for a long time, and even though it sucks now, I know this was the correct and responsible thing to do. I'm finally free to fulfill my destiny. But at this moment, I'm questioning why I wanted to do all of this in the first place. I'm wondering if I have made a big mistake.

VALENTINE'S DAY

Tonight, I'm spray painting some furniture black in my garage when she walks in and hands me a letter. She stands there silently as I read it.

Jeff—

I thought that not being with you would make me happy. I had no idea it would be this hard. I still love you so much. I miss you so much it feels like I can't breathe. . . .

I never wanted to hurt you. I feel so completely horrible. I still want to be your friend . . .

I don't want you out of my life completely. I mean, I would still like to have a relationship with you, if you still want one with me. . . . Please don't disregard this letter because it has been so hard for me to write, I write it with tears in my eyes.

Love,
Chippy

I finish reading and glance up at her. Her eyes are red and she's looking down at the carpet. Finally, I fold it up, put it in my back pocket and walk up to her. There is a sense of finality in the air. I say, "It's okay baby," and kiss her, for what I know is the last time.

Silently, she walks out of the garage.

I

ULTIMATE FRAMEWORK

I've just returned to San Francisco after a brief stint helping the RSD guys run workshops down in Hollywood. The city of fake titties and real assholes. The scene down there is everything I thought it would be and more, and I had difficulty adjusting at first. The women are hotter, the clubs are more exclusive and the guys are more aggressive. Not only that, but the guys I was rolling with all had incredible skills themselves. I was forced to step my game up in order to survive. Over the course of several weeks, however, I eventually became acclimated to the new environment.

Then I got back home.

I walk into the old El Rio like I own it. In fact, the owner is there at the door as I approach, and he says to the door girl, "This guy is here every week, he doesn't pay." I ignore this, give the door chick two dollars and tell her, "That's for you."

I take a look around. Dude. This is my home turf and it's like a child's toy compared to the loud-ass uberclubs we were at during the workshops. I'm feeling magnanimous and in complete control. My eyes go bright. I feel rooted to the ground, immovable. I sense a certain energy welling up inside me and extending out to somehow charge the air in my immediate vicinity. It feels like I am surrounded by a shimmering nimbus of golden, holy light. *I will not be denied.*

Instantly I spot my target. I've seen her here before and I've always wanted to get with her. She's not exceptionally beautiful; she dresses down but I find myself undeniably drawn to her nonetheless. She's just got a certain air, something about her that I can't pinpoint but find highly attractive. A *je ne sais quoi*, if you will. We'll call her Chess Club Girl.

There's only one problem. Whenever I see her at the Rio, she's invariably surrounded by at least seven guys, these hipster freaks who wear Buddy Holly glasses and scarves. We call them "The Chess Club" because they look like fucking dorks. I've talked to her briefly several times before, but in each case, she's been swept off by the Chess Club before I could make any meaningful headway. Subsequently, I've always been too intimidated to talk to her.

Not tonight.

I turn to Christophe and Brian and say, "Watch this. Follow me." I saunter right up to the nebulous mass that is the Chess Club, roughly push them aside ("Excuse me!") and step directly to the girl. I tap her on the shoulder and say, "HEY." She looks up at me, expectantly.

"I hate you." After I say it, I just stare at her, waiting for a response.

An odd expression crosses her face, and she looks down. "I know. I'm sorry!"

"Wait, what?"

I start slamming routines as the boys swoop in and handle the Chess Club gang. Brian is particularly effective at this as he is physically larger and takes up more space. His MO is to engage a guy, bombard him with logical questions and position himself between him and me, getting uncomfortably close while he's talking so the guy backs up. I look over and see that he's pushed one of the Chess Club members about ten feet away with this technique.

It's going well, she is my little sister, I do Alternate Opposite Sex Name and she's calling me Shannon and I'm calling her Rob. She's loving it, my body language is good and I'm doing a good job of engaging the group. I'm constantly misinterpreting things she says as meaning she wants me, then saying, "Gross! You're my little sister!" When her attention wanders, it's, "Hey! Show's over here! Are you multitasking me?" I run the Trust Test: "Are you trustworthy? Hmm . . . I don't know if I believe you. Let me see your hands." I clasp her hands, interlacing my fingers with hers, and I squeeze. She squeezes back. From there I ease into Evolution Phase Shift, then disengage hard with more false disqualifiers. Numerous alpha attacks are thrown my way by the hipsters. One guy tries to cut in and I'm all over his ass: "Wow dude, that's a nice scarf. I bet you get all the girls with that." I twirl him around by the scarf and BOOM he's deflated. I cut him out of the circle. Nice.

After a while, Christophe leaves. Brian and I can't handle all ten of these bozos alone. Sure enough, one of them latches on to the girl and gets her full attention. I manage to stay engaged in the group by talking to some fat chick. The hipster pulls my girl away to the other side of the room where a mass of Chess Club members stand with ironic mustaches and skinny pants. I know I'm about to lose her again.

Who do I see but Celine, nursing a beer in the corner, by himself. He's been there the whole time, watching this all go down. I walk over, greet him and instruct him to go occupy the guy. He refuses. I pinch his nipple and twist it, hissing, "Go bitch!"

Celine slaps my hand away and says, "No. It's over. Just accept it. You lost."

I'm furious. I spit at him, "Fuck that shit." I SLAP him in the face. "GO!"

He stands there, in disbelief over what's just happened. He says, "No, fuck you! I'm not like you! It's over, can't you see that?"

I SLAP him again and say, "Fuck that negative shit, nothing is over!!" At this point people are looking over, so I pull him away to the bar. "Dude," I say, "I'm sorry I hit you, man. But THAT GIRL IS MINE and I don't need negative shit from my friends fucking up my state." He assures me that it's okay, and seems cool, but he leaves the bar soon after. Fuck, I feel bad. Oh well.

Now I'm back at square one: completely blown out of the group. *Fuck it.* I just charge back in, singing the song "Luka" by Suzanne Vega and asking them if they know who sings it. I discover that one Chess Club member is actually cool. Apparently, he's into all the same crap music I like; he has on all these buttons for Styx, Air Supply, REO Speedwagon and so forth. I say, "Wow man, I thought you were a total fucking prick, but you're sort of cool. You should come to karaoke on Tuesdays." He agrees, and the target starts getting jealous that I'm not paying attention to her. Okay, cool. I do a takeaway and get another drink.

When I get back from the bar, I see that many more dudes have joined the group, big, tough-looking surfer dudes, and I am now all alone, as Brian too has decided to bounce. Fuck. I look around, and open another group consisting of two girls and a guy. I start asking lame questions to the guy and ignore the girls, standard shit. I ask them which ice cream flavor is the best. They list their favorites and I say, "Oh my God, you have to tell my friends, come on."

I drag them over to the Chess Club and get back in the group, pawning them off and letting them occupy some of the obstacles. Now I'm back in the mix, but I'm getting mad-aggressive-rude comments about my appearance from the dudes. IRRELEVANT. My frame is tight. I just laugh and execute picture-perfect frame control tactics:

"I love your shirt man, IZOD fuckin' rocks, I used to wear that in high school all the time."

"WHAT? WHAT DID YOU SAY? No, man, what did you just say to try to make yourself look cooler than me? Come on, man, I wanna hear this! WHAT?!"

"[laughing] You're cool, man, hipster guy, so cool bro!"

"Awesome. You're like my PERSONAL ASSISTANT, dude! Keep the good advice coming! Like *Queer Eye for the Straight Guy!*"

Handled. Other guys in the group, I just preempt by opening them first and going logical. The target, whose actual name is Heather, sees all this and is duly impressed. At one point, however, she says something that could be interpreted as negative toward me. Now, I've already told her that we should play nice and drop the ballbusting. So I say, "You're not a good little sister," and turn my back on her. I have to literally force myself to not turn back around. It's hard, but after roughly a full minute of torture, she's all up in my face again. Awesome, I've clearly passed the social hook point. She is chasing me.

The crowd thins out; it's near closing. I attempt to pull her, but it's not in the cards. She tells me that she's moving to Canada on Saturday. That doesn't give me much time to seal the deal. I throw my phone at her. She asks, "What's this for?" I inform her that she's meeting me at karaoke tomorrow. She seems quite excited about this as we exchange numbers.

I call her the next day. She answers on the first ring and is really happy to hear from me. Solid game. I meet her at karaoke on Thursday night. She shows up with two girl friends. I am alone. It goes really well, the friends like me, I am dancing with one and the other one thinks I'm cool. Heather and I even sing a duet. She's a great singer so I compliment her on that. I isolate her and run my best rapport shit. The bar closes and we go back to my place to smoke.

When we get there, nobody is awake to occupy the two friends. This sucks. I resign myself to the fact that there is simply nothing I can do. If I had come in and there were five people up drinking, maybe I'd have had a chance. I am lying on my bed with Heather, but the two friends are sitting right there and there's nothing I can do. This game is over. FUCK. They like me, so they wouldn't necessarily have a problem with their friend fucking me, but Secret Society rules state that "all persons in the interaction must be having fun." Unfortunately, in this instance, there is nobody to entertain them.

I lead them out. At the door I stop, wish her a safe trip and HUG her. Fucking lame, I know, but it doesn't seem intuitively right to kiss her at this particular moment.

She emails me a week later. "I can't wait to hang out with you when I get back . . ." Whatever. I did my best, given the circumstances, and my game should be even tighter in six months, when she is supposedly going to move back. Until then, I guess I'll just have to get by on what I have here. Which is a date with an 8.5 tonight.

HAIRPULLIN'

I'm out with Celine, for the first time since having slapped him at Rio. I buy us a round of drinks and when I come back, I find him talking to some chubby 5 with a cute face. *Dum-dum-dum . . .* I do have a weakness for little chubsters with the pretty face.

Celine's doing his usual creepy shit, leaning in and so forth, so I decide to go in and demonstrate a couple of routines for him live.

I set the drinks down, throw my arm around Celine and shout, "What's going on here? Are you hitting on my boyfriend, bitch?!" Transition into false time constraint and neutral opinion opener with good body language. I call her my "Little Sister." The chick's attention instantly shifts to me (follow the shiny thing, beeyach!), and I start blatantly narrating the pickup to Celine, like, "Okay, I'm gonna do Trust Test on her now, watch. Also, don't lean in, it's creepy." I lean in toward her and ask, "Isn't it creepy?"

She says, "Yes, oh my God, you're like Tom Cruise in *Magnolia!*" I see that I'm blowing Celine out, so I eject quickly.

Cut to closing time. I'm out front with my roommate, just kicking it, watching all the scores being settled. There aren't any serious targets this evening, so we just observe. Lo and behold, that little lassie emerges from the door and calls out to me, "HEY!" I ignore it. Again, "HEY!!" I slowly turn around and she runs up to me, and demands that we exchange numbers. I do so, just for the hell of it.

Bored the next night, I call her up to exercise my phone game. She comes to karaoke with me, bringing a friend along. I have Brian occupy the friend while I run every attract trick in my arsenal on her between songs. I debut a spectacular new hit, "On the Wings of Love," by Jeffrey Osborne. She leaves early, but not before making out with me. When I phase-shift, she says she really enjoys the part where I pull gently on her hair. She goes home. I forget about her almost immediately.

She calls me up the following afternoon. "Hey," she says, "it's Kelly . . . what are you doing tonight?" These days, I usually don't go out on Friday nights, reserving my energies for Sunday–Thursday, but I tell her to meet me at a taco shop near my house. She agrees and once there I proceed to run literally every rapport trick I know on her. I mean, I'm periodically going into the bathroom, whipping out my cheat sheet and assembling a salvo of six calculated routines or so, then going back out and delivering them over the course of an hour. Repeat until material exhausted. I venue change twice, then invite her to "Club Chalupa," the new euphemism for my home that I cribbed from the Taco Bell menu.

We arrive at Club Chalupa. She realizes it's not a club and exclaims, "This is your house? Oh my God . . . this is scandalous!"

I just say, "Yeah," and we go upstairs after a short tour of the premises. Make out on the bed. I encounter resistance, I execute a freeze-out with a right jolly game of "PIG" on the Nerf Hoop. I wash-rinse-repeat several times, humping her on the bed and then abruptly backing off, over and over. It's rather amusing; at various points she becomes indignant and gets up to leave, then changes her mind. The first time, she gives some resistance, saying something along the lines of, "It's so soon, I don't even know you."

I curtly reply, "Shut up. No more talking." She gets up and puts her shoes on, but I immediately "apologize" and so she lies back down and takes them off. I forge ahead.

She's still not with it. Getting frustrated, I say, "Look. I have neither the time nor the inclination to deal with your fucked-up emotional baggage. Get the fuck out of my house." She gets up and puts her boots and her coat on *again*, and starts to leave. I pretend to cry and say, "I knew it! You ARE fake! You were just playing me the whole time!" She takes her shoes off again and lies down.

This happens THREE times. Shoes on, shoes off. Shoes on, shoes off. She cries, "I feel like I'm going crazy! I feel hot, then cold, hot, then cold about you!" I even make my fucking CAT do a backturn on her. I tell her I'm not ready to be someone's emotional tampon or therapist girlfriend. The final straw is the time-honored classic, 100% Perfect Girl.

Aside to the audience: "I wanna lick it." Boom. I'm incorporating a new cunnilingus tactic these days; after about ten minutes of licking it, I focus on the clit and simultaneously start putting fingers in. Money. She's like, "OHH fuck me" and I do so. She yells, "Pull my hair!!" I do this as well, laughing, and I'm really getting into it, yanking her fucking hair. This makes her start squealing and shrieking in some weird rapture. I slap her ass a couple times for good measure, and then decide to experiment with some new shit. I say, "I want you to come for Daddy! Come on, come for me like a good girl!" Holy shit, the kid EXPLODES. This is definitely something I will do again.

I cuddle her, then she gets up and leaves. Even though she is a 5, I will likely fuck her again due to the freaky hair shit. I enjoyed that.

I call her the following afternoon and leave a message; she doesn't return the call. Could it be another case of total duck mind-fuck-style buyer's remorse hmmmm? I tell Jackass the story and he is upset with me, at my lack of standards. "What the fuck, man," he says, "a fucking 5? Disgusting."

I reply, "What are you talking about? I've fucked a *1* before, you've seen it! Remember Shannon Lake?"

"That's different, that's a fetish. But a fucking 5? Come on man."

It's funny, but with these 7 and under girls, I've noticed something: you KNOW they want to fuck, you KNOW you are more attractive than them, but you cannot SHOW this. No, instead, you must *pretend that they aren't easy.* I've lost average chicks many times in the past because of this. I would be thinking, "Okay, this chick must be ecstatic that a guy like me is even giving her the time of day, so let's just cut to the fucking chase, I know how this story ends." But once they catch a whiff of this attitude, they get all indignant and bail. So, this is advanced UG theory: pretend they aren't easy. Sometimes you just gotta put in your hours.

I saw railing this little tubby as an opportunity to exercise my skills on an off night, a night where I usually would have gone to bed at 10 P.M. As it were, the chick was gone and I was asleep by midnight. No concern at all about the outcome. Another thing I did was tone down the absurd clothing. That meant no ridiculous, obviously fake bling, no fucking light-up shirts, just a plain black tee and blue jeans, like a generic dode. Perfect state control because I sincerely couldn't give a fuck if this chick put out or not. I even experimented with some new lines. I mean, the whole thing was totally rote and by the numbers. I was in complete control the entire time. Not challenging at all, but a nice light workout to put me though my paces. Time to hit the showers.

APOCALYPSE '04: THE CHESS CLUB STRIKES BLACK

Funny shit. Last night at El Rio I was obliquely threatened by a member of the Chess Club. This is a good thing, as I intend to use this to destroy them even further and hopefully drive them from the Rio for all of eternity.

Ever since I swooped their girl Heather out from these guys last month, I have been corresponding with her on MySpace. She is quite infatuated with me, and the feeling is mutual. I still can't put my finger on it, but something inside is telling me that we're made for each other.

Of course, these Chess Club assholes can't appreciate our love. They began making snarky comments on her page about "light-up shirts" being "useless," and "ridiculous people who wear Journey shirts."

I responded by posting a comment of my own: "These guys are like my personal assistants! Keep the advice coming, guys, cause you KNOW I gotta impress you Valencia Street hipsters! Look at the STYLE on these guys. Fucking awesome, I can't compete!" She apologized to me for them. I sent her back the following message:

> Listen, you don't have to apologize for your friends for making fun of my blinky shirt. I know those guys are really nice people, they're just insecure. I mean, try to look at it from their perspective: some random dude barrels into their social circle and starts talking to their girlfriends. They try to shut the guy down but can't do it. They get scared for their friends, like "who the fuck is this guy and what's his angle?" They are just trying to protect you and you can't fault them for that. I'm sure if I got to know them they're really cool guys. If they ever get over these feelings of being threatened by me somehow, that could happen. Until then,

I'll continue to bug the living shit out of them at the Rio . . .
hehehehehe

Okay. While all of this was taking place, it came to my attention that the hairpulling girl, Kelly, is actually Heather's friend, and happens to be the little sister of one of the Chess Club hipsters. After I fucked her, she went psycho and confronted me at Rio the following week for being "scripted," then talked shit about me to all of the Chess Club members, saying I'm a jerk. Meanwhile, I've stayed close with all of Heather's other girlfriends, they love me, and we all go to karaoke together. The storm is brewing.

Anyways, I went to Rio last night wearing ten pounds of ridiculous, obviously fake "bling" and the "I DON'T GIVE A FUCK IF YOU'RE OFFENDED" shirt. Lo and behold, the Chess Club was there, albeit in weakened numbers.

I grabbed a couple of their girls, these two named Janet and Lisa, and waded into their group. Their leader, this little hipster punk Sonny, was giving me glares from behind his Buddy Holly glasses, smoking a Parliament. The chicks stepped away when I made them go get me beer, so I took the opportunity to approach Sonny. "Hey man," I said, extending my hand, "what's up?" He said nothing and continued to scowl at me. "You're the guy that makes the thongs or whatever, right? The butterfly knives?" I know they're actually called "Balisongs." I just wanted to tell him that he "makes the thongs."

He grunted, "Yeah."

"Do you have one right now?"

"No." Blowing cigarette smoke directly in my face.

I looked at him cockeyed and asked, "Did you get some sun today, man? You look red."

Unfazed, he just said, "Yeah, it was hot today." The guy was giving off a total "fuck you, you fucking asshole" vibe. I continued to fluff talk for a tense, uncomfortable minute.

Finally, I said, "Jeez, man, you're so uptight! What's up?"

"I don't like you." Stated as fact.

All I could say was, "What the fuck?"

He threw his cigarette down, put it out with his toe and said, "I think you're shady. I don't like the way you treat my friends."

A smirk crept across my face. I said, "Listen, man, I'm not shady . . . I'm EVIL. But seriously, I think if we got to know each other we're probably both pretty cool, so what's up?"

"I don't want to get to know you."

I laughed, "Ha! This guy! Man, you're like Bart Simpson all grown up! Fair enough." I went to shake his hand, he left me hanging. I slapped him on the arm, then turned to his friends and said, "This guy." All of them just stared at me, pissed. Finally, I broke the tension by saying, "Listen, I'll stay out of your way if you stay out of mine."

As I was turning to leave, I heard him mumble, "If you know what's good for you."

I walked off and went back to the Chess Club girls. They saw the odd look on my face and asked, "What's wrong?"

I shook my head. "I don't know, your friend Sonny threatened me with a knife. He said I'm shady and I better stay out of his way." The girls started freaking out, jabbering and asking me what happened. I said, "I don't know what's up. I was trying to talk to him and he just started acting really weird."

They said, "He's just pissed because he has a fat girlfriend, and also because you talk to Heather."

"Why? I don't understand! Why is he so insecure? What's gonna happen?" I'm such a naïve and bewildered innocent.

"I don't know. He's so lame," said Janet.

I call Christophe from work and tell him about it. He laughs and suggests I tell Heather that I can't be friends with her now because the guy threatened me or whatever. I find this to be a stellar idea and draft the message:

Heather . . . listen, something weird happened last night.
That guy Sunny was there, and I said hi to him, and he blew
smoke in my face and implied he had a knife. Then he told
me he didn't like me and called me "shady." I was like, "OK"

and then he said "stay out of my way if you know what's good for you." Janet told me he doesn't like me because I talk to you.

Dude, I feel really uncomfortable about this, and I don't want to feel that way at my own bar. I don't want this to jeopardize our relationship but I'm not gonna put myself in those kinds of situations anymore. I don't know . . . tell me your thoughts.

Within an hour, she replies with this:

RE: weird stuff

He told me he wasn't going to go there anymore, this morning. I don't really know what the hell that is all about except that Sonny and I sort of have a thing going on. I don't know, don't worry about it. He probably won't go there anymore. Sorry? I am confused.

—H

My evil plan is coming to fruition. Mwahahahahhaaa!

TWENTY-ONE-AND-A-HALFED

Christophe and I stride into the Rio like gods and start running game. I'm wearing my LED shirt that displays marquee-style messages on the front, and as usual, everyone in the bar is looking at me. I don't know why, but this shirt really seems to

PISS PEOPLE OFF, mainly guys. I get violent insults about it, nonstop. Good fun.

I open a lone-wolf 9 on the deck. The material is working; my body language and voice is good. Then some Russian meathead comes up and says, "You dance with me before, now, talking to this guy?" or some shit. I tool him away with some standard lines, and he walks off. I continue gaming the chick. Looks like I fucked up, though, by not isolating her right away, because shortly thereafter the Russian comes back. He says something about the shirt. I say, "Hey . . . I'm just trying to impress you, guy!"

He says in a thick Russian accent, "I not gay," and cuts in closer to the chick.

I say, "Oh this guy's good," and pull a fake handshake on him where I pull away at the last second. The girl clearly thinks he's a moron, but he closes in on her and blocks me off. Fuck!

Abruptly, he turns and says to me, "BLINKY SHIRT NO WORK!" He then picks the girl up and carries her to the dance floor.

I sarcastically say to her, "Nice! Have fun!" and she just shrugs as she is carted off over the dude's shoulder, giving me a look that says, "I know, but what can I do?" I'm sure all of the "buying temperature" I've built is instantly transferred to the fucker as soon as I am out of sight. Follow the shiny thing, girls! I should have cut in and got her away first. "BLINKY SHIRT NO WORK!" That's my new catch-phrase. Fuck it, I take a moment and program it so it's displayed ON the shirt.

So we're standing there, and guess who I see over across the way? None other than the leader of the Chess Club, Sonny. *Fuck this guy*, I think, *I thought he was gone for good.* I decide to go over and talk shit to him. I grab two girls I know, and roll up with one on each arm. "Hey little brother."

He glances up impassively and says, "Hey."

"Girls, this guy is awesome, he's like Biff from *Back to the Future*; he is tough. Hey dude, say, 'Make like a tree and get outta here.' I'll leave right now if you say it."

"No."

I plow on. "Wow, this guy is awesome, can you believe he's a virgin?" The girls can sense something is awry and are starting to become highly uncomfortable with the situation. I say to Sonny, "Ha, just fucking around man. Okay, well, girls, let's go." I stop and turn back to the Chess Club, saying, "Oh, not YOU girls, I meant the REAL girls. You guys have to stay here."

I go to walk off, and a Chess Club member grabs me and yells, "What the fuck is all this about?!"

I say, "Hey man, why are you touching me? I'm just introducing my friends here to Sonny."

"Why are you calling us girls?"

I put my hands up and reply, "Hey man, I'm just playing around. Why are you touching me man? I mean, do you wanna fight or something? Are you fucking serious? Don't be so insecure, dude. Just be real."

Exasperated, he says to the girls, "Nice meeting you," and drops his hand. We walk away.

About ten minutes later, I'm standing in another area of the bar, talking to a girl I know. Some random guy walks up and starts touching me and talking shit about the shirt. I ask him to take his hand off me. He doesn't. The following exchange takes place:

"Hey, dude, just stop touching me, okay? Club Gay's over there. I'm into chicks, man."

The guy, obviously drunk, becomes upset and retorts, "What?! Don't talk to me like that!"

I smile and say, "Man, I'll talk to you however the fuck I want. Now take your fucking hand off me, amigo." He becomes highly agitated and starts yelling nonsense. I tell him, "Hey man, don't try so hard, this chick thinks you're the alpha male already, dude!"

He holds up his glass and says, "Do you want me to throw this drink on you?"

I shrug and say, "Nah. Do you want me to have you ejected from here?"

The guy turns bright red and yells, "YEAH! Do it man! DO IT! Fuck it, I'll do it to myself right now!" He runs over to his friends and screams,

"FUCK IT, WE'RE LEAVING!!" He grabs his shit and storms out, yelling. I'm astounded but vaguely amused.

A few minutes later, the bar manager comes up to me and pulls me aside. She tells me that she's received two complaints about me tonight for fucking with people, and one last week from some poor woman (whom I fucked and never called back) who told the staff I made her "uncomfortable." I say, "What, so I can't pick up chicks here anymore?" The prospect is chilling, given that I've been coming here every Monday for the past seventy-eight consecutive weeks. She rolls her eyes. She also says that the guy that stormed out said I called him a "fag." Well, the Rio is run by lesbians and so naturally this raises a red flag. For the record, jlaix is NOT a homophobe. I say, "Dude, you know I'm not like that. I never said that. Look at me, I'm fucking sober."

Out of nowhere, a girl interrupts our conversation, opening me on the shirt. I turn to her, quickly run two routines, then dismiss her with a kiss. I turn back to the manager and shrug as if to say, "See? I can't help that I'm so damn sexy." She rolls her eyes again. I sigh and say, "Look. The guy was touching my shirt, and I told him, 'I'm into chicks, man.' That's it. If that guy freaked out and said I called him whatever, that's his own weird shit. As for the other guys, if someone makes fun of me when my friends are right there, I'm gonna retort. I'm not gonna fight, that's lame-ass shit, but I will verbally crush them."

The manager says, "Well, look what you're wearing." I think about this for a second, then sort of nod. "Dude, you've been coming here a long time, never had a problem before, but now these two complaints, I don't need this drama, it's my job. It's almost the same headache for me as if you WERE fighting."

I'm like, "Okay. I understand that. So what's the solution here? Am I getting eighty-sixed?"

She says, "No. In fact, I'm not even gonna have you leave tonight. You just need to fucking chill. You are on probation. Any more of this shit, and you WILL be eighty-sixed."

I say, "That's totally fair. I understand." We shake on it. I game a bit more, then go home.

I was twenty-one-and-a-halfed. If eighty-sixed is banned for life, the next level down, "forty-three'ed," is being told to leave just for the night. Well, I got half of that. I am on probation at El Rio for overzealous shit-talking.

When I dragged the two girls over to bust Sonny's ass, I think I ended up looking like the lesser man in that situation, just teeing off on the guy for no apparent reason. It's like Tyler told me once, "If the girls see you're getting a little TOO into the 'alpha battle,' like you're enjoying it, it can backfire." This was a case in point. Also, in the scenario where the little touchy guy went berserk, I could have approached things more gently. Although he was touching me in an unacceptable way and he was wasted, it sucked because the VALID complaint about me from the Chess Club lent his BOGUS one credence.

FUCK LIST

It seems the Chess Club hipsters have begun waging a full-scale campaign against me via email, and it would further seem as though Heather has been influenced. In particular, she was told all about how I "mind-fucked" her friend into having sex with me using "scripted lines from the internet."

I mean, hey, it's true. Guilty as charged.

Heather began to change her tone in our correspondence. She starting being mean to me, making fucked-up comments like, "You're just trying to get as much ass as possible, like every guy, but they're cooler (I hope). This thing you do with the scripted lines, not only is it creepy, but it would only work on someone with extremely low self-esteem, like

Kelly. This would never work on me, any other girl that I know, or anyone with self-respect for that matter."

I blew her off, telling her, "Please do not contact me anymore. I do not like you, or your Chess Club. Thank you."

She replied, "Fine," and that was that.

Sitting at home, pondering this turn of events, I begin to get pissed. A devious, Machiavellian plan begins to hatch in my brain.

Wouldn't work on anybody you know, huh?

Simply put, I am going to get back at her by systematically fucking every single one of her friends. I grab a piece of paper and draw up a list of her known female associates:

1. Kelly (DONE.)

2. Janet (A bit of a fat, obnoxious, loudmouthed cunt, but hey. A plan is a plan.)

3. Anne (Nondescript 7, should be no problem.)

4. Opal (This is the one that accompanied Heather on our karaoke date. She has a lovely singing voice, which makes her highly attractive to me. She is also hot.)

5. Lisa (Straight-up stunner 9. Red hair, glory rack, tight body, six feet tall. Has a live-in fiancé and the attention span of a gnat.)

And there it is. I put the list in a drawer beside the bed. Damn. I'm like Uma Thurman in *Kill Bill,* except I'm a dude, and instead of having a "death list," I've got a "Fuck List." I'm not exactly sure how I'm going to pull this off, but fuck it . . . it *must* be done. I need to show Heather how much I care about her.

LOUISIANA BIGTITS

Spring's rolling around and I'm feeling frisky, so I've set tonight's Dollar Drink Night up to be a fucking disaster. I heard through the grapevine that Chippy is going to be there. I invited Texas, whom I finally ended up having sex with after a few dates. Turns out she was a virgin. In any case, she turned twenty-one on Sunday, so I decided to have her join the fun. I have also invited Heather's friend Lisa.

Word is getting around among the Chess Club Girls about me. Lisa came up to me the other night and said, point blank, "I heard you fucked Janet. She said you're an incredible fuck." It's true. I pulled Janet home after a mediocre Wednesday night at the Odeon. Fortunately, I don't remember much of it; thank God I was shitfaced.

I belched, set down my beer and said, "I've been called that before. First time I've heard it said in a *positive* way, though. Nice." I wiped foam off my mouth and grinned.

Lisa narrowed her eyes at me and said, "Yeah, she said you're the best fuck she ever had. Don't get your hopes up, though; I don't fuck anyone that my friends slept with . . . for at least two weeks."

I just smiled, looked at my phone and said, "That's cool, I'm booked for three."

So, anyway, I know that Chippy, Texas and Lisa are going to be there tonight. I've also invited some girl named Brianna and this other girl whom I affectionately refer to as "Louisiana Bigtits," whom I picked up at karaoke last week. Five girls, one jlaix. Here we go!

I get there and meet Chippy. She's all keyed up on liquor, standing six foot three in heels. True to form, she is getting violent, threatening to throw Christophe in a trash can. My fear mounts. It goes up several levels when Lisa arrives. I ignore her and make out with some other girl. Then, to my horror, Chippy and Lisa begin talking to each other. I leave quickly to gather my thoughts.

I'm standing at the bar when Louisiana Bigtits shows up. FUCK. The other girls are in plain sight . . . I grab Bigtits and say, "Drink up, we gotta leave . . . something bad is happening." The poor woman literally just arrived, but she follows me, confused, as I caveman her ass out of the bar. I explain that a girl wants to kick my ass there. She downs her beer and we leave.

We go to the bar across the street. I pull her into an alley along the way, slam her up against the wall and initiate a hardcore makeout, which I cut off just as abruptly. We walk into the bar and we're the only people there. I run a couple of high-octane routines, then settle into comfort building. Chicken Dong, the bar manager, closes early and gives us a ride over to Phone Bizzle (social proof! venue change!) where we have another beer. I fear Chippy will show up, so I ask the girl if she likes basketball. She does. We depart to Club Jeffy.

Once there, it's time to smoke dope and shoot Nerf Hoops. I segue into full-blown tonguedown on the bed. There is light resistance. I do one freeze-out. Try again, more resistance. I execute the standard countermeasures.

Her pussy is dripping wet by now, yet she continues to put the brakes on when I attempt to lick it. I think for a moment, then tell her, "Listen, nothing will happen, I have whiskey dick! It won't even work!" I gesture toward my flaccid, whiskified cock. "I just wanna lick it!" She relents at this, and I, of course, resume erection during the licking and commence fucking shortly thereafter. *Ka-ching!*

JEFFY'S FIRST STRIPPER
(DRUGS SOLD SEPARATELY)

I'm headed to Las Vegas with my coworkers from the hotel for a company convention. I get into town on Wednesday afternoon and begin drinking. My friends and I get ejected from Hard Rock Cafe for throwing things and making Meat Cocktails and daring each other to drink them. A typical Meat Cocktail contains beer, beef, bacon, mashed potatoes, ribs, ice, onions, mustard, A1 sauce, salt, pepper, Nutrasweet and a little vodka. After Matt pukes on the table we are asked to leave. Like, the manager comes up and says, "Customers are complaining about your screaming," while the Nuge is bent over his Meat Cocktail, chewing on the large steak protruding from the top of the glass, and Jobski is pounding his ice cream brownie into a flat, dripping pancake with his fist. Our boss laughs and makes the HR director "reprimand" us. Dinner ends and we all go to the strip club Olympic Gardens.

We get there and I am pissed because I wanted to run game, not pay for some lame-ass lap dance. I'm always talking shit about what a great pickup artist I am to my coworkers, and I needed to show them I wasn't just talking out of my ass. Time to put up or shut up; I'd been training for this thing HARD and was, frankly, a little nervous that I'd look like a tool if I didn't pull on this trip. Furthermore, I don't like strip clubs, because I refuse to pay for sex of any kind. But I am along for the ride and I sit there with a beer while the guys have their fun. I even gave a stripper one dollar to put her ginormous fake tits in my face; they felt like concrete blocks hitting me in the fucking face, I almost got a black eye. Horrifying.

So we're sitting there and this chick sits down with us across the booth from me. Turns out she dances there and came in to work, but decided not to because there weren't enough customers and too many chicks in the place. I start running routines on her, busting her balls and shit. My friends are looking at me like I'm insane. I call her "dork" and stuff, she's getting "pissed" and says, "You are so cocky! So cocky!"

I begin unloading high-octane attraction routines. Your basic shit. She starts getting really into me as my friends watch this happen, incredulous. They've never seen me run game for real and I can tell they are starting to realize that I'm really for real, *actually*. I tell her we're going back to our hotel and she should come and call some of her "hot ho friends." She gets pissed that I called her a ho but I instantly change the subject: "Oh my God, my friend is so weird, she eats LEMONS whole, just like an orange, do you think that's bad for the enamel on her teeth?" and this makes her forget. More routines. Boom-boom-boom. This goes on for a while. We all go outside.

Outside, the manager is trying to get her to go back in and work. But I pull her away and run Trust Test, making her come closer and closer to me, saying "I'm not going to . . . I'm not going to . . ." until our foreheads are touching. We get in a cab and leave. She says, "I'm a stripper with a brain!" I call her my Little Sister and run Too Similar. I Eskimo-kiss her and then run some other game, making sure to include some passing comment about my "model ex-girlfriend." I keep calling her a "little player girl" and all this shit. Her phone keeps ringing. I say, "You are such a PIMP. All your little hos calling you . . . such a pimp!" We get back to the hotel.

I tell her we should go up and put her shit in my room. We do it. I say, "I'm so sick of dating these chicks that do drugs all the time and have plastic surgery, I mean, don't get me wrong, I love to blow rails off a shitty dive bar toilet tank as much as the next guy, but only once in while! I mean . . . you're not like that, are you?" She qualifies herself. Then I ask her if she's a good kisser, and you can guess what happens next. We kiss for a while, then I stop it and suggest we go downstairs for a drink. We do so.

Downstairs at the circle bar in the casino. I start building trust and comfort, we're walking arm in arm. I'm filling in the empty canvas of my life, telling her stories. She sees some people she knows and starts talking to them. They seem pretty cool and they ignore me, so I immediately start chatting up another girl at the bar, with my back turned on her. Shortly she runs up and grabs me. Boo-yah. I have trouble getting the bartender's attention, but she laughs. Such a feat is a trifle for SUPER STRIPPER! Amazingly, the guy comes right over. We order drinks, and the guy says, "Nine dollars." I point at Stripper-With-A-Brain. She's shocked. I laugh and say, "Hey, Jeffy ain't nothing nice, kiddo! I thought you knew! Better ask somebody!" She buys me the drink.

So we're walking around the casino and I say, "Damn, I was hoping my friends would be here so we could all hang out. But it's weird, those guys are all cool and everything, we get along great. But it's just, when they get around girls, they act all weird, like grabby, and needy, and like [imitating chode], 'You're pretty . . . can I buy you a drink? What's your name? etc.' They just can't chill and be real." She likes this. I tell her I'm tired and need to go to sleep; she should come up and tell me a bedtime story and tuck me in.

We start going up and she says, "What are we going to do? Bad things? I've only known you thirty minutes!"

"Sheesh! I hope not! I have to wake up early so you better not keep me up! Besides, I have WHISKEY DICK." Classic.

We get in the room and three bozo coworkers are in there, wasted. I hurriedly push them out of the room, suggesting they go gamble. The chick looks at the desk and says, "Someone's been doing coke here. I can tell. I'm a stripper." I serenade the stripper with a rendition of "On the Wings of Love," but in the style of Clay Aiken from *American Idol*. I tell her I want to cuddle, and we do so, just talking for a while. I then tell her I want to show her a trick. I get on her and just start making out with her. She says something funny and I do a *Saved by the Bell* aside to the audience and explain that I'm doing it. She laughs her ass off. I kiss her some more. I tell her I wanna lick it and take off her pants. No panties. I inspect her for sores, then begin the licking. She has a clit piercing, which I've never encountered before; it clicks strangely on my teeth. I put the fingers in after five minutes, and lick her into submission.

I say, "Too bad I have whiskey dick!"

She says, "It looks okay to me!" and I fuck the shit out of her.

I have never seen real tits this big on a chick that skinny. Oh my fucking God. This is the hottest chick I've ever fucked, my first stripper, and my first real 9. I cuddle and snuggle with her afterward. She expresses shock at my many injuries and scars. "What happened there?" she says, running her finger over the pentagram.

"I fell." She looks unconvinced. I kiss her tenderly and say, "I'm not an insane maniac. I'm a POSER insane maniac. I'm just dealing with the absurdity of existence by shoving absurdity back down existence's throat . . . or something."

She gives me her number and tells me to call her, she wants to hang out when she comes to San Francisco, also invites me to a party the next night. She's on the phone as she leaves. Fucking strippers.

The next evening, I am thrown out of the karaoke bar for rolling on the floor and crying during the bridge of "Separate Ways (Worlds Apart)." The asshole DJ repeatedly says, "Get back on the stage Jeffy," as this is taking place. I then belch into the mic and scream, "BEEYACH!" As security drags me out, I'm yelling, "THIS IS THE GAYEST SHIT I HAVE EVER SEEN IN MY FUCKING LIFE!!! AND I'M FROM SAN FRANCISCO!!!"

We go to Risque at Paris, and I run into my stripper there, out with her "hot ho posse." I just say what's up and leave. This is due to the fact that I'm fucking WASTED, the blinky shirt displaying the message "I gots the whiskey dick, biotch!" Jeez. I have close to thirty drinks, and two choppers of llello. I have done what I came to do and am letting my hair down. I've used the "My Little Pony" opener most of the trip ("Hey. You guys remember that shit My Little Pony? Yeah . . . did they have powers?"), but by the end of the night, I am just going up to people and drunkenly bellowing, "MAAAHH LIL PONEEEE . . ."

I end up getting thrown out of another strip club (where the blinky shirt's message of "ATTENTION WHORE" takes on a whole new meaning). The last thing I remember before losing consciousness is sitting up in my bed watching the television, confused and screaming at nobody, "WHAT THE FUCK IS THIS I AM WATCHING? IS THIS *THE O.C.*?"

I love everyone. God bless America!

WHAT WOULD TYLER DURDEN DO?

I roll in to the Rio late, with a specific target in mind: Lisa, the hottest girl on my Fuck List. I've already done three, so only two remain: the singer, Opal, and the hot one, Lisa. I've been gaming Lisa for the last few weeks, running SOLID GAME so Christophe won't get mad. Christophe disapproves of anything but SOLID GAME, and that means letting the interaction breathe, taking your time while systematically moving things forward. Honestly, I could have fucked her last week when we went on a little "date," but I was a pussy, with some inner game entitlement issue fucking me up. She was totally into me, but I couldn't escalate, on account of the fact that I felt she was out of my league.

Well, having just gotten back from fucking the stripper in Vegas, there will be no such inner game difficulties this time. It's funny how fucking a 9 makes ALL 9s seem pedestrian.

I go in and there she is, tall and beautiful with red hair blazing in the night. I walk up and lightly hit her in the stomach. She responds by PUNCHING me in the gut, knocking the wind out of me. Ugh.

I recover and say, "So whassup little sis?" and spin her around. My friends show up and I introduce her as my little sister who is a total little player girl. I continue calling her "pimp" and "player girl" throughout the interaction.

We all go out back and I start telling Vegas stories to her and her friends. I quickly isolate Lisa from the group on a secluded bench and proceed to cold-read her. I Eskimo-kiss her, telling her that it is "the custom of my native land." I do a palm reading. I thumb-wrestle her. More Eskimo kissing. This lasts roughly an hour.

We start smoking a blunt and are about to kiss for real, when all of a sudden Janet runs up, grabs Lisa by the arm and points out these guys to her, saying, "Hey it's those guys who we were gonna hang out with," or some shit. I look over and see two tall, good-looking guys standing on the other side of the back deck. Lisa snaps out of state. Her eyes light up, she gets up, runs over and starts talking to the *better*-looking one. FUCK.

I sit there, alone, and smoke the blunt. Watching them. Watching her hang on the guy, laughing. The ease with which the guy carries himself. He looks like a model. Everything is abruptly thrown into stark relief. For all my so-called "game," it comes down to this: that guy is cooler than me, taller than me, and better-looking than me, and therefore the girl is choosing him, regardless of whatever "attraction" and/or "emotional connection" I've built with her. They *just look right together,* and I cannot compete with that. This is a fact. This whole pathetic endeavor of mine, which has consumed the past two years of my LIFE, brings me no closer to making things any different when the scores are settled, finally.

Dark thoughts begin roiling in my mind. *You stupid fuck . . . you really believed she was going to fuck YOU? Hahaha . . . ridiculous. A woman like that could never be interested in someone like you. You stupid fuck.* The words echo in my brain with an all-too-familiar tone. It's the exact same voice that spoke to me years ago, back in high school, when I was infatuated with the captain of the girls' volleyball team, Anna Becker. Mocking and dissuading. *Remember who you are, and who she is. You're a short, pale, fat, pathetic loser. She's a fucking goddess. OF COURSE she's going to ditch you for that guy. It's over. She's gone.*

Christophe comes up and jolts me out of the reverie. "EY! Mahn, zees cheek is ganna fuck you," he exhorts, in his French accent. "She said, 'I'm ganna fuck Jzzheffeee!' You gatta pull to Club Jzheffee now, mahn fuck zees shit!"

I look up and say, "Well, she's with this other guy now,"

He nearly has a fit. "WHAAAT ZE FUUCK?!! Are zhou hhretarded?!! Get ze fuck up, go ovah zaire and get hair!"

Not entirely atypically, I'm confused. "What? Get . . . hair?"

"Do not fahk weeth me," he snaps, pointing in my face then pointing at Lisa, "GO GET HAIR!"

What the fuck . . . he's right. I know it's on, but I am having problems pulling the trigger. Inner game problems rear their ugly head once more. I roll past her on the way to the bar and smack her ass.

Okay. I see a little blonde at the bar and rock up. I ask her, "Hey. What do you think is, like, more romantic . . . like, which do girls like more: thug lovin' or GANGSTA lovin'?" She goes crazy, thinks it's hilarious and turns to engage me. Shortly thereafter, Lisa runs up and grabs me, totally demolishing the blonde, who scampers off, terrified of the tall drunken Lisa's display of territorialism. Here I have my chance, but I fuck it up again by not getting her out of there or at LEAST getting physical with her. She walks off and starts talking to the male model again.

FUCK.

Christophe is like, "Fuck zees guy! Go get hair!" But I'm frozen there, like a fuckin' dode.

FUCK. FUCK.

She's gazing deeply into the other guy's eyes now. It's nearing 1 A.M. and the bar starts to close, so I go for it. I say, "Come on, we're all going to Club Jeffy. It's fuckin awesome."

She says, "Who's going?"

I smirk and say, "The A-Crowd," and put on the shades, then take them off and put them on her. The dude is standing there looking like he just smelled an anus. Meaningless chatter ensues for the next few minutes, then I walk off to take a piss.

When I get back, Lisa says to me, "Hey . . . sorry, no Club Jeffy tonight, maybe another night. We're going to Phone Bizzle. Here . . . take your glasses." She hands me the shades, and sits down on the stairs between the guy's legs.

FUUUUCK . . .

I feel my heart drop. I mask my deep disturbance and talk to the rest of the group. *Fuck. Fuck.* I start busting a fatty's balls out of spite, because I'm pissed. At one point, the fatty says something to me, asking me to "show her a trick" and I reply by BOOMING out, "WHAT? YOU WANT TO 'SUCK MY DICK'? JESUS CHRIST, WHAT THE FUCK IS WRONG WITH YOU?"

Everyone in the vicinity goes, "OHHHHHHHH!!!!!! DAMNN!!!"

and the commotion is enough to make Lisa get up and talk to me again, laughing. Okay. She says, "How many times do you get hit a night, Jeffy?"

I turn to the model guy and say, "Well, heheh, the record is eighty-one."

The girls shout, "Let's break that tonight," and start smacking me up pretty good. But soon enough, Lisa's back with the dude. *Fuck.* The bar is closing for real now, and I go out front to wait and try again when they come out.

They come out, and I pick her up and spin her around. But the guy and his friend come out and pull her away. As she's walking down the street, she yells over her shoulder at me, "Come to Phone Bizzle with us, Jeffy!" I tell her I'll catch up when Christophe comes out. They continue up the street.

Christophe comes out and he's ready. "Let's go mahn!"

I say, "I dunno, dude, it seems kind of supplicating to follow her and her fucking alpha male around like a little puppy. Fuck it, maybe next week. Goodnight man."

Disappointed, Christophe tilts his head, says, "Ah . . . okay zen," and starts putting on his gloves. "Zee you next taime." He gets on his black '65 Vespa and zooms off into the night, the streetlights glinting off his chromed German war helmet with the spike on the top. I start to walk home.

My eyes start to tear up. *How could she do this to me? I thought we had something together, a connection. We were in deep rapport, she calls me all the time, how could she just go off with that guy?* I sigh, and think, *Fuck man, it's not personal. It's just the game. It's nothing different than losing a game of* Street Fighter II. *I just didn't make the right moves. Should have pulled the trigger. FUCK. What a loser I am. WHAT a fucking loser.* I continue to stagger down the dark, lonely street toward my house. I get about halfway there and just sit down on the sidewalk, sniffling like a bitch, wiping my nose on my sleeve. The outburst fails to provide any sense of release. There is no catharsis, just a stifling, throbbing pain that feels like it's being wrung out of a filthy, booze-soaked dishrag.

As I sit there, wallowing in self-pity, I suddenly envision Tyler in my mind's eye, surveying me with a look of contempt. I think to myself, *Wait a fucking minute man. What would Tyler do? Would Tyler just give up like this? Fuck no. He would plow this shit to the bitter end.* I recall all the sets I've seen Tyler do at the Standard and the Saddle Ranch, blowing out guys that make this model chump look like a fucking scrawny hobo.

And that's when it happens. I see him there, Tyler, standing before me in the street like Obi-Wan, smirking at me with his motorcycle jacket and his sunglasses. He says, "DUDE. You KNOW what you have to do. Go to that fuckin' bar, blow that moron out, pull the girl to Club Jeffy and FUCK HER, man! Eh?! OH MAN!" He brings his hands up, finger guns a-blazin', nodding wildly.

Yeah, I think, nodding along with him. *YEAH.* I rise to my feet and take a deep breath, brushing myself off. I turn around and march directly to the Phone Bizzle.

I walk in and sure enough, Lisa's at the end of the bar with the guy. I go to the other end of the bar, order a drink, and pop open a four-set with (what else) THUG LOVIN', so I'm not just standing there alone like "Follow-Man." I text message her, "Turn around."

I see her look at her phone, then she peers around. When she sees me, she shrieks and runs over. "You came!" She sits down and is quite drunk and affectionate. I start rubbing her.

I introduce her to the four girls I've been talking to. She buys shots and we start slamming them. I'm busting out CRAZY rapport shit, like getting VERY DEEP and SERIOUS. "I like you for you. You know that, I always have. Just you. You know I care about you, right? You don't have to put a show on for me, baby. You know that. I'm here for you now, and I'm here for a reason. I don't know what that is, but I just want to make you feel beautiful, all the time." BOOM. Makeout.

She's totally into it, but at the same time she keeps running back and forth between the other guy and me. It's crazy, she's literally going from one end of the bar to the other every five minutes. I phase-shift and we start making out. Yet she still goes back over to the dude.

She comes back to me as the bar closes down, saying, "I don't know who I'm going to go home with!"

I tell her, "Let's cuddle, I have whiskey dick anyway, nothing will happen. Besides . . . you KNOW I'm cooler than that dode." This might sound like I was qualifying myself, but it wasn't really the case, since the statement was in actuality *glaringly obvious*. I mean, fuck, dude . . . I'm jlaix.

She says, "Yes!" as the lights come up, but that dude is still there with his friend, waiting.

Janet's been standing there the whole time, and now she says, "This is fucking scandalous, Jeff. What happens now?"

I turn to her and say, "What happens now? Tug-of-war. Pay attention Janet, we're playin' the game!" Indeed.

We go outside, the guy and I look at each other, sizing each other up. We both know what the fuck is happening here. Heheh! Here we go, fucker! We all start walking toward Janet's car. Lisa is walking with the other guy, hand in hand. I know I have to do something. What that is, however, I have no idea. Somebody starts talking about nicknames, and Lisa says, "What's my nickname?!!"

Before anyone can answer, I blurt out, "Drunken slut!"

Everybody goes, "OHHHH!!! DAMN!!" Lisa shrieks, runs over to me and starts pawing at me. *Yes.* I put my arm around her, and put her on my back for a piggyback ride.

She announces to the group, "All right! I'm going home with JEFFY!!!"
YES.

We get to the car and the girls start making calls looking for drugs. I walk over to the guy and his friend and ask, "What's your name, man?" He tells me it's John. I shake his hand and say, "Good game, man."

He just laughs and says, "Yeah, you won." I talk with them for a bit; they are actually pretty cool. Tall, good-looking guys with no game.

Janet comes up to me and starts yapping. "Fuck you man, I ain't no second stringer. This is fucked up, doing this in front of me."

She's sort of correct, and I know it. I say, "Janet, I'm sorry, this is kind of fucked up. I respect you and shouldn't make you feel like that." Even though the only reason I even thought about fucking her was to piss off her friend, as opposed to Lisa, who is actually hot and I actually want to fuck, Chess Club Girl or no Chess Club Girl.

She says, "It's all right, man. I know you're a bad boy. But you are still the best fuck I ever had in my life." Well, I certainly try!

It becomes clear that Janet purposely tried to fuck it up for me by pointing those dudes out to Lisa back at the bar. Well, it didn't work beeyach! We get to Club Jeffy and from there, it's academic. I get her undressed, but she won't let me lick it, claiming "hair issues." She just leans back and says, "Let's see if you're as good as they all say you are."

I laugh and say, "Well, without the licking, I don't know." I let her go down on me, and she does so quite well. She tells me this will be the first time she's had sex in over a year, excluding her fiancé. I guess tonight was just "the night." I know she's wanted me for a while, maybe that whole bit with the guy was a jealousy plot line of some sort. Anyways, I fuck her twice. God . . . I love sex with hot girls.

Let me say that again: I LOVE SEX WITH HOT GIRLS.

In the morning, I fuck her again, and drive her home. She tells me, "If my fiancé sees you, you're Katie's brother." Okay, whatever! I'm Katie's brother! Great. I drop her off.

When I get home, my roommates have written on the whiteboard in the kitchen, "If you liked Jeffy's First Stripper, you'll LOVE . . . JEFFY'S DRUNKEN BAR BITCHES! Collect all four! Pull their cord and watch them:

1. Puke and roll an ankle falling down
2. Take twenty minutes to find the bathroom light
3. Reaffirm that your mind control techniques still work!"

I love this game. I love this life.

THE RETURN OF THE JLAIX

Two months have passed since I told Heather off. I have not heard from her since. In that time, I have fucked four of her friends, in a bizarre scheme to win her affection. Thus I was certainly surprised to discover a short message from her today in my inbox: "I'm sorry I was mean to you. I take it back. You're just as crazy as I am. That's why."

She cracked! Hahaha. So I sit back, pop a forty-ounce and craft a response, settling in for the following "conversation":

From: Dirt McGirt
Date: May 8, 2004 05:54 P.M.

I know. I'm sorry too. I guess this means I can stop systematically fucking every one of your friends just to spite you now. I was almost done too!
   ps: you look just like a little angel . . .

From: UniGloryCornHole
Date: May 8, 2004 06:14 P.M.

Haha, I heard. I don't care. I think you're a riot. We need to go karaoke again. That was a blast. Keep in touch. I'm coming back at the end of this month. Canada was swell but I need my friends back. I'm not going back to Pacifica, though. I'm moving to the city. See you there!
   ps: aww, thanks. But you know I'm actually satan himself, right? I scored a 93% on the evil test. ;P

What do you mean, you "don't care"? I did it all for you! In my own warped and demented way, I was being romantic.
   You think I'm kidding.

Ok, well I care. I know you are serious. I think it's hilarious that my friends are so easily manipulated. I give you props for that. I know Janet must've been an interesting taking-one-for-the-team experience. Haha. Just tell me you didn't fuck Opal. I actually do care about that one.

Easily manipulated? Are you kidding me? Some of them were tough! In one instance, I had to Tug-of-War with some fuckin Alpha Male Other Guy moron all the way to the end of the night ("follow the shiny thing!"). The Janet episode was interesting indeed; it featured me cracking a bullwhip at her while screaming, "GET THE FUCK OUT OF MY HOUSE, OR AT LEAST SHUT UP!!! LEAVE ME ALONE!!!" I was saving Opal for last. She sings really pretty, I like her.

Seriously though, I don't feel I've manipulated anybody . . . I thought you weren't gonna be mean to me anymore . . . wtf

Okay, maybe manipulated wasn't the right word. I know you didn't manipulate them. I just think it's funny that my friends all gave in to your charming ways. I'm saying you're charming. Not to be mistaken for meanness. I hate communicating with this damn intar-web. No room for sarcastic tones; . . . But, yeah, who did you have to play tug-of-war with? Haha . . . follow the shiny thing . . . haha. I'm really glad you didn't have your way with Opal, though. She's my best friend and I love her. I don't like it when anybody touches my precious gem. Besides she would've been the toughest. She don't sleep with too many guys. Janet and Kelly were un-doubtedly the easiest, eh? Ha-heh.

Again, it was not easy, I found the Janet experience to be quite harrowing and dreadful.

Anyways, I know you can't express your dulcet tones of sarcasm on this shit. But hello, you have my number

dumbass, you can call me any time. I'd really like to talk at
you . . . uh, I mean with you . . . ;P

She calls me not long after this and we chat excitedly about her return
to the city. It looks like it's on. I just hope it's not a trap.

VICTORY

Chess Club Girl returned home from Canada earlier
this week. I hung out with her on Thursday. She
brought some chump along, but I ignored him. Did some rebuilding
of comfort, charmed her with the usual gamut of Jeffyisms to "turn the
volume knob back up," as we say, but didn't close.

Tonight, she has invited me to karaoke with some of her buddies. I
work first on befriending them all, and then bust out the karaoke performance of a lifetime. Then Heather gets up there. She's an amazing singer,
and as I watch her I can feel myself falling in love. Right now, she's the
hottest chick I've ever seen in my fucking life, enveloped in magic. After
a few rounds, I isolate her out front and run a lot of deep, emotional connection stuff. We're standing close together on the stairs as she smokes a
cigarette. She takes a drag, listening to my words. Some song by Hall and
Oates wafts down from the bar upstairs. She nods at me ever so slightly,
eyes wide. I take her hands and move closer. She says, "Wait. There's
something you should know about me. I have a history . . ."

I cut her off and say, "I don't care about that." I really don't. I just
know that right now, I want this girl more than anything I've ever wanted.
We share our first kiss. It's electric. I want to stay here, in this fucking
stairwell, forever.

When I pull her, the friends wave goodbye, smiling. I drive her to my house after the bar closes and fuck the shit out of her. The culmination of a six-month project. I feel like I'm walking on sunshine. She is so special to me. Just look at her.

It will be interesting, however, to see what happens when she returns to Rio on Monday, and how the Chess Club will react to her giving me attention. She even said, "I'd be kicked out of the Chess Club if they knew I fucked 'the enemy.'" My strategy will be to straight-up ignore them and talk to her directly in their midst. Perhaps I'll even make out with her in front of them. I know she's fucked Sonny, so it would crush the poor chump to witness this. Oh well. To the victor go the spoils.

FULL-BLOWN ONE-ITIS

This sucks. I'm in love with Chess Club Girl.

Last week, we were chilling at her house when she suggested that her little fuck buddy, that asshole Sonny, might come by. She was concerned that he would find out I was there and drama would ensue. I said, "Okay, cool, I'll leave," but she ended up pleading with me to stay with her, so I did. The rest of the night, I hoped he would show up, just so I could kick his ass.

She was supposed to meet me at the karaoke bar a few nights ago, but flaked. I waited for her to show up for over an hour before I gave up hope. I didn't call her to find out why she didn't come, and I then proceeded to pick up a different chick there, who was actually hotter. Yet when I brought the new girl back to my house, I started crying and kicked her out because I was plagued over thoughts of Heather banging some dude.

What the fuck.

This is not cool. I need to shake this. I resolve to not call or contact her in any way. I need control. I need to break her. I must break her will. Usually, these chicks pine for *me* and try to get *my* time and attention. I am not accustomed to being on the other side of the equation, and it's not a good feeling.

Obviously, these feelings are a function of the vast amount of time and investment that went into this pickup. That much is obvious. What's funny is that even though, intellectually, I know that's what has happened here, the net effect is the same.

What I find amusing is how the one-itis of the player is different from that of the chode. Had she flaked on me back in the chode days, I would have just gone straight home and cried; in this instance, my reaction was to first pick up a hot chick, drag her home, kick her out and *then* cry.

She comes over to my place today, apologizing profusely and telling me some drama tale explaining her absence. I tell her what I did when she didn't show, the pickup, the crying, the whole bit, and confess my feelings to her. "I've been with a lot of girls, and you know that. But something is different. I just want to be with you. I don't know why, and I know it doesn't make any sense, but . . . *I love you.*"

She doesn't even flinch. She tells me that she feels it too.

Everything is fine now. I spend the entire day with her. We fuck five times. We even go to the park and let balloons go, just like in my Balloons in the Park routine. There is no more pretense. Now she is fully in love with me, and I will most likely become bored with her in a few days. I feel so much better. I am back in control.

JEFFY'S FIRST THREESOME
(SCOTCH NOT INCLUDED)

There have been a lot of threesome reports popping up on the seduction forum lately. It's high time that I got in on the action, and guess what? It just so happens that my new girl is into chicks. Then again, aren't they all?

Heather already knew that I was deep into the game, and that I was skilled at it; after all, I did systematically fuck all of her friends just to spite her. But it wasn't until recently that the full extent of my involvement came to light. She found out about "jlaix" in a weird, roundabout way. I was out with Lisa one night at the Starlight Room when some geek from the forum rolled up on me like I was a rock star and started yelling, "Oh my God, you're jlaix aren't you! Oh my God dude!! jlaix!!!" Understandably, Lisa found his behavior to be quite unusual. Subsequently, she went all Nancy Drew on my ass and discovered the forum, the lay reports, my involvement with Real Social Dynamics, the whole enchilada.

It wasn't really that big of a deal at the time. But after Heather returned from Canada, I dropped Lisa like a hot rock. I had grown tired of her attention deficit disorder, and besides, Heather had been my original target all along. Possibly out of annoyance, she went ahead and told Heather all about the legend of "jlaix," in an apparent attempt to salt my game. It looks like it had the opposite effect, as Heather, instead of getting pissed, became fascinated and now wants to master game and even become an instructor. Point blank, she asked me if I could teach her some moves so we could pick up chicks together.

I said, "Do you really want to do this? Because I *can* do it. I know how. If you're serious, we can make this happen." She assured me that she was, and so I gave her a quick rundown on inner game, routines, etc. At El Rio on Monday, I ran some interactions while she watched, then I got her participating. She made some errors at first, but she's a quick learner.

It also helps that she has a certain alpha-female vibe about her. In any event, she's down. She's even begun participating on the forum.

Her handle is, of course, *ChessClub*.

Karaoke time. I'm peacocked out with the blinky shirt displaying the message "TRYING TOO HARD." ChessClub and I meet some friends there and settle in for some karaoke action. My free drink bartender isn't here. No shitty scotch for jlaix. Awww.

I'm sitting there with my beer, scoping about for targets. Nothing. Just as I'm about to give up hope, some gal comes in all by herself. She looks kind of cute. I tell ChessClub to have a look at her. She does so, then says, "That could work."

I open with an old-school favorite, Dental Floss. I say, "Oh my God, you gotta tell my friends," and pull her over to the group. After introducing her, I start blasting out a fusillade of routines. Blam blam blam.

I take Chessy aside and tell her to run some routines on the girl as well. She calls her a "total badgirl." She runs Fat Girl Personality: "Lemme ask you a question, and bear with me 'cause it's kind of weird. Were you a fat girl in high school? Because it's like, in high school, the beautiful people didn't have to do anything to be popular, but if the FAT GIRL wanted to be popular, then she had to have a real SPARKLING personality. I guess what I'm saying is . . . you have a fat girl personality." I also tell her to use the chick's name a lot.

Chessy layers all this into the conversation while I spool off some more shit. I tell the target, "Before we go any further, I just wanna let you know, I'm Not Boyfriend Material. I won't take you out to dinner, I won't bring you flowers . . . I'm not going to cheat on you with your best friend, I'm not gonna break up with you on your birthday and I'm not bad in bed. I'm just *not boyfriend material*." I Eskimo-kiss her and call her "The All-American Girl" then run Sincere Compliment ("Are you the kind of person that can take a sincere compliment from a stranger? Good . . . so am I . . . shoot") and Total Weirdo ("You know, I don't know about you . . . you're either super super cool, or a total fucking weirdo. Maybe both."). Just a straight-up barrage of canned material. During this, our body language and voice projection are tight as fuck, we're cutting the fuck in, HARD.

I make the girl qualify herself on my standards: "I'm so sick of dating these chicks with plastic surgery who do tons of drugs. You're not like that, are you?"

She says, "No, that's why I LEFT L.A.!" Whatever. I ask her if she's a good kisser, and she says she is, so I check for myself. Then ChessClub kisses her. She tells ChessClub, "You're a better kisser than he is."

A few minutes later, Chessy pulls me in close and tells me it's ON. "Okay then," I say, "now we get her phone number."

She replies, "Fuck that shit, let's extract that ass!"

I raise my eyebrows and laugh. This girl has the killer instinct. "Okay," I say, "watch."

We return to the table and I tell the target, "Do you like basketball? Yeah? Wow, that's awesome, because I have a basketball court in my house, yes it's FUCKING AWESOME! Holy fuck, you HAVE to see it! Let's go right now, we'll shoot some HORSE. It's SO COOL!! Let's go, we'll come back and sing more after. I live a couple blocks away." She agrees, and we get in the car.

On the way there, the target says something about how she went through a breakup recently, and that's why she went out to the bar alone. "I needed this," she says.

Holy fuck, this is gonna be too easy.

Upon arrival, I bust out some Two-Buck Chuck merlot and we begin shooting Nerf Hoops. After a game of PIG, I run So Genuine. Then I take a deep breath and prepare to launch a new routine from the forum, one that I've never run before: the Dual Induction Massage. My heart is pounding. Once I start saying this, there's no going back. I begin.

"Wow, I had the most awesome experience last week. I was visiting my friend Steve in San Diego, he's this really cool shaman/guru/transformative healer dude, and he showed me this *awesome* new massage technique. Two of his students did it to me, it is called the 'Dual Induction Massage.' What it is, their hands move on you *simultaneously* with the exact same movements. It's so awesome. Here, let me show you."

I lay ChessClub down on my bed and we start massaging her as I instruct the target on the "proper form." Then I say, "My turn," and take my shirt off and they do it to me. I say, "Oh, it is so relaxing. Oh." Then, I say to the target, "Your turn. Take this shit off," and remove her shirt. ChessClub and I start in on her, but this time we make it more sexy. Rubbing her tits and ass. I start making out with ChessClub while we massage her. We almost start laughing, as it just seems so absurd that this is actually working. I move ChessClub's head down and she starts making out with the target. I take off the target's pants because I wanna lick it.

From there, it's academic. I fuck ChessClub from behind while she eats the target's pussy. Both of them suck my cock. We do a three-way makeout, then I fuck the target while fingering Chessy, who is kissing her. Holy shit, this is incredible. I bust off like a truck bomb, then fuck the target again while ChessClub watches, coolly smoking a cigarette.

We lie there for a while. The chick is in a dazed state, having just had the living shit fucked out of her. "Wow," she says, "when I went out tonight I didn't think *that* was gonna happen!"

I reply, "Yeah, me neither!"

After a while, the girl gets up, gets her things together and leaves. Jeffy's First Threesome. Chessy gives me the high-five. What a flawless execution. I love this silly little ChessClub girl, she is so awesome and special to me. I say, "We're gonna have to do this again, except next time, with a hotter chick." She was like a 7, but hey, whatever. I snuggle and cuddle with ChessClub, then go to sleep. I dream about picking up chicks.

MÉNAGE-À-CANUCK-STRIPPER

At the door of the Rio, the guy is refusing to let Chess-Club in because it's after midnight. Not thirty minutes have passed since I left this place, picked Chessy up from her bartending gig and brought her back. I start haranguing him. "I've been here every week for the past consecutive ninety-three Mondays, and you won't let my fiancée in? This place is like my home. I can't bring my fiancée into MY HOME? What if I was President Bush and she was First Lady Laura Bush?!! Would you let us in then? Huh?"

He starts laughing a little. "She's Laura Boosh?" he says in an indeterminate Caribbean accent.

I say, "This guy is hard, he's like those Buckingham Palace guards with the big hats." He laughs more and waves us in.

Unfortunately, there are no worthy targets in sight, so we're back out the door almost as soon as we came in. We decide to go to Kostume Karaoke. We've had a good week, pulling off another threesome just two days after the first one. We aren't planning on doing any pickups, but sometimes God just drops shit in your lap. As we're picking our songs, the door opens, and in walks a 9, surrounded by six chodes. Quite a rare specimen for this particular bar. Just goes to show, you have to be ready to act *at all times*.

I shrug and turn to Chessy. "Okay, so there she is, I'm going to run Dental Floss, then Little Sister, then A-Crowd." The bartender, who by now is well acquainted with my antics, just laughs and shakes his head as he overhears this. A couple of seconds later, the girl walks over to us to look at the karaoke book and BAM! I'm in.

I'm spitting the hot fire, and she's loving it. Within seconds, Chessy's chiming in, building rapport and getting rather touchy-feely with her. She's eating it up. We find out that she's Canadian. A fortunate coincidence, as Chessy was just there, and I'm about to go there myself to conduct a workshop. We explore this further for a while, using the commonality to build more comfort with her.

She asks Chessy to sing with her, and requests that I join them onstage to "be her little bunny" while she sings "White Rabbit." During the song, she begins getting freaky with ChessClub, rubbing up on her leg and dancing suggestively. Meanwhile, I'm down on my hands and knees in front of them, behaving like a weird animal, screaming and clawing at the crowd with a pair of bunny ears on.

After the girl's risqué performance, ChessClub deduces that she's a stripper, and asks her about it. Confirmed. Then it's my turn to sing. Chessy convinces the chick to get up there with her and do a bit of "backup dancing" for me. I'm putting my heart and soul into the track, belting it to the rafters. The crowd goes wild, cheering for me. I surrender to the moment, and something inside ignites, surrounding me with that shimmering nimbus of golden, holy light. It's like a drug. I am the fucking shit, invincible.

I turn around to sing to the girls for a bit, and to my surprise, they're eating each other's faces off. Turns out Chessy had pulled the old Spin Kiss Maneuver, and it worked like a charm. And here I thought that the crowd was cheering for me. I laugh, turn back to the audience and dig into the song even deeper, soaring through the final chorus, exploding in love and magic.

The song ends and the karaoke host announces, "Ladies and gentlemen, how about a hand for Jeffy, and his little sister, and what appears to be his girlfriend. Who says you can't get laid at the Odeon? It's like *Deliverance*."

The stripper approaches me and says, "Uh . . . that's not your little sister, is it Jeffy?" I spit beer on the floor, laughing.

Meanwhile, these proceedings have garnered the attention of the chodes, and they seem worried. They appear left and right, trying to cut us out of the group. Her roommate is first. Chessy distracts him while I run the Trust Test. Another chode jumps in. I tool the fuck out of him, mocking his shirt as Chessy starts up another makeout session with our lovely stripper. He tries to come back at me with some witticism. I ignore it and say, "Hey man, look, why don't you just go get some crayons and a helmet and go draw me a picture of that fuckin' shirt so I can buy it," followed by an immediate backturn. He's done.

I stand there, on fire, staring around at them, basically daring them to fuck with me. Some other dude, who appears to be a steroid abuser of some sort, tries to talk shit. I immediately begin talking over him, acting as though I am mentally retarded, hitting him and repeating the phrase, "Oh my God, you're cool, you're cool, oh my God, you're cool," over and over. I drag the guy aside and make him dress in some funky-ass costume featuring an extremely gay wig and force him to dance around for me. Tooled. These guys are simply outclassed. They're literally speechless, unable to think of anything to say as they try to cut in.

This goes on for a bit, and then it is my turn to sing once more. Again, the girls get up and dance behind me. Suddenly, the stripper *rips off her shirt* and is wearing this ridiculous gold, sequined tube top bra. She gets down on the floor, grinding out some little striptease bullshit. We're trying not to crack up; this girl is fucking superhot and getting damn close to naked on the stage of the shittiest loser dive bar I know. We start a three-way makeout as the entire crowd gapes at us, in shock.

I'm thinking, *Damn, I'm pretty drunk and so is Chessy, we should go before this ends up being another whiskey dick situation.* Apparently, Chessy's thinking the same thing, because she tells me, "Come on, let's extract. It's on." She says to the stripper, "Yeah, you like basketball?" She says no (that's a first). Unfazed, Chessy continues, "Well I didn't either at first. But, dude, we have to go to Jeffy's house, he's got this basketball court and we'll play PIG. It's really fun. Let's go. It's right around the corner and we'll come right back."

She's interested, but not fully there yet. Knowing that she's a stripper, I decide to intervene with a different approach. I say to her, "Come on, let's go smoke drugs." Now, by this, I'm clearly implying that we're going to go smoke crystal or some shit, but in actuality I have nothing back at Club Jeffy save for a bit of rather pedestrian, garden-variety cannabis. However, when the girl inevitably complains about this "misunderstanding," I'll be able to take refuge in the ambiguity of the statement.

She immediately perks up. "Okay! Can my friend come?" She points at her roommate, roid-chode.

Chessy's got this. "Sure, of course he can!" Yeah, right. We leave. We're all walking to the car when Chessy abruptly turns around, puts her hands on the guy's shoulders and tells him, "Dude, you stay here, we'll be right back, it's right around the corner! Don't worry!" She spins him around toward the door. With a strange, dazed expression on his face, he complies, slowly walking back into the bar.

We get to my house. One more shot of whiskey. She's not into Nerf Hoops at all, so we go straight for the Dual Induction. I start in with the routine, but before I can get into the meat of it, the stripper cuts me off and exclaims, "If we're doing the massage thing then I'd better take off my pants!" Woosh . . . off they come, she flings them into the corner. ChessClub and I share an amused glance.

We massage her for about two seconds before we start making out over her back, then ChessClub flips her over and starts eating her pussy. She starts hollering, "Oh my God, you're incredible! I'm cummmmmmm- mming!" I'm fucking Chessy from behind, watching the stripper writhe under her ministrations. I get up, walk around the bed and roughly shove my cock in her mouth. Hardcore porn ensues, I'm switching girls and ripping condoms open in a blur. This chick is so hot, it's like I'm fucking a cartoon. Finally, I come all over ChessClub's tits, and the crazy stripper bitch goes all porntastic and starts frantically licking up my semen and rubbing herself in it.

I get up to take a piss, and when I come back in the room, the chick is on all fours on the floor, backing her naked ass up into me, literally begging me to fuck her again. "Ohhh please fuck me!" I'm just stand- ing there, stunned. ChessClub insists that we kick her out, because she doesn't want to sleep with this fucking drug-addicted (albeit superhot) slut and so we give her a ride home.

It was the smoothest lay yet. Chessy and I are going to be pulling hot-ass within minutes, if we keep this shit up. Good, clean fun indeed.

It was *so fucking easy.*

Unfortunately, the goddamn tweeker whore stole my bunny ears.

POUTINE DREAMS

I've been traveling a lot with RSD lately. I can literally feel the difference in my perceptions as a result of all these excursions. Until last year, the only time I had been out of the United States was on a road trip to Tijuana to get drunk when I was eighteen. I've been to several different continents now. Exposure to other cultures has made me more attuned to the human condition; the differences highlight the ways in which we're all the same.

I've grown accustomed to the intricate dance that is frequent air travel. Everything has been systematized. I breeze through security lines while others fumble and stumble with their belts and change. I have acquainted myself with the different quirks of each airport. The hardass TSA agents at Austin, the dumb fucks at Miami, the mile-long security lines at Heathrow, the filth of JFK, the seemingly endless walks from gate to gate in Phoenix, the numerous uncovered electrical outlets for charging the laptop in Denver, the golf-cart based "Fat-Mobiles" (as I like to call them) whipping by at George Bush Intercontinental in Houston with their idiotic drivers screaming at people to get out of the way.

And who could forget the sneering Canadian customs officials. Christophe and I are dealing with one of them right now, having just landed in Montreal. I'm doing a workshop here this weekend. I've remained gracious throughout the interaction, but Christophe is losing his patience. The official asks him, "What are you going to be doing while in Canada?"

"Getting drahnk," he replies, clearly annoyed.

She's not amused. "Where exactly?"

"Ahhh, I dohn know . . . A BAR MAYBE?"

"And where are you staying?"

"Weev sahm guise I meet on the intairnet." Although she's not pleased with his tone, there's really nothing she can say. We're allowed through.

There are some real fucking hard cases on workshop this time. I barely squeek by. My game is tight when solo, but this workshop game is a whole different animal. It's a whole new skill set that I'm just starting to understand. I don't have a drink the entire weekend, and by the last night I look super fucked up, like I've been blowing rails all night, exhausted and red-eyed.

Fast-forward three days and I'm back in San Francisco. Last night, Chessy and I "ordered in" because we were resting up for El Rio tonight. But the bitch we called didn't show until 2 A.M., so I ended up pouring a glass of whiskey on her head and kicking her out without sex.

I feel like I've become incredibly stupid, and I like it. It's by design. I've already tried being thoughtful and intelligent. I know all about it. The only thing thinking ever did was make me angry. Somebody asked me the other day, "What's the point of this pickup crusade of yours?" To me, the question itself sounds suspiciously like thinking.

In my mind, right now, I look at it like this: There is no point. There is no purpose. It is pointless. *Life* is pointless. That's *why* I do this, fucking all these sluts. We'll all be dead soon. Fuck this silly bullshit. For me, this is about sex, plain and simple. Some people study pickup hoping it's gonna change them into a magical butterfly of delight. I harbor no such delusions. I'm still the same fat drunk, except with more and hotter sluts.

I have taken several days off in the wake of the Canada trip, to recuperate. Tonight I will go out to pull ass for the first time in a week. I am ready. Drunks ahoy! Thar blow bitches!

ANOTHER WHORE GETS FUCKED

Last Friday, while I was away in Montreal, ChessClub gamed up a girl at some party and got her phone number. According to her, it was an extremely solid interaction, and she had every expectation that the number wouldn't flake. She called her up on Monday, made some small talk, then invited her to karaoke. She had to work the next few days, but promised to get that day off.

Thursday rolls around and Chessy calls her up again. The girl is very excited on the phone, saying that she already started getting loaded off Jameson and intends to show up drunk, and that she can't wait to see Chessy. "Oh man," I say, shaking my head, "we are so banging this chick tonight."

I debrief Chessy in detail as to which routines she's already run on her, so there's no overlap. There's nothing more cringe-inducing than running a routine on a girl, only to hear her say, "You said that before." We work out a basic game plan and depart for Kostume Karaoke.

When we arrive, Miss Jameson's already there. We go to the bar first and greet the bartender and the karaoke host. Chessy spots our girl and makes her way over to greet her. She makes some apology about not being able to take a shower before she came, then tells her that she was just in the process of breaking up over the phone with this dude she was seeing. When Chessy asks her why she broke up with him, she replies that it's because he never has sex with her. Chessy looks disgusted and sneers, "How lame!" She tells her to wait there for one second while she picks a song. She immediately tells me what the girl just mentioned to her.

I laugh and say, "Money!" This shit is going down. Chessy brings her over to the bar. We make some small talk, and she introduces me. I'm wearing the blinky shirt, and Jameson goes straight for it, obviously fascinated by the bright lights and moving letters. She asks how Chessy and I know each other, and Chessy tells her we're friends. I say, "Yeah, we tend to hang out a lot because we're both always at karaoke."

I sing. Chessy sings. Everybody drinks. We start busting routines. We're in the fucking zone, and it's flowing like smooth butter.

I go outside to smoke bomb, and this cute little metal/punk chick with long black hair and bangs rolls up to the door with some dude in tow. Since I'm feeling officious, I decide to card them. They take out their identification and show me, at which point I reveal that I am not actually employed by the venue. They laugh. ChessClub comes out at that moment and asks the girl for a cigarette. She pulls out her pack and they both light one up. I start in on the girl hard, machine-gunning routines at her. She's reacting well, and this sets the dude she's with on edge. He tries to intervene in our conversation, and I curtly interrupt him. "Hey . . . wait a minute . . . are you guys brother and sister?"

He looks at the girl, then back at me. "No, we're . . . friends."

"Oh man," I say, "you totally look like you're brother and sister. If you guys had kids they'd come out retarded. . . . HURRR DURRR!" I wrench my face up into a grotesque, pinched expression and start clawing at the guy's chest. "HURR DURRRR!"

After this he goes silent, and just stands there as I continue to mack on his girl. At one point, Chessy grabs his head and pushes it down, and says, "Suck your own dick, dude! Suck your own dick!" He's bent over double in an apparent attempt to fellate himself, while the girl watches, amused.

"I . . . I can't," he pleads. Chessy lets him up. He says, "I'm going in now," and heads into the bar.

Now, this girl is hot. Chessy and I both really want to take her home. But my field intuition tells me that it will be difficult. So we decide to isolate her at another time and stick with sure-thing-Jameson back inside. I instruct Chessy to get her phone number before we eject.

Okay, now it's time to get Jameson. Chessy walks right over to her after the punk girl's number is in hand and says to her, "Come on, we're leaving. We're going to Jeffy's house. Do you like basketball? Because we're going to play PIG and smoke some bomb. Let's go!"

"Okay! But we have to stop and get some liquor too!" I let out a short guffaw. This chick totally knows what's happening.

We arrive at Club Jeffy after purchasing the liquor . . . Jameson, of course. We play some basketball. Take a few shots. Smoke a bongload. Play some more basketball. She's admiring my pellet gun, going off about how much she likes guns and this and that. So I decide to bring out the Mossberg. Almost a bad move. Upon hearing the distinctive *click-KLACK* of the shotgun, she has a strange reaction and seems disturbed. I immediately put it away. Fortunately, she's easily distracted, and begins rubbing ChessClub's shoulders. Seeing the opening, I launch into the dual induction.

"Ooh! Awesome," she shrieks, "I wanna go first!"

We're massaging her. We start to make out over her. Standard shit. I go for the pussy lick, then it's ChessClub's turn. Fucking commences. ChessClub is lying there getting her pussy eaten while I fuck Jameson doggy-style, and she's literally smiling from ear to ear, looking like she just won the big game. She's right, it's the best feeling ever. We switch it up, and now Chessy's riding me standard cowgirl style, while Jameson sits on my face and makes out with her. Completely fucking awesome.

She leaves shortly after we finish, grabbing a cab out in front of the house. I notice she has left her skateboard behind; I have to wonder if this was done intentionally to ensure "round two."

I was fucking ON tonight. After a week of tending to business and resting, I was ready to fucking rock. I was really "seeing the ball." Tight frame. Like, I just KNEW that I would hit every note perfectly as soon as I walked out of the door, both onstage and in my interactions. I find that I'm able to tap in to that "nimbus" state more and more easily now. Went out, served some bitches on the mic, then we bang some broad. And here ChessClub was complaining because we weren't going out last week. Sheesh, kid, you have to rest sometimes. Three in one week, and then we take a week off and she's tripping. Sometimes in this game you've got to be patient and look at the big picture. One particular night, or even week, means little in the overall scheme of your ongoing development.

Also interesting was the fact that ChessClub got pissed off this time, when I came in the chick. Actually, it was more like "annoyed," because according to her, I was fucking the chick too long while she was sitting there doing nothing. Honestly, this was only because I was starting to get a case of "condom dick" with "whiskey overtones" and was afraid that I wasn't going to be able to finish. Hell, I had been trying not to get drunk, I even dumped a cup of the Jameson into the potted plant in the corner of the bedroom while we were shooting hoops. Anyway, it is agreed that I won't come in these bitches first anymore, unless she tells me to. It would seem I'm entering the realm of "high-quality problems" now. Woe is me.

Yet another bitch got fucked. In the morning, I'm hungover in bed, so ChessClub writes and posts the report on the forum. Various members express concerns that she is not in fact real, and that she is merely a figment of my imagination, a bizarre alter ego that I've developed as I sink deeper into psychosis. Hell, maybe she is.

CLUB JEFFY

ChessClub is now my official intern, a position that entails many responsibilities. She makes phone calls for me, following up on numbers while I play nerd games on the internet involving things such as "drakels" and "the Zardmaster" (I recently got enough gold pieces to purchase the Vampire Blade and Undead Puppy). She writes the lay reports for me when I am hungover. She cleans my house to prepare it for extraction before we go out. She goes to the store to get me beer and ice cream sandwiches. Everyone needs an intern; it's very helpful. God bless her.

Anyway, a couple of days ago my roommate Catherine informed me that it was her birthday on Friday, and that she invited some friends over. "Great," I said, "whatever."

Tonight, after a long day of fucking about town, I take a little disco nap. I wake up and go downstairs to discover the furniture has been moved around, and some dude is setting up turntables in the living room. Oh. I see. Before you know it, a *massive* line of people starts filing into the house. Shit, I go upstairs and get ChessClub . . . we've got a full-blown party on our hands here. I take my shotgun out to the car and put it in the trunk. Then I start drinking Pabst Blue Ribbon out of the Tiffany mug. I wander around my house scanning for targets in a flagrant manner reminiscent of Tyler at Mel's, except with less squinting. One little cutie is giving me an approach invitation, but she's not *that* hot, so I defer that for now. There are mostly 7s here. There's maybe one 9, but she's my roommate's girlfriend, and as such she is off-limits.

As I stand in the kitchen and harangue the crowd, I notice something strange. Some chodes appear to be discussing me, gesturing toward me and speaking to one another in an odd, conspiratorial manner. I roll up hard and fast and thunder some genial bullshit at them. There are a couple of guys and a couple of girls.

"You're the guy!" says one dode. "I AM YOU!"

I demand to know what the fuck he's talking about. They explain that they are acting with Catherine in a play about a guy's quest to get laid or something. Apparently one of the characters is some kind of seduction coach. Catherine told them about what I do, and so now these *thespians* are fascinated and want to hear all about it. I throw some openers at them. One dode pipes up, "I would never take your workshop because I have game, but it's interesting."

I take a look at him; he looks like he could easily apply for Chess Club membership with his glasses and argyle sweater. I laugh. "So, you have game, huh? Do you do cold approaches on groups of strangers? You know, like the hottest chick in the club there with her steroid boyfriend?"

"Uh, no."

I go, "Oh, so you just do social circle stuff?"

"Yeah."

"Oh . . . that's cool. Right on man!" Backturn.

As I walk off, one of the guys catches up, the guy who "portrays me," as he put it. This guy is practically pleading with me to expound game to him to help with his character development. Since there are no girls around, I decide to indulge him in exchange for free tickets to the show. I go upstairs with him and shoot the Nerf Hoop while ChessClub sits to the side, looking pretty. I give him the standard jlaix speech while the guy sits there in awe. ChessClub appears very bored. Finally she just gets up and walks out of the room.

Less than five minutes later, I'm blathering on to this guy about phone game or something when the door opens. ChessClub enters with some little girl in tow. She announces, "Here's another candidate!"

I start to laugh and say, "Another candidate, all right." The girls sit down on my bed. I give the dude eye code to leave, motioning to the door. He misinterprets it, and he gets up and moves to the other side of the room. Finally, I get up and say, "Hey dude, come here, let me show you something," and walk out the door.

He follows me out into the hall. I say, "Look, me and my girl are gonna bang this broad, so uh, see you later."

The guy actually has the balls to say to me, "But I want to see how you do it!"

I laugh, slap him on the arm and say, "Read the fuckin' report tomorrow, buddy." I go back in the room.

The chick appears drunk. I cut the shit and almost immediately begin the dual induction. She's a good masseuse. She keeps saying retarded shit like, "I am soooo drunk I have a boyfriend . . . I am druuunk," and all this bullshit, which we ignore. Finally, we get her shirt off and start making out over her. All systems go.

Now it's ChessClub's turn to start making out with the girl. But for some reason she won't do it. She's hesitating. I think she's had too much to drink herself. Finally, she goes ahead and puts her lips up to the girl's, but she still seems to be holding back. This sort of fucks up the flow and the chick starts saying shit like, "I love you guys but we're not gonna fuck tonight I'm on my period . . . I love you . . . please, don't hate me!" Jesus, bitch, we've known you for ten minutes! What a life.

I take the chick's shoes off. ChessClub is not helping at all. I know that if Chessy starts a hardcore tonguedown, the chick will get horny, I'll get her pants off to initiate the licking and she will be compelled to fuck by her own biological imperatives. As it is, I am encountering some serious resistance as I try to take her pants off.

I'm snarfing and snuffling at her pussy like a demented animal when some random chick walks in the room, holding her coat. She takes one look at the tableau before her, says, "Oh my," and walks right back out.

I start busting out my last-minute-resistance shit, I keep telling her, "Shhh. Shhhh look here shhh . . . slow your mushkin speed slowwwww. Shh . . ." as I kiss on her. I pace and lead; I'm about to bust out the real nuclear stuff when I notice that ChessClub is just sort of sitting there like a puppet, doing nothing; in fact, she looks like she's on the verge of passing out. The realization hits me that without her participation, this thing is sunk. I become enraged. I jump astride ChessClub, straddling her on the bed. I start yelling, "Bitch! Do something!" and slapping her across the face, back and forth, hard. She does nothing, her head goes from side to side, she just appears kind of loaded as the head lolls to the right, to the left. She is stunned by the blows.

The target's inexplicable reaction is to lie there next to us and start repeating, "No . . . don't hate me! Don't hate me! Guys please don't hate me!" ChessClub snaps out of her fugue state and gets the number from the girl, who then leaves. After this, a drunken anger-fuck ensues. We pass out.

I'm not sure about this one. I know it would have gone down had our game been on point. I would even go so far as to say that there might be a chance yet. The comments about not fucking us "tonight," the leaving of the shoes, the number, the shoving of my tongue down her throat; there were all these little indicators that suggest to me this may still be a go.

Even if it's not, though, I don't really give a flying fuck. I can think of a lot worse ways to spend an evening than by drinking free beer, basking in nerdy fanboy adulation, having my girl walk downstairs to pull ass, getting a massage from a pair of hot chicks, and engaging in three-way tonguedown. Anyways, a swing and a miss for Jeffy and Chessy. There's a first time for everything.

SWINDLING BITCHES OUT
OF THEIR DREAMS

ChessClub and I have developed a fairly consistent modus operandi. We call it "tandem hunting." On the forum, guys have come up with differing ways of going about this sort of thing, but I think that our model is more fun. It's predatory. I love that we can go out, have a fun night of pickup and swindle some little girl out of her dreams, leading her toward the bedroom so we can run the Dual Induction on her before she even knows what's happening, then dump her out on the street. We're using these other girls to enrich our sex life. That's what gets Chessy enthusiastic about it; it's about *our* relationship, not about me fucking other girls.

Yet I'm beginning to suspect girls like ChessClub are born, not made. I mean, certain girls are just going to be predisposed to this sort of thing. I got lucky. Story of my life, right? But, if I had to deconstruct how this whole thing has gone down, I think I can identify some guidelines:

1. I didn't *tell* her that I was some player, pickup guy. She found out about it on her own and became fascinated by it. That is, she heard through the grapevine that I fucked all of her friends to piss her off, then Lisa told her that I was an internet celebrity slash pickup artist. You must allude to the fact that you are special and can pick up any bitch you want.

2. Once she started asking about it, I was very reluctant to reveal anything. I kept this up until she was begging me to teach her. Then I started running game in front of her to show her how it worked. This made her even more fascinated. That was when she suggested we pick up together. Once she saw the power that a skilled pickup artist wields, she wanted to possess it as well. You plant the seed, they make decision. It's just like trying to tell a guy about this stuff: most likely, they'll think it's retarded. People have to seek it out for themselves.

3. I made it clear that she was my primary girlfriend. I also made it clear that she was my student, and must defer to me in all scenarios in the field. Now it's set up so that she understands and appreciates that she is learning life lessons that she will take with her even after we go our separate ways.

4. Each time we have been successful, the target has either been a lone wolf or with a bunch of guys. I suspect a chick there with her female friends would be more difficult. Much more difficult. You could possibly extract the entire group back to your place and have your wings occupy them there. ChessClub and I have done this with a pair of girls before.

5. ChessClub runs comfort-building stuff while I do the attract stuff. It's just like a regular pickup, except we split the duties. The bonus is you can get the target's head fucking spinning because you're hitting her from two sides at once. You also have an extra set of eyes, ears and arms to deal with interlopers and other obstacles. The flip side of this is that since there are two of you, there are double the chances of fucking it up by doing the wrong thing.

6. I usually approach first. I think this works better, for reasons I can't entirely explain. We've also found that if Chessy enters the interaction too soon after I open, the target assumes she is my girlfriend, and backs off. If she comes in too late, the target views her as competition and tries to blow her out. This is easily solved by doing an accomplishment introduction as soon as Chessy enters set. Chessy then immediately states that she is "an old friend" to eliminate any misconceptions like this.

We have developed a standardized "fuck positions sequence," which we use to optimize the threesome experience. First, I eat the chick's pussy. Next, ChessClub eats her pussy while I fuck ChessClub. The look on the target's face when I make eye contact with her while fucking Chessy is priceless; it's like I'm saying, "You're next!"

After this, we have her eat ChessClub's pussy while I fuck the target from behind. Then we segue into a three-way makeout while I fuck the target missionary and finger ChessClub. Finally, we execute the coup de grâce, the "Triangle of Love" formation where ChessClub fucks me on top while the target sits on my face and they both make out. Then I bust inside ChessClub. This seems to be a solid sequence, lasting about thirty minutes or so. Everyone gets fucked twice (except for me, I'm fucking the entire time, ha) and everyone's happy.

When I started this shit two years ago, the idea of me being with multiple hot chicks at the same time and having fucking threesomes every week was preposterous. Now it's just my life.

TICKING TIME BOMB

I'm home sick from work today, and I think it's time for ChessClub's first "time-out." She went to some hot chick party last night at "Dr. Coke's." This is some radiologist guy, who has this luxurious, five-thousand-dollars-a-month flat downtown and allows demented drug ruffians to party there. Not a bad setup for him, I suppose, but I'm concerned that ChessClub is getting too involved with drug people. I mean, I've certainly done my share of dope, but now I'm simply too old for this shit. I'm over it, and I don't really wanna be with someone who does hard drugs all the time. I have no doubt that she did blow, perhaps sucked some manner of cock, who knows.

Particularly galling to me, however, is the fact that she told me she was coming by afterward and failed to do so, leaving me waiting up for her in a state of semiconsciousness as I administered Advil, Listerine, and lidocaine hydrochloride in an attempt to assuage the symptoms of this fucking throat infection. I'm actually kind of pissed.

So fuck it, I'm gonna just go fuck someone else tonight and ignore her calls.

Let's make one thing clear, however. I'm pissed that she's doing drugs and not keeping commitments, *not* worried that she's hooking up with other guys. In fact, that isn't really something that bothers or concerns me at all. The parameters of our relationship are well defined: we can both hook up with other girls, but not other guys.

Sounds pretty good for me, huh?

I'm convinced that I could take any girlfriend of mine to a gathering of top-notch players and leave her there alone, and she wouldn't bang anyone, because my mind-control tactics are too powerful. I'm on some fucking Jim Jones types of shit, they're drinking the Kool-Aid. Maybe I'm wrong, but I sincerely believe this so it might as well be reality. Even if she did suck a cock, who fucking cares? I really don't care about much of anything anymore. Except possibly my cats.

I presume it would be somewhat difficult for the average person to imagine how they'd present such an agreement to a girl without coming across like a hypocrite or an insecure little fool. As in, what would the word-for-word conversation sound like? In actuality, there is no conversation. It is all subcommunicated. I simply *do not care* if she thinks I'm a fool. The boundaries were made clear from the beginning, and she knows without a doubt that if they are crossed, I am gone without so much as a second thought.

With Chippy, when she would threaten me with the idea of her committing some indiscretion, I would always say, "I don't give a fuck WHAT you do." Invariably, this would make her cry. Of course, she wanted me to give a fuck. But at the same time, my tonality had a backhanded edge to it; while I truly didn't care one way or the other, at the same time, if she crossed the line I was DONE with her, and that was evident. My attitude was, "I'm banging chicks, you bang dudes and you're gone. Call it hypocritical if you want, but I don't give a fuck. If you don't like it, get the fuck away." Mind you, I think these things were minor in regard to the larger context, which was the fact that I had her completely wrapped around my finger through my relentless emotional manipulation tactics. The only thing Dad left me. My inheritance.

With these, I can keep any chick (postfuck) as my fucking slave who will do anything for me for a good, long while. The problem is that it's not exactly "healthy" and it corrodes the relationship over time. Yes, they will do my bidding unquestioningly, until they reach the breaking point where the relationship is totally poisoned. At that point, the switch is flipped and they then hate me (yet still find themselves calling me on occasion). It takes years, but they all get there sooner or later if I apply these techniques, which are brutal emotional mind-fucks.

Unless I ditch these behaviors I will never have a relationship that lasts. But I can't seem to stop. I know it's wrong, and I am disgusted when I find myself doing it, as I can actually feel it eroding the relationship.

But it appears as though I'm addicted to control.

HUSTLER HONEY, EUROTRASH

newsgroup: alt.seduction.fast.general
author: "jlaix"
date: Fri, 10 Sep 2004 10:40:02 PST
subject: 3LR: Hustler Honey, Eurotrash

It has come to my attention that certain community faggots be talking shit. You know what they say? They say jlaix has no game, except to get wasted, sing monster ballads, and fuck repulsive warpigs.

Look, this is not revelatory information. I do bang the occasional hoggie, this is well-documented. I get drunk. I sing karaoke.

But what these keyboard-jockey bitches forget is that jlaix knows how to bring the muthafukkin pain! What, don't you remember me? The guy that brought you "What Would TD Do?" The player behind some of the hottest girl-on-stripper action since your mom's house? Hahaha, you little fucks. I don't respond to flamers on some dumb fuck's muckblog, I PRODUCE. THIS is my response.

So thanks bitches, you put a fire under my ass to show you up, and I ended up having a threesome with a fuckin stripper 9. Let's see you talk some more shit. Please.

Me and Chessy go out to a LOUD dance club for 80's night, with Christophe and a couple of students. I say to Chessy, "Don't these motherfuckers know who the fuck I am? Memories are short. Fuck this shit, tonight we approach only the hottest chicks in the club. I've been resting on my laurels lately with these 7s and hogs. Tonight is 9 night." She agrees.

We go in and they're playing my favorite music from the 1980s. I'm wearing my favorite item of "chodelicious attire," my Journey T-shirt. Bon Jovi comes on and I sing along.

Anyways, it's UGFest Deluxe in there. We just drink, dance about and wait. And wait. Soon, the hotties start piling in. We pick three targets, and decide which one to hit up first.

It's this little blonde thing; she looks like a little porno doll. A solid 9, in the corner with a couple of friends, a mixed set. I tell Chessy, "HER. Let's go. Salad opener."

This is a new thing we've been experimenting with, using the most retarded opener you can think of. The salad opener would certainly qualify. You go up and say, "I like salad." That's it.

So we roll up. Chessy says, "I like salad!"

I say, "I like salad too."

Chessy asks her, "Do YOU like salad?"

Now, I've been using this fuckin salad opener for weeks, and I've never gotten a very good response. Usually, they just stare at me all weird and I have to plow. Not this chick . . . she starts laughing her ass off. Beautiful. I KNEW I could get it to work. I think this time, our sub-communications were down pat, that's why it worked.

After this, I stack it with another retarded opener . . . "What's better, walnuts or eagles?"

Standard game, as usual. I tell her, "Shut off your Social Program. There . . . now you're you." I cut out the guy, make up different nicknames for her, Eskimo Kiss. I say, "Come here, let me tell you a secret," and then put my mouth to her ear and whisper, "Nevermind." All-American Girl, abbreviated Trust Test, Little Sister, Too Similar. She loves me, she loves us. I make sure to pay attention to Chessy so she knows we're a package deal. I qualify her hard. "Are you emotionally mature? Are you a cokewhore?" Yes and no, she assures me.

She goes off to dance. I'm not worried. I'm sure she'll come back. I see these two gays grinding up on her and shit. She's getting all freaky with them. Turns out they're not gay, they're just Eurotrash. Chessy goes closer to get the score. They say their names are Ron and Don. I consider blowing them out, but Chessy stops me. "Look, they're slowly blowing themselves out with their grind game. It would be try-hard to blow them out; they're chodey." Sure enough, the chick leaves them and runs to me, asking me to shelter her. I get her against a corner and start some real work. Proof that those guys you see dancing with the girls aren't going home with them. They're just placeholders for the REAL players. Let them occupy her for a while; less work for me.

Chessy gets some dude to buy us all drinks, and as they're at the bar getting them, I roll up behind them and grab them. The chick turns to Chessy, horrified, and says, "HE'S not buying them, is he?" Like all worried, that I turned out to be a chode. Chessy laughs and assures her I'm not, that some other guy bought them. She looks relieved.

I go chat some other people for a while. Suddenly Chessy comes up to me and says, "Do you know what she does? She's a stripper, she works at the Larry Flynt Hustler Club. I told her what we do, that we're pickup artists and she thinks it's awesome." She rolls up and I confirm it, then I start talking social dynamics with her, and how it relates to the strip club, with the needy losers and their habits, etc. Huge rapport boost.

She tells me how she gets so turned on by confidence and good game, she could tell I was different as soon as I stepped up. "It takes a lot of balls to step to the hottest chick in the club like you did." Humble too!

We have a three-way kissing match. Not too much, though, lest I become tacky club makeout guy. I want a T-shirt that says that, like with a Superman-style logo . . . "Tacky Club Makeout Guy!" That would be tight.

The girls start dancing with each other, and it's all erotic and shit. Every dumbass chode nearby is nutting in his pants. I'm just watching it in front of me like the king; they occasionally come up and hug me/kiss me. The social proof is palpable. I swear to God, one chick, like a solid 8.5, walks by and looks at me like I'm a rotisserie chicken or some shit, with this smoldery look. She might as well have mouthed, "I want to fuck you," it was that crazy intense. I turn to some chodes who are drooling off to the side and say, "My life is very complicated."

I go to take a piss and get my coat. Then I see some guy whom I don't remember having met, and he says, "Hey Jeffy!" I look at him, and he's standing there with some chick.

I say, "I am a hunter-killer macrobe," and walk away.

Pull time. I have Christophe handle the debrief of the students, and bounce with my girlies. We go to Club Jeffy. No dual induction. I rarely use it anymore; it was like training wheels. I think that in a lot of ways, it was more for MY benefit, to make me feel comfortable in such an alien situation. I'm beginning to think this same logic can be extended to ALL routines. Don't get me wrong, dual induction still has its place, but a lot of the time it's just unnecessary. You just lie the chicks down (no chairs in the bedroom) and start making out with them. The biggest part is making sure that EVERYONE IS INVOLVED. Nobody can be ignored, at any time, otherwise it fucks up the vibe. You have to keep your wits about you. You truly have to be the conductor and direct the girls. Be the *man*, man.

I start getting impatient to fuck, though. There is a lot of foreplay, and I keep motioning Chessy to take her pants off and escalate. But then I remember all the threesomes I fucked up by pushing too hard, and I decide to ease up for a second. When the chick goes to the bathroom, I tell Chessy, "We're gonna do this one your way this time. You feel the girl-vibes and escalate as YOU see fit." She agrees.

Long story short, eventually we all got it on. Fucked the shit out of them both. Hot as fuck. This chick had a perfect ass; it was like a magical dream. They nuzzled up on either side of me tightly and we all went to sleep, drifting off with "Save a Prayer" playing quietly on the stereo.

This morning we went to brunch. We have so much in common and the vibe was perfect. I told her she had a fat girl personality and she said that was the nicest compliment she's ever gotten. Pretty little stripper girlfriend sounds nice. We dropped her off at home and she said, "Call me when you guys want to get a drink." Now, four hours until Bootcamp starts back up. I'm gonna get me a power nap right now.

So, to all the haters: you can suck my muthafukkin' DICK, and we still smokin' . . . WHAT?!

—jlaix

what's the difference between us? we can start at the penis; or we can scream "i just don't give a fuck" and see who means it.

DINNER WITH EX-GIRLFRIEND

"Eh, I liked it," I say as we walk out of the theater.

Tonight, a "date" with my ex-girlfriend, Chippy. She called me up during the week and suggested we do a little catching up. I figured it couldn't hurt and thus far, it hasn't. We head to the bar and have some food and drinks.

In the middle of dinner, we start to argue about RSD, a typical occurrence. When a relationship ends, it's usually for a good reason, and right now it's all coming back to me. Nevertheless, I'm trying my best to keep things civil. She turns to me and says, "I have to confess, since we broke up, I slept with someone else. He's from Mexico and he's very athletic."

Okay, so this brings her grand total of sexual partners up to TWO. That is, if it's even true, and not just some sad attempt at a "jealousy plotline." I take a bite of crab cake, slam down my glass of scotch and say, as calmly as I can, "I have to confess as well. Since we broke up, I slept with forty-two girls."

There is a brief lull as this statement hangs in the air and begins to dissipate. Chippy appears nauseated and somewhat incredulous. She tells me that I am "fucking disgusting." We finish dinner and leave.

We get to my house. I make her smoke weed, which she rarely does. She becomes spontaneously violent and starts to beat me up. She's drunk and wild, and I'm getting hurt. I put some distance between us and yell, "WAIT WAIT WAIT . . ." She stops in her tracks, hand cocked back, growling. I say, "Baby, let me ask you a question okay? Shhh . . . okay. Let me ask you a question. Have you ever . . . in your life . . . been pepper sprayed?" My hand comes up with the spray, directed at her face. Reluctantly, she calms the fuck down.

I take off my pants and initiate fuck. She embraces me with a certain desperation, and it startles me. Something's different, she seems insane . . . she tells me to choke her out and shit. I'm not sure what's going on here. In the four years that I've known her, she has never exhibited this sort of behavior. I lecture her on the dangers of erotic asphyxiation. It's as though she wants to be degraded by a scumbag. *This is what I have become.* Somewhere in the back of my mind, my inner child recoils in horror and disgust. I dismiss the implications of this before they can fully form, and honor her request, occasionally smacking her ass.

In the morning, she calls me a "ho." As she leaves, I casually tell her I won't sleep with her again because she "fucked a Mexican, and I don't want to get a disease." Nothing against Mexicans; it just happened to be the most absurd thing I could think of saying at the time, given the circumstances. I mean, fuck, *I'm* the one that slept with over three dozen people. In any case, sitting here now and reflecting on these events I am ambivalent. I'm either at the top of my game, or have hit a new low. Probably both.

BRO DATE

ChessClub and I go to Zazie for brunch. It's a beautiful day. We leisurely drive up Castro Street, taking it all in: the gargantuan rainbow flag at the top of the hill, the fat bull dykes with mullets, the shirtless boys holding hands, traipsing down the side-walk in love. There is an idyllic, somehow pastoral quality to the scene. I turn to ChessClub in the passenger seat, and gesturing around us, ask her, "Do you identify with all this? Like, do you think of yourself as 'gay'?"

She says, "No, I just like to bang hot chicks."

Chessy is quite literally the strangest girl I have ever met, for a num-ber of reasons. NOTHING makes her jealous. For example, she'll ask me what I did while she was at work, and I'll casually say, "Oh, well I called some ho over to suck my cock," and she'll just laugh. She truly does not care. Additionally, she's a straight-up maniac when we hit the club. One observer called her "a newbie gone wild." She will approach every feasible target in the club until something sticks. Her zeal and dedication surpass that of most people I have met in the scene.

After brunch, I take her home, then I head downtown to meet up with my best friend from high school, Hudson. He's in the city this week for an IT conference. I haven't seen the guy in about eight years, but it seems like longer. I find him at the base of the monument in Union Square. I don't recognize him at first; he is wearing a full beard and has gained at least seventy pounds. Jesus Christ. *What the fuck happened?* He looks like shit. I'm embarrassed to admit that I actually feel a tinge of contempt as I greet him, throwing him a hug. There's a sense of unfamiliarity, like we're meeting each other for the first time, or like I've just come back from Mars. We sit down at the cafe, and I can tell that he feels the same way. He orders a straight whiskey. It's two in the afternoon.

The conversation gets around to game. During one of our infrequent phone conversations, I told him a little bit about what I've been up to, even going so far as to direct him to the forum. He expressed a passing interest in it at the time, but I've never seen him post. I excitedly explain the latest developments with ChessClub. He listens for a while, then raises a question. "I'm not quite sure how you're training this girl without her being suspicious of how you manage her," he says, narrowing his eyes in the sun. "I mean, what's your approach been? I'd think the less you talk about game the better . . . teach just what she needs to know."

"Yeah, I like the need-to-know frame. But my approach with Chessy has been to openly tell her that I am mind-fucking her in this fashion beforehand. It's not like it's some clandestine thing I'm trying to pull off."

He takes a gulp of his drink, finishing it off. He waves the waitress over and orders another. "Here's the thing though. Seduction was invented by men, right? They invented it to put them on parity with a woman's natural attraction and relationship skills. Most women are driven by their emotions and if they ever want to try and control you, which is just a matter of time, they will put that knife right in your back and use it as a lever."

I laugh and dismiss this, saying, "I highly doubt it. I simply will not permit a frame where this is even a possibility. Do you think I didn't foresee this possibility before I began doing this with Chessy? Do you think I'm fucking stupid? Is that what you're saying to me?"

He just rolls his eyes. "Do you really want me to answer that?"

"Look. I've arranged it so that the kid can not countermand my wishes without experiencing severe cognitive dissonance. Like, her game is booby-trapped, and if she ever tries to use it against me, it will blow her fucking head off. This is accomplished by means of a series of emotional switches I have installed in her head over the course of the relationship. This gives me the control I need, but unfortunately limits her gaming skills to a degree and prevents her from reaching her full potential."

"Dude," he says, "calm down. I'm just thinking out loud. But you do have to consider that you might have created a monster here."

I scoff. "This concerns me little. I am not worried about 'creating a monster' due to the fact that I'm a monster myself. If this bitch gets out of line I will fucking crush her." I reflect on this momentarily. "When it comes down to it, it's more that I don't see how this chick could possibly hurt me on any level. Maybe that's a concern for other people, people who are still capable of 'feeling,' but personally, I couldn't give a fuck less if I tried." I break off for a second, and stare at him across the table.

Hudson is probably my oldest and most trusted friend. I realize that, despite any present sense of unfamiliarity, when I look at him I might as well be looking in a mirror. I reconsider and say, "I don't know. Maybe you're right. One day I'll be in the street drinking Mad Dog 20/20 because of what I have done . . . then I will say, 'YOU WERE RIGHT! I AM RUINED!' "

He chuckles, then his face turns more serious. There's an interlude, as if he's measuring his next words carefully. Finally, he says, "All right . . . but lemme ask you this: if you're dead to feeling, then what's the point of living?"

"Self-preservation is a strong impulse, dude. What, I'm gonna snack on buckshot just because I don't give a shit about anything but myself?" We sit there. A bird lands near the table and I shoo it away. Hudson just looks down at his drink, stirring the cubes, then sits back and starts to watch some kids playing in the square. He looks almost . . . wistful.

ANOTHER BORING THREESOME

My pickups have taken on a mechanical, rote quality. I'm not really having a great deal of "fun" anymore. I instead find myself robotically hammering stale, scripted routines at the women, one after the other, then going home and robotically hammering my cock *in* them. One after the other.

Unfortunately, this trend seems poised to continue for the foreseeable future, as ChessClub and I continue to engage in paint-by-numbers threesomes. One after the other. I have some special new technology I've been working on, a plug-and-play "insta-set" that runs Attract, Comfort and Seduction material concurrently (instead of in a linear fashion), eliminates pattern recognition on the girl's part and allows for cut-off threads with fallback material. This makes my routines flow very naturally, no more "this guy is some kind of weird comedian" shit. Now, it just seems like I am a supersmooth conversationalist, and I can really focus on *cutting the fuck in*, and on my facial expressions and tonality.

Additionally, I've gotten ahold of some boner pills. I'm sick of seeing that disappointed look on my girlfriends' faces when I bust . . . threesome over! But with this shit, what the fuck, it's like high school again. My cock is now a weapon: I can hurt girls with it. I feel like I could fuck through two layers of Sheetrock. Upon waking, the morning wood is so extreme that I can barely walk, and must angle myself in a "Superman" pose in order to piss. Highly recommended.

Christophe brought an interesting sticking point to my attention the other night. He said that I tend to stay in the attraction phase too long, just making the girls laugh and giggle at my awesome lines. Interactions should be twenty minutes, tops, before phase-shifting. Chessy agreed with his diagnosis. This is something I've been aware of. The thing is, I like watching the material hit, I find it gratifying, and so I'll often just blast attract shit without escalating enough.

This goes against several "rules." Rule 1: Use the least amount of material necessary to get to the next level. You don't want to exhaust all your shit early (admittedly, this would be tough for me since I have literally three hours of material teed up at any given time, but still). Rule 2: PULL THE FUCKING TRIGGER WHEN IT IS TIME.

With all of this in mind, I begin preparations for tonight's Kostume Karaoke. I dig out my old Ultra-Sexy Teen Jihad Martyr Belt. It's an elastic back support belt, to which I have affixed a large analog clock, numerous red sticks of "dynamite" with wires sprouting in every direction and several flashing LED lights. I strap it on, and Chessy and I venture out into the night.

We get to the karaoke bar, and no chicks show up. There's only one decent girl in the entire place, a bare-minimum 7.5 wearing kitty ears. Acceptable. Chessy opens. I roll in and she fails to introduce me, so I take her aside and upbraid her for this transgression. I reopen the girl. Turns out she's there alone, and just moved to the neighborhood. She'll do.

Dallas is bartending tonight, and I notice that he's shaved off his luscious locks. We inquire about the dramatic change, and he gives Chessy a lock of his hair that for some reason he has saved behind the bar. I thank him and inform him that I am going to use it to clone him, raise the clone as my child, and make it my servant. He gets a very disturbed look on his face and walks away.

I sing some bullshit and crush the motherfucker like a Barry Bonds steroid homer. Chessy gets up to sing some classic Cyndi Lauper, "Girls Just Wanna Have Fun," replacing "have fun" with "suck cock." Naturally, during the bridge, I run up, mount the stage and whip out Puff the Magic Dragon, shoving it in her mouth. She proceeds to suck my cock in front of the assembled crowd, who stare on with various expressions of shock, horror, dismay and amusement. I pull out just in time for Chessy to resume singing the second verse, and leap off the stage, returning to my bar stool.

Dallas gives me a thumbs-up and pushes a free glass of scotch across the bar at me. I wink at the target, who doesn't know whether to be impressed or terrified. I engage the girl, hard. Sexual vibe from get-go. Cocky shit, lots of staring at her up close, with a dumb smirk that the average person would want to slap off my fucking face. When Chessy gets back, she settles in on the other side of the girl. I unleash a salvo of predetermined bullshit:

Thug Lovin'
Little Sister
High-Five
(fluff talk)
Total Badgirl
Social Program
(fluff talk)
All-American Girl
Too Similar
(fluff talk)
Trust Test
So Genuine
(fluff talk)
Eskimo Kiss
(fluff talk)
Not Boyfriend Material

The target talks about the Burning Man festival out in the desert, which she just returned from, and how she took a "kissing workshop" there. "Okay," I say. "How were your skills before and after the workshop? What do you rate yourself?" She says she's a 10. "Hmm, I don't believe that . . . let's see." I kiss her. "Hmm. Okay . . . making me feel emotional! Here, Chessy, you kiss her and see for yourself." ChessClub kisses her.

The girls get onstage and sing a song together, while they dance about and grind on each other. Dallas and the karaoke host both glance at me with that *"Haha you fuck . . . not again . . ."* look on their faces. I say, "YUP . . . you know how this story ends, guys," slamming down my glass of booze. All the regulars here know us as That Comical Couple That Picks Up Chicks. I'm fully comfortable with the role. I don't give a fuck.

The girls get offstage. Chessy plays "Fuck, Marry, Kill" with her, picking out three random guys in the bar and making her choose which one she would marry, which she would fuck, and of course which she would kill. Afterward, the target insists that I play a round. After she picks the three girls, I think for a moment, then announce, "Easy. KILL THEM ALL."

Chessy starts digging deep, taking her to the restroom for the obligatory "girl time." While inside, she hatches a brilliant plan and shares it with the girl. "Let's play a trick on Jeffy," she says, conspiratorially, "We'll swap shirts and see how long it takes him to notice!" The girl agrees, and they come out wearing each other's shirts. I act like a moron (not much of a stretch) as they giggle.

"What are you girls up to?" *Tee hee, he's so dumb!* Finally, I "realize" what's happened and say, "Oh, you guys," wagging my finger at them. Now, we've gotten her accustomed to removing her clothes in front of Chessy. Furthermore, if she wants her fucking shirt back, she's going to have to come back with us to the pad.

I finish off with Too Similar and give her a quick backrub, qualify her on my standards, then we extract to Club Jeffy, under the pretense of "smoking weed." Dual Induction is initiated.

Fucktime! Your basic triple-X hoedown ensues, with one funny incident. We're all fucking, and I go to eat the chick's pussy. But ChessClub beats me to it, and starts munching away. She then PUSHES me to the side and won't let me participate. How do I handle this? I get up and announce, "Okay, you're irritating me now, so . . ." While she continues to snack away at the chick's cunt, I grab some lube and spurt it all over my cock, then ram it into ChessClub's ass. "This is what you get, bitch!!" I roughly fuck her in the ass while she finishes licking and nuzzling the chick's pussy, causing a multi-orgasmic freak-out. I bust a nut, and then after a brief rest, we fuck again, finishing this time in the favored Triangle of Love.

We permit this one to stay the night, because she is a nice, normal person, not a bizarre stripper on drugs or some weird shit like they usually are.

In the morning, I'm getting ready for work and the doorbell rings. My roommate Ben answers it to find two police officers standing there. "Are you Jeffrey Allen?" one of them asks.

Ben replies, "No, he's my roommate."

Pause. The other cop asks, "Is he stable?"

"You mean . . . right now?"

I come downstairs in my business suit, looking relatively normal and well-adjusted. The police escort me out to my car, which I apparently parked in the ten-minute zone of a nearby business. There are four squad cars, two fire engines and an ambulance all parked around it; the gas station across the street has been shut down as well. About thirty people have gathered to see what's going on.

It turns out that while the parking enforcement guy was writing me a ticket for violating the ten-minute zone, he noticed the bomb belt, which I had left sitting conspicuously in the backseat, and called in the fucking bomb squad. Fantastic. I groan and exclaim, "Oh my God, I'm so stupid. . . . it's not a bomb, it's a prop that I use for karaoke."

The cops appear even more confused. "Take it out," one of them orders me. I remove it from the car and proceed to explain myself further. It takes forty-five minutes before the issue is resolved to their satisfaction.

The sergeant approaches me after consulting with the rest of them and says, "You're lucky we were able to find you through your registration. If not, we were going to either break your windows and flood the car with a fire hose, or just blow it up. Would have been Baghdad in San Francisco. You're also lucky we're not going to charge you for the response." I thank him, sheepishly. They confiscate the belt as evidence and give me a receipt for it, indicating that after a month, I can go down to the station and recover it. I imagine how that scene might play out:

"Good afternoon, Officer. Yes, I'm here to retrieve my fake suicide martyr belt please, here is my receipt, thank you very much."

Yeah . . . I don't think I'll be doing that.

THE HOUR OF CHRISPY

I'm in a cab, headed across town to the Marina (aka "L.A. Lite") with Christophe and ChessClub. We have developed a nickname for Christophe. It is "Chrispy," and he despises it. "Thees ess whaht mah name would bee if I wahs to be gay," he says. No matter, he shall henceforth be referred to as Chrispy.

Anyway. I received a call from Tyler down in Hollywood the other day. He had a mission for me. Whenever Tyler calls up with a "mission," I know it's likely going to entail something unpleasant. "Dude," he said, "there's a sea change coming in the pickup world. This shit we're using, the routines and all of this, it's about to become VERY public. There's reality TV show offers coming in every day now, a book is being written, it's gonna blow up man. This stuff is about to become the 'What's your sign?' of the new millennium. We need to start moving away from this shit NOW if we want to stay ahead of the curve."

I wasn't sure what to make of all this. "What do you want me to do?"

"I want you to go FULL IMPROV. I want you to do it for two months. No more routines. We have to make the transition to full natural game. It's not going to be easy. I've been doing it for the past couple of weeks, and it feels about as uncomfortable as going out with no pants on. It made me physically ill, I was actually nauseated as I approached. You don't get that instant validation from the girls like you do with the material. It's tough. But the good news is that it autocorrects all of your subcommunications. Anything internally that wasn't fully dialed and was being covered up by the routines will be brought to light. Have fun, man."

I know that this is going to be a challenge. I've had such massive success with canned material that I know it's going to be difficult to give it up. But I also know that he's right. Soon this crap is going to be all over the place, and my precious scripted witticisms will be issuing forth from the fetid pieholes of legions of douchebags all over the globe. Anyhow, I know that what's important aren't the lines per se, but the TYPES of communication that are involved. Taking things to a flirtatious level, putting sex on the table in a smooth, fun and playful way, etc. I've been doing this so long that I should be able to make the transition to complete spontaneity without too much difficulty. Christophe was enthusiastic when I told him about the new mission. We've decided to begin using the most banal, "chodely" openers imaginable, and try to make them work.

We arrive at the Matrix. Chrispy is wearing a shirt with a stylized image of Lionel Richie on it. I approach a group of three women, bust my opener, they start cracking up and we're in. They particularly like Chrispy, they're stroking his head, they're in love with him. As they're doing this, I say, "Hey, do you know who this guy is? He wrote Q-PLAYER." They stare blankly at me, having no idea what the fuck I'm talking about, then continue hugging him. For some reason they tell him he "should be on the radio." ChessClub and I laugh as we attempt to come up with a title for the radio show. Finally, we settle on "The Hour of Chrispy."

I go into the mode; my algorithm starts running. Like a heads-up display, I can see the game and the energy around me. This shit is a fucking joke; I could be a soldier getting fucking *shot at* in Iraq. This little "game" bullshit is NOTHING. I start working the bar in slow motion; there are several sets happening at once. Women I've fucked are all over the bar, some of whom were among the friends of ChessClub that I banged in order to spite her way back when. A couple of girls roll up and attempt to talk shit. I ignore it, run my new improvised game on them until I win them over and then BACKTURN them, hard.

Earlier this evening, Chessy and I called a couple of girls whom we had met last night in the Mission, and told them to meet us out at the Matrix. They said they might show up. When we first picked them up, I was continually making offensive comments to them throughout the night. They were just 7s, and I wanted to see if I could get away with saying super-fucked-up shit to them. First, I asked our target if "she ever got sweat on her chode." She appeared sickened and disturbed. I frame-controlled it away, though. Next, after we venue-changed them, I called her a "incontinent cokewhore," for absolutely no reason whatsoever. She became incredibly pissed off, then I just changed the subject and plowed through it. We venue-changed them a second time and at this place, I went right up to her and said, "Hey, guess what? My cock is immense."

She just looked at me and said, "Really?" Meanwhile I'm just nodding and smiling like a fucking moron, standing in the middle of the club with a huge boner from pills.

So after all this shit, we just left them, and called them tonight as a sort of Hail Mary play, not really expecting them to follow us all the way across town.

Surprise, surprise, they ACTUALLY SHOW UP.

Bam. We start in on them heavily. Chrispy takes the Asian one with the borefriend, we take the blondie. Drinks. I kiss her neck and pull her closer. She talks at me about my fucked-up comments the other night. I slip into rapport mode and show vulnerabilities, about how "I put on a persona because I'm insecure, and that's why I go around with all these girls," etc. I kiss her. We extract them to Club Jeffy at the end of the night, no problem.

Here's where things start to go wrong. Everybody goes upstairs. The plan: Chrispy will isolate his chick downstairs with a cigarette, then we fuck our chick. Well, that doesn't happen, they all pile on my bed. Worse, the girls all start singing the theme song from *The Little Mermaid*, at TOP VOLUME, in unison, at three in the morning.

This is almost too much for me to bear. They sing the song in its entirety, despite my cries of anguish. It feels like I'm having a panic attack. Finally, I pull the bullwhip off the wall and CRACK it several times to shut them up. This works, but I have to excuse myself for a long while to calm myself. Too late: this has put me in a weird mood, and I'm all angry and on edge now.

I go back in the room, and we're all on the bed. Now, five people on a queen-sized bed is not kosher. I'm getting pissed, and finally I kick Chrispy and the Asian out of the room. I guess they went to her house, which happened to be up the street. I'm thinking, *It's about time, Chrispy, you bastard, you were supposed to isolate, not sit up in my room for a fuckin' hour.*

Next thing you know, we're making out with this chick, and it's getting intense. Clothes start coming off. Girls make out while I fuck Chess-

Club. The chick gives me an EXPERT blow job while fingering Chessy, whom I make out with. I'm all fucked up on wiener pills, so I stay hard the entire time this is going on, like an hour or so. Fuck, get sucked, fuck some more. Then, finally, I go to fuck the chick.

She gives resistance. What the fuck is this bullshit, you've got to be kidding me. Okay, it's now 4 A.M. and I have to be at work in three hours. I do a hardcore freeze-out and just lie there. The chick starts sucking my dick again. It goes well, but then ChessClub, who is wasted, says some stupid comment and the chick goes out of state again. I get pissed and start yelling at them. "What the fuck! I have to work in THREE HOURS. One won't shut up, and the other won't put out! You need to get with the fuckin' program, or both of you have to get the fuck out of here. Please, leave immediately."

They refuse, I threaten to get crazy and get the water gun out, etc. The target, after a while of this, says, "Okay, we can bang."

I start in on both of them again. This time I put the condom on and finger the chick, and she has a string dangling out of there . . . apparently she's on the rag. I say, "Take care of this," and she goes in the bathroom to take care of it.

She comes back in, and I go to stick it in, but she refuses AGAIN. She proclaims, "You're not getting any from me, you're an asshole, I'm done with you."

Well, that does it. She has no idea what an asshole I am. I get up and get my clothes and boots on. It is now five in the morning. I turn on the bright lights and start lecturing her about her "weird games." I tell her she's being extremely disrespectful of the fact that I have to work in two hours and is keeping me up with fraudulent promises of fuck. Any other night, I could have plowed through it, but I seriously don't like going to work on one hour of sleep. She gets her shit together and I escort her to the door. She refuses to leave. I lock her out on the front porch. I go back to my room.

I look out, and she's still there. Fuck. I have to go to sleep, and I can't afford to babysit and watch this chick all night to make sure she doesn't smash my shit. I go down and let her in, and tell her she can sleep on the couch. She tries to get me to lie on the couch with her, saying she wants to fuck, but I've had it with this bullshit. I'm not going to reward this fucked-up behavior. She can't fathom she's done anything wrong. Just a dumb ho on her period. Fuck it. I lock the door to my bedroom and go to sleep.

When I leave in the morning, she's still on the couch. In retrospect, I should have just yanked the mouse tail and started railing. I secure all valuables and go to work, telling ChessClub to ensure she leaves promptly. Who knows, maybe I'll put my cock in this one yet, but I'm definitely not holding my breath, and I'm certainly not staying up all night to plow through BULLSHIT from an idiotic 7.

DISCIPLINE AND SHARING

I'm standing in front of the mirror in my bedroom, tying a half-Windsor knot. It's Friday night and Chessy and I are headed to some chick's birthday party. We met her at the Rio, this law student and her friend, both midlevel 8s. I'm in a pinstriped suit and a pink shirt; I put on the bunny ears. Chessy decides to wear adorable kitty cat ears and a furry bow tie, along with some flashy attire. This isn't even a costume party or anything; we just treal like that.

We get there and the law student chick greets us. I present her with the bottle of Veuve Clicquot I brought; we pop that shit and drink it down. The chick is looking hot, hotter than I initially thought she was. A high 8. She is clearly attracted to me. She begins asking weird invasive questions about the relationship between Chessy and me, like, "Have you stuck your penis in her?"

I shrug and say, "Yeah, of course." This despite having represented that we are "karaoke friends" up to this point.

I work the party and the target by turns. Several halfhearted attempts are made to tool me, which, predictably, fail. The whole party venue changes to a bar in the Haight, Murio's Trophy Room. Again, I split my time in half, paying attention to the target and the rest of the crowd in equal measure. ChessClub is going nuts at this point, opening groups left and right. She opens a tall blonde woman who sort of reminds me of Chippy, but wild and demented. I step over to them. Turns out this chick is there with some dode, who just stands there looking like a dumbass while Chessy and I take turns making out with his girl and videotaping it, along with his dumbfounded reaction. The chick is very drunk and claims to be a stripper. I look at her closer and think, *Okay . . . a low-grade stripper, but sure . . . I can see that.* Her insane demeanor is sort of endearing, in that whole psycho-cat-eviscerating-a-bird-and-eating-its-entrails-in-a-gleeful-fit-of-bloodlust kind of way. Chessy busts out a couple of routines on her unnecessarily. It would be quite simple to fuck this chick. However, the other target is marginally hotter, and after all, it is her birthday. It would be just plain mean to ditch her for a demented strip-ho like that. As we walk off, the dode is visibly relieved. *Enjoy her while you can, buddy, we have her fuckin' phone number . . .*

The party thins out and we move to North Beach. After the clubs close, we end up at some dude's house. I maintain a close rapport and physical escalation with the lawyer girl. But Chessy doesn't seem to think the girl is into her, and so she starts wrestling around with this other blonde chick who happens to be there. She starts making out with her, right in front of our target! She moves her up to what the host called the "chill room," which should more accurately be called the "fuck room" since it's just a big room filled with mattresses and pillows. She makes out with her, gets her pants down and is about to go to town when her god-damn boyfriend calls. He's downstairs. She pulls 'em up, runs downstairs and lets him in.

The boyfriend is a chode and Chessy can very easily blow him out. It's obvious that she can fuck this girl in the bathroom if we stick around, but the lawyer is ready to be pulled and we're all in this together. We head out.

Unfortunately, things start to unravel, which sucks because it seemed so solid. The lawyer keeps asking me, "Can I spend the night at your house?" We get to Club Jeffy and all get in bed. She looks at my sheets and says, "Clean your sheets Jeffy." There's a huge jizz stain on them. OOPS! Good thing she didn't bring a UV lamp, because I've been painting the fucking walls in here. She puts her hands on her hips and says, "I'm not going to fuck you guys. You don't know how many couples have tried this on me." This is where I should just pull out the standard tactics for dealing with this shit, but I'm too wasted and drop the frame. I just give it to her. Fuck. Then I pull out the most clumsy, stilted delivery of the massage routine ever. She doesn't go for it. She just looks at me blankly.

We all get under the sheets together, anyway. In a Jeffy sandwich. We are belligerent. All of us. I decide to just start making out with her and shit, because I know she wants ME. My line of thinking is that I'll get her worked up, then Chessy will join in. Only this leaves Chessy laying there like a tool, at least for the time being. She tries to get me to include her, but I ignore her. So she gets pissed, leaves the room and goes downstairs. I know what she's thinking: she should have stayed and fucked the other chick and now she's stuck here and this is lame. Eventually, however, she decides to come back up and attempt to join in again. When she walks back in the room, we're laughing. "Great, now it's a fucking joke?" She's clearly not pleased, but she lays down anyway.

Now, our little attorney goes all "Dr. Phil" and decides that it's therapy time. She proceeds to sit on top of both Chessy and I and tell us how we have some kind of fucked-up relationship and that we both need counseling and so on and so forth. We endure this for a while. Finally, she lays back down. I start fucking with her some more; again Chessy is laying to the side, silently staring at the ceiling. She pinches me to indicate her annoyance. I respond by playing footsie with her, which apparently pisses her the fuck off because she gets up and goes for the door again, grabbing the comforter off the bed. I sit up and say, "Don't go, it's late, it's not safe, just come lay down and we'll all cuddle." Yes, I tell her that it's "not safe" downstairs. In the *house*. And it works.

"Fine."

She gets back in bed and it's the same thing: her lying there while we mess around. She finally says, "Dude . . . this is cool and all, but can you at least include me?!" She's frustrated as hell, emotional. Drunk and emotional because I'm there fingering this chick, which I guess is justifiable. In any case, the girl has had enough. She obviously thinks we are total freaks. I have no idea why she's stayed as long as she has. She says she is leaving. Chessy gives her money for a cab. I just want her to be gone and the night to be done.

The next morning, I'm mad at Chessy. I tell her she shouldn't have gotten emotional and that she fucked up the lay. I say that I had a plan, that I was going to get her hot and then include her. She thinks this is retarded. She gets mad. "You should have at least warned me or given me a sign!"

"I tried, with my footsie."

This enrages her more. "Footsie!? That's ridiculous. What, you don't have two hands?"

"She would have known," I say, realizing it makes no sense the second it comes out of my mouth. Chessy is extremely upset. She can't understand why I'm being so harsh on her when she's the one who was being ignored. I say, "You're overreacting," and leave the room.

Shortly, Chessy comes downstairs and embraces me from behind as I stand in front of the stove. "I've been thinking," she says. "You are right. I did overreact. I shouldn't have let my emotions get the best of me. We both fucked up. Let's just both cut our losses and take this as a lesson." I turn around and kiss her. We go upstairs and go back to sleep.

Later in the day, the chick calls me. She debriefs me, saying that she didn't think Chessy was attracted to her. "That girl is in love with you, Jeff, and you're being an emotionally abusive asshole by ignoring her like that." She begins to interrogate me and make all sorts of assumptions about our relationship.

I just get pissed and say, "Okay, you wanna know? Here." I tell her the entire story of who we are and what we do. The forum, the threesomes, all of it. She sits there on the line, astonished. I tell her to call ChessClub and talk to her. She says she won't. I say, "Okay. Here, hold on," and hand the phone to Chessy.

Chessy grabs it and says, "Hello?"

"Uh . . . hey," she responds, cautiously.

"Hi!"

"Have you been standing there the whole time I've been talking to Jeff?"

"Yup."

"Wow, you guys are a couple of mind-fuckers, aren't you?"

Chessy just laughs. I pipe in, "She thinks I abuse you. She wants to help you get away from me. She says I don't treat you well."

Chessy asks her, "Is this true?"

"Well, no, that's not exactly what I said. I said I think he doesn't treat you well, but I don't know . . . maybe I just don't take things the way you do."

"Different strokes for different folks," replies Chessy.

"Yeah . . . well, I better get going . . ."

"Do you want to say bye to Jeff?"

"No . . . that's really okay." She hangs up. It comes down to this: we made so many mistakes that it wasn't even funny. I should have paid attention to Chessy, who should have paid attention to the target. Main thing we could have done? Not gotten wasted. Period. We're staying in and resting tonight.

On Sunday, Chessy sends a text message to the crazy stripper chick from Murio's. A little text conversation ensues:

Chessy: wassup!?

Stripper: just faden a beer.

Chessy: mmm . . . sounds delicious. We are going to the Mint Lounge and would love for you to join us.

Stripper: where's dat?

Chessy: Market and Guerrero, I'm eating and will call you when I'm done.

We get to the Mint and decide to play this shit straight. No getting wasted like last time. United front. Stick to the fucking script. This game requires *discipline*, and sometimes it takes a brutal fuckup like the other night to make that clear. When you stick to the script, shit gets done. *Intent*. This is how you get shit on the scoreboard.

The chick shows up at the bar. She "forgot her wallet," so I buy her a drink. The rules exist so you know when to ignore them. This was one of those times. I qualify it by running Not Boyfriend Material. She busts the fuck out laughing, "You're so funny! So funny!" and all this shit. After this, I covertly give Chessy some cash to buy her the drinks from now on.

So, this chick is fucking nuts. Wild child. Within ten minutes, we are all very close, the girls are kissing again. Dancing around the bar. Getting freaky. Making fun of dorks. Typical crazy party girl stuff. We're having a lot of fun. We all sing "Love Shack" together, I do the affected male vocal part, except instead of the actual lyrics, I just start spitting the lyrics to "Straight Outta Compton" in the same weird voice. We're going off, the crowd is loving it. The vibe is very comfortable, and we just know it's time to extract, which we do effortlessly. No overselling basketball, just "We're going to Club Jeffy."

We arrive. Blaze some bomb, mix some drinks. Commence Dual Induction Massage. You know what happens now. PORNO. She makes ChessClub come five times with her mouth and it's probably the best threesome, sexually, that we have ever had. Afterward she asks if we do this with a lot of girls. I say, "We have before, yes." Asks me if we've ever filmed it. Hahaha. YUP. Then she tells us that she's a porn star. Holy shit. This bitch is crazier than I am. I think I like this one.

She asks Chessy if she's into fetish. She says, "Hell yeah." They spank me and tell me to be good and shit like that. We go another round this time with biting and violence involved. WOOO. Finally, we all go to sleep.

In the morning, I wake up, and the chick is GONE. *Okay,* I'm thinking, *she left sometime during the night, whatever.* I get up and survey the room. The floor looks like a fucking minefield of used rubbers and sticky juice. Literally, there are like fifteen condoms scattered all over the fuckin' floor. But that's not what disturbs me; the chick's clothes are still there, her pants, her shoes, everything. *What the fuck, is the bitch in the fucking closet? Is she under the bed?* I start getting freaked out, I look all over the house, she's nowhere to be found. Was this an alien abduction? Was it all a dream? *What the fuck?!*

I go back to bed. About half an hour has passed when I hear a knock on the door. It's my roommate Gabe, looking for the bong. I give it to him, and he's got a strange smirk on his face. He says, "Hey man, thanks for sending us that chick, dude."

"Oh God . . . what happened?"

He tells me that in the middle of the night, the chick walked, butt-naked, into the room where he and his girlfriend were sleeping and got into bed with them. They asked her, "Are you lost?" She said no. "Did Jeffy send you down here?" She said yes. He and his girl kind of looked at each other for a second, then shrugged and just fucked the shit out of her.

"Thanks again, man. We were having a fight and we really needed that," he says. I guess this was their first threesome. The guy looks like he's GLOWING.

"Sure, bro, share the wealth, any time, dude."

The chick comes up a little later, and I ask her what happened. She says she must have got lost when she took a piss, or sleepwalked, because when she woke up she didn't know where the fuck she was and who these people were that she was in bed with. As she prepares to depart, I am amused as I listen to her take a call from her father and lie to him, informing him that she is "out handing in job applications." Yes, that's much more palatable than telling him, "Well, Dad, actually, I got fucked six ways to Sunday by four strangers last night."

Later, in the evening, I come home and discover that Gabe and Catherine have bought me a small gift and an elaborate, embossed thank-you card.

All in all, this weekend was quite a roller coaster of emotions for myself and my young protégé/weasel ChessClub. Many lessons learned and many game points earned. Two pickups we played to the hilt, one of which resulted in a colossal fuckup, the other of which resulted in an incredible night of weird wild porntastic adventure. The stripper left a bunch of her shit over here, probably in a bid to get the do-over.

SMASHED AGAIN

I flew to Detroit this past weekend for some RSD business. While I was out there, I encouraged Chessy to pull a bitch from the club by herself and bang the shit out of her at my house (hers is a squalid, prisonlike edifice that reeks of cigarettes; I figured it would be easier for her that way). Sure enough, she did so on Saturday. I returned to San Francisco the following day and congratulated her on a job well done. She'd hit a game plateau recently and this solo pull was just what she needed to jump-start her ascent to the next level.

Tonight, we're reunited and the dream team is back in effect. We saddle up and mentally prepare to destroy shit, as it's Monday Dollar Drink Night at El Rio. We roll in, and guess who's there? The chick she fucked.

I look at the chick. She's good. Definitely fuckable. High 7, low 8. Okay. The plan is to get introduced and just get myself grandfathered in by vibing and being a cool-ass guy. Which is pretty much what happens. All of the girl's friends are apparently some strain of lesbian; one of them obviously dislikes guys in general and myself in particular. Doesn't matter. I start layering in sparse attract stuff. The El Rio liquor is taking hold. The ladies are getting fucked up. Rio closes and we venue-change our target, making sure not to let her out of our fucking sight during the critical thirty-minute period between last call and the scores getting settled.

The scene out front is somewhat chaotic, with a fucking Italian dode trying to pick up both Chessy and the girl. They diss him and ChessClub mocks him, picking at his shirt and saying, "Damn, look at the style on this guy!"

He becomes incensed, in a greasy, European sort of way. "Are you lesbians?"

Chessy says, "Your mom's a lesbian," and the girls laugh and kiss.

The guy becomes apoplectic. "I GOOD ITALIAN BOY!! My momma not a lesbian!!! WHY YOU SAY THIS?!" He's screaming on the street, freaking out.

Chessy takes a soothing tone, trying to calm him down. "Oh, I'm sorry, I'm sorry, I was just joking around. Actually, MY mom's the lesbian . . . and she wants to FUCK YOUR MOM." The Italian goes through the roof, several men are restraining him . . .

I go up and say, "Dude, are you okay?"

"Why they have to say that?!"

"Dude, are you okay man? You seem tense . . . you look tired dude . . . are you okay?" He's all discombobulated, yelling, the chick's friends start yelling in his face. This goes on for several minutes until it somehow ends a little ways down the street. We venue-change to Phone Bizzle.

I run several sets in the Bizzle and then return to the target. Start escalating on her and win the friends over, even the man-hating one to a degree via some commonalities. Extract to Club Jeffy.

Once there, it's pretty standard stuff: slowing things down, having some drinks, etc. Dual Induction. The girls make out. "I wanna lick it." I do so while they make out. I fuck Chessy while she eats the chick out. I eat the chick out while Chessy rides me. Various permutations. Then I go to fuck the chick. She tenses up and says, "No . . . no."

I sense it's not token, and she's like, a full-blown lesbian and her decision is final, so I just get up. It's not a freeze-out, I just get up and put my shit on. I'm not upset. I can think of a lot worse ways to spend a Monday night than by getting massaged by two hot chicks and quasi-threesome-ing them. I'm totally cool with it and just say, "All right." I'm very normal about it, very calm and polite, yet the chick assumes that I'm pissed, and has a bizarre air about her. I offer to give her a ride to her car, or get her a taxi. She vehemently refuses, insisting on walking. I go to give her a genuine hug goodbye, and she gives me the man-slap on the back. It's bad social vibing; this woman is acting very strangely.

She leaves and then SLAMS my front door. I am bewildered. About two minutes later I hear a loud CRASH outside. I jump up and thrust my head out the window just in time to see the chick running away from my car. I leap for my keys ("FUCKING BITCH!"), throw my shoes on and run the fuck outside. My car's windshield is shattered, and there's a big potted plant smashed on the ground next to it. Holy shit . . . I search the neighborhood for the chick, but she is nowhere to be found. Her ass must be hiding the FUCK OUT.

I go home and call the cops. They take a report. After they leave, I call the chick's phone. Super nonchalant and breezy. "Hey Rachel, what's up, it's Jeffy. Uh . . . that was . . . unnecessary . . . I don't really understand what your problem is. I was cool about everything and I was being genuine about that. Aaanyways, called the cops, you're now a wanted criminal being searched for right now, they know your name and description, the make and color of your car and where it's parked, so I hope you get home okay . . . so I guess I'll talk to you later . . . probably in court . . . all right, take it easy."

The following morning, I continue calling her incessantly, leaving essentially the exact same message dozens of times. She ends up calling Chessy and telling her she will pay for the damage, if Chessy will please just make me stop calling.

I will not stop. I have researched her. I have discovered her full name and address. I leave another message informing her of this with the suggestion that police involvement will be unnecessary provided she brings me the money by tomorrow. "I don't dislike you, okay? I've been super fucked up before and done stupid shit like that myself. You know maybe one day we'll all laugh about this, like, 'aww shit, 'member that time you was all crunk and smashed my shit after we tried to fuck you haaa,' but that cannot happen until I am compensated for the damage you did to my car. Let's just get this fucking bullshit HANDLED." This chick better come correct.

On the one hand, I kind of have to laugh, because this is classic jlaix drama, right? Haha, that old bastard and his wacky adventures! But frankly, I'm getting sick of this shit. I've had a string of these types of incidents recently involving psychopath low self-esteem cases: some chick having a freak-out at the Odeon, yelling, "What are you guys doing here?!" when Chessy and I walked in, bitches gaffling my shit from my house. Some have even gone so far as to form a conspiracy group dedicated to fucking with me on MySpace. Literally, several girls who did not previously know each other have banded together in their hatred of me and formed this group, going so far as to stalk me at the bars I frequent, harassing ChessClub and me by snapping pictures of us and yelling insults like some kind of paparazzi terrorists. One of them, this chick Lauren whom I used to fuck with a fair amount of regularity, *really* has it in for me. She's even gone so far as to post FLYERS with my photograph on them around the neighborhood, indicating that I am an "STD-Infested, Whiskey Dick Wanker." It would be funny, if it wasn't so fucking creepy. I'm thinking restraining order maybe if it gets out of hand . . . ? I don't think these chicks have the intelligence to really fuck me over, but they apparently have the desire and I think it could become extremely annoying. I've even had to change my phone number to stop all the damn prank phone calls.

I mean, it goes back further than that, almost to the very beginning. I know the glass repair man on a first name basis, for Christ's sake. Hell, every window in that car is aftermarket glass, except for the left rear one. But there have been a lot of incidents in a short time span recently and it's gotten me to thinking. When I started this shit, I always envisioned it to be a four-year course. Maybe the lesson of my junior year in the game is that my game needs to mature more. Like, okay, you have all this power you didn't have before, now learn to control it better. Fuck, it's like some dude riding a Ducati superbike for his first motorcycle.

It's time to implement some changes. Keep shit on lockdown. Just be more cautious in general and do a better job of screening more thoroughly for head cases, deranged drug maniacs, etc.

Chessy suggested that the chick was abused as a child or some shit, and I agree it's likely. Frankly I don't give a fuck about her motivations,

I just want my money. Fucking ridiculous. Seriously, I was on my best fucking behavior with this chick last night. Perfect gentleman. No guns, no hosing her down and kicking her out, none of that shit. And THIS is the time the chick freaks the fuck out and goes psycho. Of course, right? Un-fucking-believable. Maybe the real lesson here is: virtue well punished.

TEEN DUFFER AT THE TACO SHOP

I'm sitting in the Phone Booth, drinking scotch, neat. I'm fucking bored. A few of my friends are here, gaming up some girls, and I watch them, disinterested. Finally, I ask Chessy which ones are available for gaming (i.e., not my friends' targets). She sighs and says, "Only the chubby one."

I perk up immediately. "Perfect!" I go in with my standard shit. She's some kind of golfer. What the fuck. Calibrate value. Increase physical contact, slowly but constantly. Fun fun fun. Cool cool cool. I can see the cylinders tumble into position in the girl's brain. She stares at me, hopelessly attracted. I try to pull, expounding the magic of Club Jeffy. This is to no avail, as her peer group will not permit it. I get VERY close and ramp up my sexual state; I'm getting wood and shit. I make weird kitty cat noises and Eskimo-kiss her, then take her phone number.

Okay, whatever. But when Chessy and I get back home, the chick calls me. She says, "Hey I couldn't go with you tonight, but I really wanted to. Call me soon!"

I say, "Right. That's hot. Bye."

• • •

I go up to Tahoe the following week, and I send out a mass text message to several chicks, including her: "Hey what's up . . . I'm in Tahoe until Friday . . . what are you up to?"

She calls me back while I'm in a casino. I have a twenty-minute talk with her, during which I just do a lot of push/pull. "You're awesome . . . sort of." And my new favorite: "You are SO adorable. It's sickening." We make tentative plans to hang out on the weekend.

I call her up on Saturday, while I'm taking a shit. She says she's going to see a basketball game that her school is playing in. In other words, she's FLAKING. I say, "Ohh I'm so disappointed. I hired a limousine, had flowers flown in from Bolivia, and a concert *penis* from France, to play the piano. I guess I'll have to send them back. Or just ride around in the limo and play with my pianist."

She's indignant. "Don't bullshit me! I can tell!" *Wow, we got a genius here!*

I say, "How cute, going with your classmates to cheer the team! Rah Rah! GOOO TEAM!"

"Whatever asshole, you're THIRTY." Okay, now this chick is pissing me off. She's eighteen, sure, but I'm only twenty-nine . . . not thirty.

I remain calm. "Touché. Tell you what, when you get back from your game, call me up if you're not too wasted, and I'll come out and meet you okay? Cool. Have fun!" She agrees and I hang up.

I'm out on the town when she calls me up at around 11 P.M. She tells me where she's at, and I go to meet her. I bring Christophe along to take care of the peer group. We get there and the chick charges up to me. Holy shit, I knew it was ON, but I can tell by her demeanor here that it is "ON ON." She ignores her friends. The only strange thing is that she's giving me a lot of shit about my age, as well as continual heavy sarcasm. I attribute this to her youth and insecurity; she's using tests as a way to hold on to her fragile reality. As such, I take these comments for what they are and largely ignore them.

I suggest we go to Mel's to get something to eat, as it is right up the street. She tells her friends and we leave. We get in my car and I drive to the taco shop by my house instead. She says, "What the fuck, this isn't the way to Mel's!"

"I changed my mind. I want a taco. You will like it."

The taco shop is across town and she keeps saying shit like she's going out of state, "This is BORING!" and so forth.

To combat this, I make bizarre nonsensical comments and noises. "WOOP WOOP! Magical Mischief Midgets in the night! You're a plasma baby!" This does the trick. Finally, we arrive at the taco shop. Time for the heavy shit. I do some generic cold-reading on her and she says it is "incredibly accurate." Hmm, interesting, what better time than now to run INCREDIBLE CONNECTION? It has the desired effect. We finish eating and return to my car.

"Do you wanna go to a party? My roommate knows where it is, it's underground." I drive to my house, right up the street. When we get there we go straight up to my room. Mix drinks, play basketball. I sit on the bed. She's nervous. She keeps saying shit like, "I'm not gonna fuck you tonight," and all this nonsense.

I just say, "Yeah. Yeah," and ignore it. I tell her to lie down by me, and that I wanna show her something. She does. I lie next to her and chitchat about bullshit to slow things down and get her comfortable with just lying there. Then I kiss her ("Are you a good kisser?") and things start to heat up. I do this for twenty-five minutes, then I go for the pants.

RESISTANCE. "You're thirty" comes up again. Ignore and plow. "We shouldn't be doing this."

I pace and lead. "Yeah, we shouldn't do this, but it feels so good . . ." Wash-rinse-repeat. I'm in no hurry; I know I can do this if I play it right, due to how ON it has been thus far.

Suddenly she sits up, puts her hand on my chest and throws a major test. "What exactly do you think is going to happen tonight, Jeff?"

"Hmm. Well, basically, I'm going to fuck you until you cry." With that evil smirk on my face.

She is incredulous that I would say something like this. "Not on the first date," and so on. I ignore this and stick to the script. Her friends keep calling her. I tell her to ignore it. She finally answers and I can hear them asking where the fuck she is. She says, "I'm at that guy's house . . . I'm sleeping on his couch . . . I'll call you in the morning."

I try to take her pants off. "I wanna lick it." She refuses, says she's self-conscious about it and everything. I say, "You'll like it, I am the best. Nothing bad will happen. I just wanna lick it." I keep saying this over and over, "Nothing bad will happen, it's safe," and, "Nothing is wrong. Everything is fine." Over and over I repeat this. This lasts quite a while. I'm about to bust out 100% Perfect Girl, but decide to give it another shot at taking the pants off, saying the same stuff. This time she relents, and I start to lick it. Get the fingers in. Advanced methods are employed, deep-spot shit, she orgasms. I say, "We're gonna fuck, it is gonna be sooo hot . . ."

Finally, I go to fuck her. More resistance. I kind of just caveman her. She says, "I'm stronger, you can't force me."

I say, "What the fuck are you talking about, I'm not trying to force you to do anything!" For some reason, this is what clicks . . . she opens up and what do you know, it's fucktime. While we are having sex, she continues to bust on me about my age. My penis is inside of her, and she's still saying, "YOU'RE thirty."

"That's right," I say, feeling demented. "Who's your Daddy?" Good times.

Her phone rings at nine the following morning. She answers it and talks to someone a bit before saying, "No, I didn't fuck him!" She hangs up and says, "Oh my God, I lied to my best friend." I tell her she is a degenerate liar, fuck her again, then I take her to Sunday brunch, as Chessy is out of town, and I dislike being without female company. We go to Boogaloos and are able to get a table, surprisingly. I order the Desayuno Tipico with a side of bacon and two mimosas. During the meal, I lecture her about how her sarcastic temperament is characteristic of a weak frame and insecurity. I get the feeling that I will never see this girl again, and I do not care.

COCAINE RAPS

Chessy and I are posted up at the Rio, slamming booze and getting straight smashed. The place is basically a fucking cockfarm. Then Chessy spies a pair of young-ass bitches up in the corner. "I want that one," she whines.

"Well fuck it, have at her. Go pop it if you're so into it. I'll come in thirty seconds later." She walks off and opens them up. As promised, I roll in shortly thereafter. "Are you bitches hitting on my girlfriend?" It's slightly off-calibrated, they eye me weirdly, but I correct this by adjusting my body language and facial expressions to appear more disinterested, then start riffing with Chessy. There are two girls. They appear extremely young, probably eighteen or so. Definitely not old enough to be in the bar legally. They're both cute, but one of them is significantly hotter. Doesn't matter, both are duly gamed. Fuck it.

One of them screams, "LET'S GO DANCE!!!" and tries to pull the other off.

Chessy says, "NO," and holds her. They're having a tug-of-war. Finally Chessy lets go and the chicks go flying. We share a laugh. Then, inexplicably, one of them runs back up to us and kisses us both, on the mouth, then runs off to go dance. Holy shit, all right. We high-five.

We pound a few more dollar drinks, then decide to check out the dance floor. Sure enough, the chicks are there getting all freaky. These chicks are fucking wasted; now they're dancing with these chode-ass motherfuckers who appear to be gay. I know better. They're trying to mack, dance-floor style. Chessy starts getting nasty with the girls. I do as well, but then I pull her away. "This shit is quicksand. Let these squids have their fun and keep their buying temp up . . . we'll just drink more and wait till the scores are getting settled out front, then blow 'em out like a fuckin' candle."

I go and chill with the doorman for a while. I tell him what the scenario is with the bitches. "Me and the fiancé are gonna pull that ass."

He smirks. "Going for foursome, eh? You will be very in demand, my friend!" he says in his Caribbean accent.

Foursome . . . I hadn't thought of that, but fuck it. "Dude bro, I'm gonna need some boner pills."

Closing time. Sure enough, the chicks come out with those losers in tow. I just roll in and swoop them away. Literally, these guys must have no game whatsoever; they don't even put up a fight. They didn't even SAY anything. So now we're walking down the street with these chicks, allegedly to Phone Bizzle. We're pumping their buying temperature with piggyback rides and other nonsense. We pass a drunken bum reclining on a couch in front of a smashed television and alternately pose for photographs and hurl fistfuls of change at his head. The dorks from the club ride by on bicycles and yell, "Bye BITCHES!!" Ohhh sour grapes? Morons.

We come to the street that Phone Bizzle is on, but just continue to walk by, because, of course, we're actually on the way to Club Jeffy. One of them notices and says, "Hey this isn't the way."

"It's a shortcut," I say as we continue to walk. "Have you ever been to Club Jeffy? It's fucking awesome." The hotter one, by this time, is way into Chessy and as such urges the friend to come along. This works for a couple of blocks, but then the friend pulls her away. I just continue to walk to Club Jeffy.

Chessy is nonplussed. "What are we doing? Shouldn't we go after them?"

I laugh. "Silly girl. We're going to get my car and go to Phone Bizzle . . . it'll be easier to pull them that way." We retrieve the chariot and drive back to the Bizzle. By the time we arrive, they're already there. I walk up to them and say, "You guys went the long way." This of course makes absolutely no sense, seeing how they got there before us, but it works. Somehow it explains everything, and we're back in set as though nothing unusual has taken place at all. They are with a new guy, apparently their friend, some effeminate dode. He's harmless, but I sense a logistical problem.

It's not long before the bar starts shutting down. This time, we pull them all to my car, including the guy, and go to Club Jeffy. We get there and I make the guy a drink and sit him down in front of the computer, encouraging him to "check his email." He does so. Meanwhile, Chessy and I lay both of the chicks down on my bed and start making out with them. The guy just sits there for a while, then leaves the room. He is not seen again after this; he must have left the house. It's weird: he didn't even steal anything.

Shit starts getting heavy. The hot one's clothes come off. Chessy starts banging her. Now, I know this is gonna be a problem, because the moment I take attention away from the 7 she's going to fall out of state and pull the friend away. Even though I know this, the temptation is too great and I start to go down on the hot one. She resists. This is nothing that an hour of standard last-minute-resistance-busting wouldn't fix, but I don't have an hour . . . this shit is not solid, these are some chicks we met forty-five minutes ago. Anyway, as predicted, the friend gets jealous, gets up and pulls her away. "Let's GO," she says.

We escort them out. Hell, I even give them cab fare. Whatta guy. These chicks are fucking wasted. One of them gets in a cab and speeds off, leaving the other one wailing incoherently in the street as she staggers out of sight. I wait two minutes, then start putting my boots on. "What are you doing?" asks Chessy.

"Come on, put your shit on, we're gonna go get her."

We pile back into the thugmobile and start driving in progressively larger concentric circles around Club Jeffy. Sure enough, we discover the girl waiting at a bus stop. I drive onto the curb accidentally, right in front of a cop. Miraculously, he just drives by. I roll down the window. "HEY!" She looks bewildered. "Go get her," I say to Chessy. "Tell her it's not safe."

Chessy gets out and walks over to her, telling her that she should come with us, that it's not safe for her to be out on the street like this. Chessy grabs her arm and starts pulling her toward the car. She appears reluctant. Just then, out of nowhere, this big Impala rolls up filled with black dudes. They stop the car and start to holler at the girls. Chessy yells, "SEE?!! OH MY GOD!!! LET'S GO!!!" and runs to the car. The girls get in as the Impala drives over to my car. The guys start to spit more game.

I scream at the top of my lungs, "HOLY FUCK!!!" and slam the car into reverse, flip it 180 degrees and peel out on the wrong side of the street. "IT'S EASTSIDE!! EASTSIDE!!!"

The chick is hysterical. "Oh my God! What's happening?!"

I turn to the backseat, still driving reckless, not even paying attention to the road. "Eastside rappers! It's coke wars! COKE WARS!" The chick is straight freaking the fuck out. We drive a few more blocks and get to my house, but she ain't having it . . . she literally jumps out of the car while it's still moving, flags down a cab and gets the fuck out of there. Chessy and I nearly piss ourselves laughing. Back at my house, I find the hot one's panties on the floor. The 7 left her orthopedic insole behind, inexplicably.

In retrospect, we could have easily fucked either one of the chicks if they were alone. But the door guy at Rio had me all up on the foursome tip, so rather than get someone to occupy the obstacle, we just went for broke, put all the chips on black and said fuck it.

This is pretty typical El Rio game, not solid in any sense of the word whatsoever. Meet, game game game, pull, then caveman. I mean, Chessy and I are relentless. If we haven't orchestrated a pull by the time last call rolls around, we'll just run up and down the street out in front of the bar with a permanent marker, yelling, "AFTER PARTY," and scrawling my address on the arms of every hot chick we see. Invariably, SOME-ONE shows up at the house. We pull every night. Now, we don't end up FUCKING all of these girls. Think about it: they arrive to the so-called after party and it's some empty house with a weird couple who immediately tries to fuck them. But we do *pull* every night. No intelligence required. It's what I call junk game. Like junk food. It's tasty, but offers little sustenance, if any.

EASTSIDE!!!

DUMP TINA

I am in the airport in Auckland, New Zealand, being threatened by a security officer. Frank warned me about this in Sydney, right before he gave me the pill. We had just completed another RSD workshop, and I was in no mood to stay awake for the duration of a trans-Pacific flight watching *Shall We Dance*. "If you take it with alcohol," he said, "it gives you a buzz and amnesia before you pass out. It's the same stuff that the singer from REM took when he was arrested at the gate after going on a rampage on the plane. He couldn't remember anything."

I proceeded to drink a shitload of liquor prior to taking the pill. Next thing you know, the airline had seated me next to a screaming infant. After this, they made everyone deplane because of a mechanical problem. I started muttering curses, and apparently this was enough to have me taken aside and admonished by security. After several apologies for my language, I am given a different seat and told to behave.

Sixteen hours later, I get home to my pad in San Francisco. I walk into my room and drop all my shit. It is dark and smells like unfamiliar pussy. Chessy is asleep in the bed. I wake her up and start regaling her with Aussie tales, like how I got with my first British chick there, and all the crazy times we had with the students.

Turns out Chessy's been up to some mischief of her own while I was away. Apparently she had gone to some fashion show with a couple of her hot ho friends, picked up some designer chick and had a five-way strap-on girl gang bang. She has large bruises all over her from the mania. Holy shit . . . I know of these chicks she's talking about, and they're hot. I'm not even back in town for five minutes, and looks like my dance card is already full for the week. We're gonna bang one of the girls each night. We fuck and I go to sleep, exhausted.

• • •

Flash forward to the next day. Rio Dollar Drink Night. Chessy arranges for the fashion show chick to meet us there. Now, Chessy said she's been banging this broad all over town in the brief time she's known her, including at my house. The chick knows she has a boyfriend, and also knows about the game, and even about RSD.

We used to do this whole "covert commando" shit (where we tell the chicks we're just "karaoke buddies"), but I've found that when we do that, we get more cases of the chick freaking out back at the pad when we spring the threesome on them. The girl we're picking up has to IMPLICITLY understand what is going to take place before we extract. The key word being *implicitly*. We don't want to trigger anti-slut defense by being explicit and coming across as the creepy predator couple, but we make sure that they understand on *some* level that we're a package deal.

The old model was this: I run attract, Chessy runs rapport. Not anymore. Now we make sure the target knows that we both like her, and we also make sure she's attracted to BOTH of us. I run my usual game, and Chessy runs her "chick attract" game, which consists of compliments and shit like, "You're so pretty, let's make out." This way, she knows what we mean when we say, "Have you ever been to Club Jeffy?"

My plan tonight is to lay back, be a chill cool guy, pepper some high-octane shit in there and get grandfathered in. We arrive late. The chick is already there, I get drinks, then Chessy introduces me. I start off sort of aloof, but quickly gear things up where I'm in her space, I'm smiling brightly, my eyes are bright. The nimbus takes hold. I move us to a more secluded area in the back where we can work.

I plan to go very light on the routines, using them very strategically, merely peppering them into the conversation from time to time. Vibe vibe vibe. Drink drink drink. I run Sincere Compliment. Buying temperature spike. Vibe. Little Sister. Vibe. I am in total control.

I'm wearing a pin on my lapel that says, "DUMP TINA," and the chick asks me what it means. "It means tweekers suck," I say. "Tina" being slang for crystal meth. It's my little antidrug statement. "I mean, hey, I like to blow rails off a shitty dive bar toilet tank as much as the next guy, but I kinda frown on meth. I'm too old for that shit."

Two giant black dudes roll up all of a sudden and start gaming both of the girls. These guys are fuckin' HUGE. I throw my arm around the one on the left. "I LOVE THIS GUY! He's like my little brother! Just look at those wittle cheeks!" I pinch his cheek and go "booboooboo-boo" and start laughing. The one on the right starts to move in. I shout, "WHOA! These guys are good! Hey man, pick these chicks up man, let's see this shit!"

The guy says, "Yeah, yeah, look at you, man, look at your hair!"

"Hey, just trying to impress you, man!"

He goes, "Well, it works! I'm impressed!" Ha, this dude obviously understands game. I like these guys, they've got class. I continue . . .

"No way, man, you're the master! Look at the STYLE on this guy!" plucking at his shirt. "Dude, these girls are my little sisters, they just broke up with their boyfriends, you should talk to them!" The guy on the left tries to cut me off, but my elbow "somehow" gets in his way.

"Awww shit, he's givin' me the elbow! He's givin' me the elbow! This guy!!" He's laughing.

"You know, man? You guys make a cute couple," I say, gesturing at him and then Chessy. "You should kiss him. I love it when two chicks make out." Meanwhile, the other one tries to cut in on me more . . . I turn around and see a few of the boys from the Lair, who've been watching the whole time. I wave them over. "Hey guys, I want you to meet my friends!" As soon as the player dudes turn to see who I'm talking about, I backturn them and cut them out of the group.

"Aww shit!! He gave us the backturn!! The backturn!"

The other one says, "Fuck this, let's cut."

As they leave, I'm like, "I like you guys! Fair play, man, fair play!" This was pitch perfect. Very jovial, just like busting around with your buddies. These guys could have pounded me into a fine red mist, but they didn't. Fuck, I PINCHED HIS CHEEKS. The key? My frame was rock solid, and I was making them laugh, not trying to "humiliate" or "destroy" them. This is why these sorts of tactics get a bad rap: people don't understand the distinction, then they run around insecurely chastising people and wind up getting their teeth punched in. At any rate, the chick is clearly more attracted to me after this.

Chessy goes to get drinks, and I do the Trust Test on our target while she's gone. Perfect execution. It's fucking on. I do a takeaway and let her talk to some gay guys she knows. Chessy takes me aside and says, "Listen, we should pull her now, to go do drugs at your house."

"She has blow?"

"No, she has meth." Oh brother. No wonder she seemed kind of tepid when I explained the pin to her. Fuck it, let's go. I can pretend to sniff it. No way I'm doing that shit. I can't bust a nut on it. I'd just sit there pumping away for hours and hours to no avail.

We walk out, Chessy, Tina and me, arm in arm. The door guy gives me that sly old look again. I tip my invisible hat to him.

Back at Club Jeffy, the chick goes to bust out the meth, and . . . there's none left in her little satchel. Boo fucking hoo. Awesome. Segue into the girls making out on the bed. I just join in. BOOM. The chick is hot, huge tits, but I don't like the way she kisses. Too aggressive. She reminds me of the stripper who wandered downstairs in the middle of the night and fucked my roommates. A total cokewhore.

So there we are, straight FUCKING, busting out all these different positions, full-blown porno time. We go into the triangle position to finish off. Right then, Tina's phone rings. She stops *midfuck* and answers it with some lame excuse: "It's this guy I've been trying to bang forever, I have to take this!" She goes off to the other side of the room and takes the call.

I tell Chessy, "This is fuckin' rude, let's kick this bitch out." I call over to her, "Do you hear, bitch?! Fuckin' rude. Taking phone calls while we're having sex?! What the fuck."

She finally gets off the phone, then continues making unconvincing excuses for her behavior. "I just feel weird getting between some couple, being the third person."

I chortle and spit. "What the fuck? You're not the third person, okay? You're like the fifteenth person. You think this is the first time we've done this? *Oh, I'm so nervous! Oh!* Hahaha!"

She says, "I'm so sorry, it's just this guy . . ." I deduce what's going on. The guy is her dealer and she desperately needs her shit.

I cut her some slack. "Listen, I understand, okay? It's just sort of disconcerting when you get up abruptly during sex like that. We like you. It's cool."

She brightens up and hugs me, saying, "Oh my God, I'll be back and I'll fuck you guys better than ever, I promise! I just have to go now! I'll fuck you so good, I promise!" She pantomimes this, to my amusement.

She puts her clothes on and I say to Chessy, right in front of her, "It's only one-fifteen; we can go out and pull another if you want." She agrees. We put our clothes on and all walk out together.

Tina hops in a gold Datsun 280Z that pulls up and says, "I love you guys!" as she speeds away to get her fuckin' tweek. Chessy and I, on the other hand, go to the Phone Booth. What could be more delightful than two threesomes in one night?

Not many targets there. We open all the viables, using a new opener. Chessy approaches and asks them, "Hey guys, we need a female opinion. Does his face smell like pussy?" Then I shove my face up in theirs so they can assess it. One woman runs off in horror. Others laugh and concur that yes, it does in fact smell of stank-ass pussy. We don't end up pulling, but we sail off into the night regardless, singing Journey at the top of our lungs, high on life. And scotch. And weed.

BLOODY MURDER

A succession of months fly by. I've been taken to task at work, transferred to the hotel out by the airport, the equivalent of Siberia. I now manage a paltry staff of fourteen people.

I pick up my phone and begin making calls to the girls currently in my rotation. Nobody answers. I plan on going out tonight, yet am oddly uninspired by the prospect.

My game sucks ass lately. I never approach unless I am highly motivated by the woman's appearance. I used to be a fucking monster, approaching every chick in the club, because I was building the skill set. Now that I have it and have done all these crazy things, I no longer care to approach unless she is really something special, unless she truly captures my imagination in some way.

I fear this has had the long-term effect of dulling my game. Ironic, because I know this could hamper me when I finally do see that special girl. I'm talking about the finely nuanced shit, the details, the lightning-quick intuition that comes from 24/7 gaming like I used to do. When gaming a 9 or 10, there is no margin for error.

My "meta game" isn't as good either, and by that I mean my game infrastructure. Like, before, I was up on my motherfuckin' numbers HARD, every day. Boom boom boom. Now I kind of fuck around with the phone halfheartedly, but typically end up going out to dinner with ChessClub, getting drunk, then coming home, watching a movie and blowing bomb till we fuck and/or pass out. The Rio is still in effect, of course, but it has sucked lately, with a higher thug element and fewer hot young girls. They charge more for the drinks now. Simply put, the Rio's not what it used to be. When I go there now, it just makes me sad.

I don't go on many dates anymore either. I just resurrect ancient fuck buddies from beyond time (at this point there are so many, it's not difficult to conjure up a long-dormant 7, like some kind of disgusting pickup necrophile).

My "relationship" with Chessy becomes increasingly annoying and similar to a typical relationship by the day, despite the fact that I'm allowed to bang other girls and that she bangs chicks with me. It's still a relationship; she's still a chick. Her behaviors have begun to irritate me, deeply. Several months have passed since we fucked Tina the drug maniac, and Chessy now spends the majority of her time fraternizing with her and her clique of deranged cokewhores.

I've told her to stop hanging with those bitches, because I am worried about their influence on her. These girls do shit like get double-penetrated by cops and lay down rails like the Manifest Destiny is depending on them. She's become swept up in it, and I've had to play Captain Save-a-Ho and "rescue" her from a number of bad scenarios.

When she's not doing drugs, she's asking me for money and rides to various places. We argue pretty much nonstop. Consequently, our close rate has dropped to levels that I consider abysmal. Something's got to give.

I drive out to the club to meet ChessClub and a couple of her crack hos. I can tell as soon as I look at her that Chessy is whacked out of her fucking skull. She's slurring and stumbling and hanging on Tina, spinning around and around. "Heeyyyyy baby," she exclaims when she sees me, her eyes barely able to focus. Inside, my heart drops. This is not the girl that I fell in love with in that stairway last summer. It's someone else. Or is it? Tina smirks at me in the background; she looks proud, like she's mocking me. *See what I did to your bitch? She's not yours anymore. She's mine.* I feel the hate welling up, seething.

"You're fuckin' wasted. This is disgusting. I told you about this shit! Fuck it. I'm leaving." Chessy's eyes widen, like she can't comprehend why I'm saying this to her. She just sort of teeters in front of me.

I turn on my heel and briskly walk out of the venue, ignoring her cries from behind me. I hear Tina saying, "Let him go, fuck him, let him go." I drive back home and go to bed.

I wake up when someone starts insistently ringing the doorbell. It's 3 A.M. I wait to see if one of the roommates gets it, if they're expecting someone perhaps. But I know who it is. Finally I get up, throw open the window and look down. ChessClub is standing at the top of the stairs, pressing the bell over and over. "HEY!" I yell down at her, "What do you want?!"

She looks up. Even from this height I can tell she's obliterated. "Lemme in motherfucker!"

"Fuck that, you're off your shit. Get the fuck out of here. Just go home!"

She starts yelling at the top of her lungs, "ASSHOLE!! FUCKING OPEN THIS DOOR ASSHOLE!! FUCKING DICK!! LEMME IN!!!"

Again, I refuse. Undeterred, she attempts to climb over the front gate, but in her condition ends up falling backward and tumbling down the concrete steps, landing in a pile down on the sidewalk.

She starts shrieking bloody murder, undoubtedly waking everyone within a two-block radius. She gets up and starts pacing back and forth in front of the house, wailing incomprehensible gibberish. I can see she's bleeding heavily but can't tell from where. Now I'm conflicted . . . if I let her in it's going to be a shit show for sure, but if I leave her out there she's going to get victimized. FUCK.

I go down and let her in. It starts.

She's cut on the elbow, and bleeding all over the floor, but appears otherwise unharmed. This is miraculous, given that she fell backward eight feet and then down a flight of concrete stairs. I'm honestly surprised she's not dead. As it is, this is a fucking nightmare, as she continues to scream in my face. "YOU ARE TRYING TO CONTROL MY LIFE! YOU DON'T WANT ME TO HAVE ANY FRIENDS, SO YOU CAN CONTROL MY LIFE!!!"

"Uh, babe, newsflash: those chicks are NOT your friends."

She doesn't listen, can't. "YES THEY ARE!! YOU CAN'T CON-TROL ME!!!!" She's completely berserk, alternately crying and physically attacking me. This goes on and on and on. I decide to remain silent and ignore her, let her wear herself out. I get into bed and stare at the ceiling while she continues to berate me. Finally, after what seems like hours, she passes out. I continue to stare at the ceiling.

CHESSCLUB R.I.P.

This is hard. I don't know exactly what to say.

I broke up with Heather this week. For real and for good. Somehow, the relationship lasted over a year. Which is funny to me, because when I started this whole "game" shit, I resolved that I would never have a girlfriend ever again. And sure enough, every girl I slept with was on borrowed time. It didn't matter how interesting, rich or even how hot she was, I would invariably become bored with her and cut it off after two or three fuck sessions. Most women, most people, just don't hold my interest.

That being the case, why did I become involved with Heather? It wasn't because of the whole "tandem hunting" thing, as that didn't even come up until about a month into the relationship. Before her, I wouldn't DREAM of being with a girl for a month, unless it was on a strictly "booty call" basis.

Looking back, the reason I felt differently about her was that the initial pickup took so much time, planning and energy. I plucked her out of a group of ten defensive guys, then she moved to Canada for six months, during which time we had a falling-out that I responded to by systematically fucking all of her friends. That's a lot of INVESTMENT. When it paid off, I was understandably reluctant to simply jettison her like all the others; it seemed a waste. Then she expressed interest in threesomes, and I was hooked.

For the first six months, it was incredible. Threesomes left and right; it seemed like I had found the Holy Grail of pickup. I took her on as a student of game because I saw a lot of potential in her. And we rocked shit . . . we would enter the club and tear the motherfucker apart. Bam bam bam, like clockwork. Clowning on dodes and high-fiving, we were an unstoppable team.

But when the fairy dust cleared and we started to get complacent and annoyed by each other's bullshit, it went downhill FAST. She stopped listening to my advice. She thought she was hot shit. We didn't go out as much. We started to get laid less and less, until it got to the point where we could only pull on workshop. It felt like I was back at square one, as far as game was concerned. And that's when the real arguments began. Those arguments where you say the things that you can never take back, things that will *never* be forgotten. The fights got more intense. We couldn't go out and game anymore, because we would invariably get in an argument that would in turn blow both our states. Even on autopilot, the tension would be simmering right below the surface.

Then there was the bloody screaming episode. I was so shaken by it that I called her *mother* the following morning, and told her that she was sick and needed some serious help. Mom came and got her, took her up to Napa where she recuperated for a while, got sober. When she came back, she got sick and had to have surgery, so I reluctantly took care of her. After she got better, we tried to go out, but it was the same old shit. More, I learned she was still in contact with Tina and the Cokewhores, despite her claims that she would cut them from her life. I finally decided that this was not healthy for me to be around. I hadn't had a fresh lay in *three months*. With Heather around, my game went to shit. I felt suffocated. Moreover, I kept thinking back to that crazy night . . . If the cops had come, they probably would have taken one look at the bloody screaming woman attacking me, hauled me off to jail and sorted it out later. No way I am gonna jeopardize myself like that.

She claims to have changed, but I don't see lasting change. Just superficial. I don't want to end up like Che's brother; his wife started out the same way, and now she's a full-blown raging alkie, who will stay up for three days drinking varnish, and at one point even attempted to kill his dog. I refuse to let ChessClub drag me down any longer. I tried to be the hero, to be supportive. I really tried. But I can't do this. I can't be around her unless she gets her shit together . . . and I'm not holding my breath.

I was weak. I allowed myself to love this girl. This only serves to reinforce my belief that everyone is a fucking creep and you can't trust ANYONE. Or rather, you can't EXPECT things from people.

Things are getting nasty, predictably. She's been harassing me and issuing thinly veiled threats, coming by my house with her buddies in tow for backup. I cannot be around her anymore. This kills me, because I thought she was gonna be a superstar, and she let me down. I would have done *anything* for this kid, would have given her the world. Just like last year when I spent months schooling my roommate Brian in the game— then he fucks the first scallywag who gives him the time of day, and he drops out of the program—I am let down again. Except this time it's hitting WAY closer to home. Lesson: no more fucking apprentices.

I suppose now that it's all over, I will go back to the method I employed previously to fill the need for intimacy: serial one-itis. Where I fall in love with every girl I fuck, but only for three days. Method acting. Then move on to the next and repeat the process. "Date, fuck, win," right? I live by the sword, so I guess I'll die by the motherfucker then. This is my gift, and my curse.

OFF NIGHT

I feel like shit tonight. I'm standing out back at the Rio, two vodka tonics in each hand, stacked on each other precariously. I've been sick this week. Several times tonight, I've coughed on girls, causing them to become upset and leave. Burning the candle at both ends has weakened my immune system; between RSD and the hotel, I've worked twenty-four days straight and counting. Not to mention the fact that I've been going out, getting hammered, and making out with strangers practically every night for the past three years.

Come to think of it, I've been getting sick a LOT lately. This isn't good at all. My voice isn't as crispy and hitting; people are able to talk over me. Beyond that, I'm just fucking things up in *general.* Last weekend, I conducted a workshop in Chicago that culminated in a drunken fight with a frat boy in a pizza shop during debrief. He threw a slice of pizza at me and I ducked, causing it to hit one of my elderly students in the face. A fucking disaster.

Earlier this afternoon, I called up a few chicks whose numbers I got over the weekend. All of them were flake; this was mildly upsetting since at the time, they had seemed fairly solid. Just goes to show, *you never know which numbers are going to flake.* Like, the one that you had screaming and pawing you for two hours can straight flake, and the one you talked to for three minutes on a bus answers on the first ring and screams, "Oh my God, I'm so glad you called, let's hang out!!" Knowing this, it didn't really bother me all that much, but it's sort of set the tone for the evening.

Christophe is in Europe, so in lieu of a solid wing, I invited a "civilian" friend, Pasquale. He's a youngster who has a lot of potential, but not much else. He has no finesse; he blurts a lot of counterproductive nonsense. No concept of wing tactics; he has a tendency to contradict me, making me look like some chode in front of the girls. Social pressure I can handle, but when your own "wing" is undermining you, that can take a toll. I would have been better off going solo.

It's also clear that we arrived too early. El Rio doesn't even get cool until eleven, but we rolled in at nine. That's TWO HOURS of dollar drinks before the targets arrive. By the time eleven rolls around, I'm already wasted. I usually take a disco nap, wake up at ten, get ready and roll in stone sober to go to work. Not tonight. As a result, my calibration is WAY off; I'm yelling stupid shit and acting a fool.

I'm standing on the deck leering around, wasted and coughing. I see four girls that look okay, and open them with Dental Floss. It goes fine, until Pasquale comes in and blows it by saying, "Why are you asking them about floss?" Fuck it, I just plow. More women enter the group. One is an 8, probably the hottest chick in the place. I ignore her and game the peers. She starts busting my balls, I bust her ass back, but my delivery and rhythm are off and it doesn't work very well. They're not entranced like they usually are. I feel like one of those random Lair guys I see out sometimes, where you can tell the chicks are just humoring them and waiting for them to leave. It's a bizarre feeling and I am NOT used to it. I continue to game the less-hot friends, but then I cough in their faces and they get pissed. I mention Journey and one of them becomes all excited. I sing a few bars of "Faithfully," but my voice sucks. Pasquale says, "Nobody wants to hear that," and the hot one starts to tool me. I make a lame comeback and basically get blown out. Shit, I haven't gotten blown out in a long fucking time, and it sucks.

I shake it off and turn to see an ex-student and his bro just standing there doing nothing. I tell him to go talk to some girls. He approaches a couple standing off to the side; meanwhile his friend asks me what I'm doing. I shrug and say, "Eh, not much, there's no hot chicks here."

He says, "What about that set?" indicating the one I got blown out of.

"That was a warm-up."

He says, "Pretty hot for a warm-up."

I resist the urge to kick him in the teeth. *What the fuck have you done tonight but sit there and watch me?*

I reply, "Yeah."

Eventually, I decide that it's probably best to fold 'em and pack it in. As I'm leaving, I see Nikki and Deb, these two hotties I met last week.

They're standing in line, and they call my name. The hotter one, Nikki, is on point as *fuck*, and during the initial interaction, she was super into me. Apparently, they've come specifically to see me, and now I'm fucked because I'm already leaving. What, am I gonna go back in and game them all fucked up? Not gonna happen. I weakly tell them I'll "see them around" and I go get a taco, head home and pass out. I wake up the following morning in bed fully clothed, with my boots on.

This was my first "off night" since getting back into the game for real (i.e., breaking up with Heather). I've been having all this great success, I was riding high, and I forgot that this kind of shit is inevitable. Part of the game. So, rather than beat myself up over it, I'll just do up a quick postmortem, file it and let it go. Every failure is a brick in my palace. I'm taking the next couple of nights off, going to bed early and taking my vitamins to shake this sickness. Next week, I won't go early, and I'll leave the civilians at home. Stick to the fuckin' script, get some more numbers and work that shit. As long as it doesn't become a trend, one night is nothing.

AULD LANG SYNE

A Monday sometime in September. It's a warm night . . . Indian summer. My venereal tests came out clean. It's like I won the sexual lottery. Strong like bull! For now at least. I have some vegan Sloppy Joes at Che's house, then bounce to the spot. I get there and there is a LONG LINE out front. Holy shit. I haven't seen a line here since the old glory days of Rio. Awesome.

I walk directly to the front of the line and push my way through. But the timing is wack, and right as I get up, the door guy is yelling at people to back up, and I get rebuffed. I'm stunned, I walk back outside and pretend to be on my cell phone so I don't look like a chode. Lame.

Heather walks up while I'm standing in line. It's been a month since I broke it off with her. This is the first time I've seen her in a social setting since the breakup. I say hello. I ask her if she wants to try some game out together; if it doesn't work out, we'll split up and it's every man for himself, no hard feelings. She agrees.

This other chick appears, some girl I opened a long time ago, whom Chessy and I had been trying to bang. We call her "FakeBi." Sometimes you get one of these chicks who likes the *idea* of a threesome, but when push comes to shove, she will not do it. Like, every time we would have her meet us, she would have at least one friend in tow. The sister, the coworker, sometimes even the boyfriend. The chick gets off on the *whiff* of kinky sexuality, but is in reality a fucking pussy. Sure enough, tonight she's here with four guys, including the boyfriend. After we greet her and she wanders off, I turn to Heather and say, "Fuck this chick, I've had it. Fresh chicks only tonight. GANGSTA!" This will be my catchphrase for the evening, along with "Need mah DRANK!!"

But I'm still stunned from not getting in, and the fact that I'm stoned out of my fucking mind isn't helping either. I call Christophe, who's already inside. "Wherrre ze fuck ahr zhou?" he says. It sounds superloud in there, like an F-16 taking off.

"I couldn't get past the line, what should I do?"

"What ze FUCK mahhn, just walk past ze lahn! What zze fuck ahr zhou theeenkeeen Djzhefphheee?" It occurs to me that he is correct, and simply walk up again. Thugs are staring me down as I brush past.

I just shout, "GANGSTA! Need mah DRANK!!!" The door guy sees me this time and lets me slide in, along with Chessy. We leave the FakeBi outside. "See you in there!"

It is *packed*, nice. Hot fun in the summertime. I get two vodka tonics, two dollars.

There are tons of "pickup guys" here. Looks like El Rio has garnered quite the reputation as a result of my online reports. I am amused as I watch all of them greet "Chessy" quite warmly. "Heeeey girl!!!!" Big hugs. Funny, I mention the breakup offhanded once in chat and somehow everyone knows a day later. Hey, it's all good, they can have at it . . . if they dare.

We post up out back on the deck and start scanning the crowd. FakeBi finally gets in, and I'm being fairly dismissive of her. Some dude she's with asks me how we know her. I say, "Her? We fucked her." He looks really disturbed; hopefully he will tell the boyfriend. I laugh, then we start scoping targets.

Christophe is in a mood. He shouts, "Hey mahn, peek zee hardezd set een hair, I don geeva FUCK!" I point, he shoot, and he blows some dumbass out. I laugh and stop paying attention after that, opening some drunk chicks halfheartedly.

Time passes. We're just standing there. I haven't really done shit all night. Meanwhile every other pickup dork is deep in set, they're probably thinking to themselves, *jlaix ain't shit, he's all hype, he's just been standing there talking to guys all night.*

Yeah right.

A little hottie in a sundress walks by, an 8, and I bark, "HEY, HEY," at her. Opened.

She asks, "Where can I find a lesbian?"

I tell her, "Shit ho, you're in luck. I'm a lesbian." She thinks I'm just a dumbass until I follow up with, "Allow me to introduce myself: k. d. lang." I sing a few bars of "Constant Craving" and she cracks up. Then I say, "And this bitch here," gesturing to Chessy, "well, she's not a lesbian, but she does lick a mean pussy! Ain't that right?" I sock her on the arm. The target laughs. I say, "So, are you like a straight dyke or what? Do you bang guys?"

"Only in threesomes." *Boom.*

I start stacking game. She's starry-eyed. I command them to make out. They do it. I spit some more game, then I kiss her. We go out back and meet her friends. We find out the chick just turned eighteen; I choke on a piece of ice and get pre-cum on my boxers.

Some big thug-looking dude walks up to me and starts to compliment me on how I cut the line. "Were you in here before? 'Cause I was like yo, they was in here, before so I didn't trip on you."

I tell him that no, we had only just arrived. "Just be confident, man!"

He laughs and says, "Yo mayeng, I like yo style mayeng!"

"GANGSTA!! Need mah DRANK!!!"

Time to venue-change. I suggest we go to Phone Bizzle. She protests, "My friends are going to give me a ride home!" I tell her I will "give her a ride." She finds her friends and tells them she's leaving with us. What the fuck, this seems too easy. Gotta love the power of rudimentary game on teenagers.

As we walk out, the FakeBi comes up and says to me, "You guys are a piece of work."

I wink and say, "Right back at ya." Buh-bye!

Bizzle. The girls sit, I get drinks. I force her to make animal noises in exchange for the drink. I languidly reel out gibberish; there's no passion behind it. The girls make out. Then I make out with the target. Then we have a three-way makeout, and after this, we take turns attempting to throw popcorn in each other's mouths. The bar closes.

Club Jeffy time. She's like, "I have to go home!"

I keep saying, "Yeah, later." When we get there, I basically go *straight* into it. The girls start making out, but something's not right. The girl claims to be a virgin and puts up massive resistance when I go for her pants. The vibe sours. I try to turn it back around, without much enthusiasm. Finally, the girl gets a call from her friends and takes this opportunity to leave. Numbers are exchanged, but I know it's not going anywhere. She's gone. Heather and I make uneasy conversation for a bit, then she decides to go home as well.

Sitting alone, I type up my customary field report of the evening. When I get to the part where the chick leaves, however, I can't continue. I pause for a moment, then write an entirely different ending, one where Chessy and I actually fuck the girl at the end. I post it online. Immediately after hitting the "submit" button, I am overwhelmed with a sense of shame. In the thousands of reports I have posted, never *once* have I deviated from my policy of telling nothing but the unvarnished truth. Why I decided to violate my code now, I have no idea. Regardless, I leave the post as it is and prepare for bed. As I brush my teeth and stare at myself in the mirror, one word continues to reverberate through my skull:

PATHETIC.

DOUBLE VISION

Since I ditched the girlfriend, my game has come back like a fucking locomotive. It's not just the freedom either. It's the fact that my *intent* is back. I feel excited as fuck. I feel like the baddest motherfucker. I feel alive.

When I go out now, it is with the frame of looking for a new primary. She must be hot, smart as fuck and successful. With that in mind, there is no fear or approach anxiety at all. I just go up, and I'm screening them hardcore, right off the bat. Like, when I do the whole "you'd make a nice new girlfriend, can you cook?" bit, it's not a scripted routine, it's REAL. That's right, jlaix is in the market for a new primary. Desired qualities include: tall, blonde, big tits, bisexual.

Another thing that's been helping me lately is the fact that I've been getting back into some really intense rapport shit. I've been running so many RSD programs that I developed a tendency to just blast chicks with attract material, because on workshop one can't get too deep in set; you just do some quick demonstration for the students, but you can't sit there for two hours. As a result, my rapport game has atrophied, so I've been boning up.

It's Sunday, so I call up a girl to set up a Day 2, this tall skinny chick who works at the club we go to on Thursdays. I tell her to meet me at the Mint for some karaoke. I go to my boy Che's house to blaze some bomb and fuck with my iPod before I hit this shit. But right before I'm about to leave, the chick calls and flakes. Since I'm stoned, I don't ignore and go relentless as I usually would. I just kinda smile into the air and say, "Oh cool, yeaaaahh, tha's cool." I know that I've blown it as soon as I hang up, but I think, *FUCK IT,* and decide to go to the bar alone. Che decides to come along.

We get to the karaoke bar, and there's not really anyone in there. There is one set, consisting of two 7s and some guy. I open with Thug Lovin'. I am OWNING these fucks. They think I'm drunk or high or something, because I am. I win them over. I start telling them how I'm looking for a girlfriend. Then it comes my turn to sing. I get up and I'm nervous, because my voice is sort of fucked from the weekend, and I'm singing a brand-new song, "Juke Box Hero" by Foreigner.

I DESTROY it. Not the most technically adept performance, but it was GUT, which is more than enough to devastate the casual bachelor-ette-work party karaoke-goer. The crowd is high-fiving me left and right as I walk off the stage.

This other chick approaches us, a petite little Latina chick in a mini-skirt, smoking. Adorable. A low 9. I start stacking game, routines mixed with vibe, then the hardcore qualifying. I'm going overboard, I can sense I'm in the danger zone, but it doesn't matter, she qualifies herself to me on everything . . . EVERYTHING. I'm asking her all this absurd shit like, "Are you successful? What are you doing with your life? I can't have a scrub," and "You're very pretty. People envy you because of the way you look. But you're lonely. You're far more lonely than you deserve to be. I know how it feels." I escalate HARD on her and she reciprocates, oh my God.

I get called up to sing again. I do "All Out of Love." I actually cry during it, because I think about Heather and the breakup. When I get offstage, the chick is rubbing her legs like a cricket. I do a takeaway and hit the restroom.

As I'm walking back to the girl, the guy from the previous set, whom I've merged with this chick, comes up to me. He sort of takes me aside, like he's about to tell me a secret. "Bro, you're looking for a girlfriend? This chick wants you, she told us. You can get her number!"

I laugh. "Get her number? Cool, thanks man!" He nods and walks off. *Get her number.* I just pull her after that. We go straight to my house. She's saying, "You're gonna make me do bad things." Yes.

We shoot some hoops. We smoke some bomb, then I lay her down. This is going so well. She is smoking hot, and she seems so perfect, we are just vibing so naturally and having a great time. It is ON. Then I notice she has a raging cold sore on her mouth. *FUCK.* Well, this means no kiss-ing obviously. I just start on her neck. Then we get naked. I start eating her out, because "I wanna lick it."

She loves it. She tells me I "eat pussy like a chick." I guess that's a compliment. I know my pussy licking is my only legitimately redeeming quality. But it seems weird, because there's no kissing, that intimacy is missing. I can feel it, feel the weirdness. Without warning, she stops everything cold, right as I'm about to rail. She says, "Can we just be friends?"

Now normally, I would just whip out the old tactics and proceed to defuse it in a very methodical fashion. But I'm so drunk that I just don't give a fuck. I say, "Get out of here." Just like that. INSTANTLY slam from deep rapport and oral sex to chilly cold blood.

"What? Are you serious?"

"Yeah, this is bullshit. Leave."

She says, "Okay." She gets up and gets her shit together. Before she leaves, I ask her to do me a favor, to not smash my windshield or slash my tires. She says, "What the fuck. I would never do that." She leaves, I pass out.

In the morning, I go outside and look at my car. She kept her promise. The window is fine, the tires are fine. But she kicked the SHIT out of the quarter panel. Well played. If I ever see her again, I'll just laugh; she gets props for working within the parameters. I just can't get mad at this kind of shit anymore. Still, I am particularly aggravated due to the fact that it was *so on*. Had I simply hung in there and been patient, I would have smashed, but fuck it. I don't have time to fuck around with bullshit.

I WANNA KNOW WHAT LOVE IS

I wake up from my disco nap on Monday night at around 9 P.M. I drive to my dealer's place and pick up a twenty of chronic, a handful of Vicodin, and some boner pills. He gives me five Cialis. Nice . . . brand name. I tuck them in my pocket and then decide to make my way to El Rio.

Some of the guys online have been clamoring to hear a jlaix report where I stay sober during the pickup. Well, too bad. They can go fuck themselves. What is this, prison camp?

I convince Che to come along. We get there, and I'm superexcited, on the prowl for my new girlfriend. I step to the first group of girls I see, without thinking. There are three of them, two 6s and one 8 wearing a cowhide skirt. They open instantly due to my nonchalant yet supremely confident demeanor, then I slam them with some high-octane material, which I deliver impeccably: I AM IN STATE. The nimbus, the zone, my calibration is on. I'm in the homestretch, riding that shit on the very edge, knowing just how much to let it out.

I befriend the peers first. All of a sudden, one of the girls asks me, out of left field, "Are you the dating coach? We heard there was a dating coach here and we came to find him." Somebody's been telling tales out of school.

I say, "What the fuck is that?" They say it's like *Hitch*, that movie. "That's absurd." I finish my drink and order another.

Then I isolate the 8, Cowhide. She tells me her name is Ellen. We go out back to the deck, and as I'm gaming her up there are several thugs milling about, sort of shooting glances at her like they're gonna roll up and steal her from me . . . yeah right! These thugs are so cuddly and adorable, they act all hard but they couldn't even pick up their own balls. Chodes in Roc-a-Wear.

I run the usual shit at the appropriate times, but mainly I'm getting close to her, in her face, touching her, and using my voice and facial expressions to hypnotize her; it's the training taking over, total unconscious competence. I am aware that she is a low 8, as opposed to, say, a 9 . . . where my margin for error would be substantially less, but I suspect I am "on" enough to handle even that challenge, should one present herself. It seems so easy. Then a couple of 9s walk in and I am VERRRY tempted to eject and hit them up, but things are so obviously on with this target that I demur and decide to play it to the hilt. I'm not a huge fan of the "short set method" these days; sometimes when you hop from group to group you spread yourself too thin and end up with nothing. Then again, there is something to be said for not being afraid to "trade up" midgame. Regardless, I make my choice and stick to it.

I do a takeaway and make a round, chat with an ex-student and exhort him to "stop being a faggot," right before I shove him right into a pair of girls. I lecture someone else about something for like five minutes. I sell one of the Cialis to some guy in the bathroom for ten bucks. Then I see that little lesbian "virgin" that I almost fucked with Heather a few weeks ago. Some Fan Club President is talking with her.

I stroll up and just stand between them. Ignoring the chode, I say very calmly, "I hate you," with this smirk on my face. The chode is blown out and looks indignant; at least that's what I assume he looks like, as I do not look at or acknowledge him at all. I then punch the chick lightly and say, "Hahaaaa just kidding, you know I love you. So what's been going on?"

She's acting very cold toward me. I think she's embarrassed or something; it's clear that I'm freaking the hell out of her. After our initial encounter, she called Heather and basically told her she wanted a relationship with her and NOT ME. Lesbian Virgin apparently wants nothing to do with jlaix. Okay, I chat her friends for a bit and then leave.

Back to my other chick. Some dumb fuck is there, and I just ignore him, he's a complete "doojz bahg" as Christophe would say. He makes some very weak attempt to make me look bad, but I just use standard "display of lower value" tactics and he is suitably tooled. He's dead on his feet and doesn't even realize it. He makes some other quip, and I come back at him with, "Wow, bro, you're fucking hilarious. We could team up . . . you'll be my sidekick like Ed McMahon, I'll say something and you'll be all up my ass." Not a challenge, but I respect the fact that he even tried, so when he goes for rapport with me later, I chat with him for a while, as he seems intrigued by the "dating coach" shit. I cop to it to the girls, and they start busting my balls for it, but I just act sad and say, "Hey, don't make fun of my job. I don't make fun of yours. That's really mean." This seems to completely disarm them; this somehow makes it "okay" that I'm a professional ho-bag.

By this time, I'm into the hardcore qualifying again. Jesus Christ, this is powerful stuff when applied at the right time, which I'm learning is fairly early—but not too early. In my opinion, this was the main problem with the old model from the early days of the pickup scene, where these weirdos would roll up and immediately get the girls to visualize golden bubbles of desire and a unicorn from beyond time.

Anyway, things are going along nicely when all of the sudden, Lesbian Virgin rolls up all serious and says to my target, "I need to talk to you."

Cowhide is taken aback by her grave demeanor, and is like, "Who the fuck are you?"

After a pause, I figure out what's going on: Lesbian Virgin has mistaken my target for Heather. I laugh, because they do look somewhat similar. I say, "Oh, you thought she was Heather! Nah, this is Ellen! That's funny." Then I turn somewhat "apologetic" and say, "Listen . . . I'm sorry I flaked on you yesterday." She just stands there looking embarrassed.

Cowhide says, "Who's Heather?"

I say, with Lesbian Virgin standing right there, "Oh, Heather's my ex-girlfriend. We fucked this chick last week." Everyone laughs, and the little Lesbian Virgin slinks away, her face red as a beet. Fuck her. *Try to front on me? I'll own your ass back to the stone age.* It's kind of fucked up how well a brutal owning like this can skyrocket attraction, but it certainly does the job in this instance, as well as letting the target know that I expect threesomes if she's gonna fuck around with me.

Closing time. I venue-change Ellen and her friend to Phone Bizzle. That chode tags along. I try to offload a creepy old gay guy on him, but he is able to escape. We all end up going together. Fine, he can occupy the friend. At the Bizzle, he tries to tool me again by saying, "She's going home with you man!" all loud and shit.

I look at him like he's crazy and say, "What the fuck dude, that's gross; this chick is my little sister!"

After Phone Bizzle, I give the chicks a ride home. I decide to play solid game on this one and get the number. I get it solid as possible and drive them home. As they get out, I help Cowhide out of the car and hug and kiss her lightly. Magical.

The next day, I call her after work. She answers on the first ring as instructed. I do a quick callback humor bit, then tell this story about an incident at the hotel's restaurant where a guest had complained to the waiter, demanding that someone "toss his salad" over and over, very loudly. I let her talk for a while, then I think, *fuck it, I'm going for the meetup.* "Meet me at karaoke later. We'll have fun, it'll be cool." After some mild convincing (basically just strong frame and leading questions like, "What are you doing AFTER that?") she agrees to meet at nine. I apply a soothing gel mask with antioxidant green tea extract and clean up my house. Vacuum, bathroom (ensuring toilet paper levels, cleaning piss off the floor), dim the lights, set the music, put a glass of water next to the bed so I won't have to get up after I fuck her to get a drink. I pop a Cialis and leave.

She's already sitting at the bar when I arrive. I greet all the staff, get a drink, then approach her. She looks good. It seems a little awkward at first, but I think it's just in my head because I notice her facing me. I withhold my body language for a while, then turn to face her and start in. A couple of minutes pass, then I find my groove. I stare into her eyes and slowly I feel the serial one-itis coming on, like good blotter acid. *Love, ohhh love* . . .

I look down and my eyes go wide; she is wearing a tiny black leather miniskirt. I told her on the phone to "wear something cute . . . so we match," but this is going above and beyond the call of duty. I am mesmerized by this for a while, but I get it under control.

Now the qualifying and rapport begins. I find commonalities and do a bunch of other stuff like philosophies and identity grounding. At some point, after I sing "Can't Fight This Feelin'" by REO Speedwagon, but *before* I sing "Juke Box Hero," I get the feeling I may be going overboard and I simply move into vibing and start grabbing her, rubbing her. I say, "Let's get out of here."

Where are we going? Club Jeffy. Usual routine. Pretty straightforward after that, "come here let me show you a trick" and tonguedown. Soon I wanna lick it, and proceed to do so. There is mild resistance. I just say, "I'm the best, you will like it," as I snuffle and snort around at her crotch . . . finally the gates open, and holy shit whaddya know she's not wearing any panties. My already painfully throbbing, pharmaceutically enhanced wiener becomes harder by several degrees on the Mohr scale. Guess what comes next? I eat it and then FUCK THE SHIT OUT OF HER.

After I finish, I drink another beer. We talk a little about the pickup, debrief. She says she wasn't going to sleep with me, that she didn't want to be "the next number on my scorecard."

"Is that how you feel? Come on," I say, "it's not like that."

"Yeah, but I know about you, they talk about you. They say you are a walking STD. How many girls have you been with, Jeffy?"

"Oh, I don't know . . ."

She doesn't stop. "No, really . . . how many?"

Well, she asked for it. I say, "Your new name is 85." I wave at her, "Hi, 85!"

She starts giving me shit about being this notorious player, so I tell her, "Oh, I see how it is. You're just another Jeffy curiosity seeker . . . you just wanna poke at the freak with a stick." I look sad. "You don't know what it feels like to be treated like an object!" I turn away. She starts laughing. I turn back. I get on her, and fuck her for like an hour and a half straight. We go to sleep.

When I wake up, I'm late for work, because I forgot to set the alarm. Nevertheless, the Cialis lasts thirty-six hours, so I fuck the shit out of her *again*. She takes the legendary "walk of shame." I don't know why they call it that; there's no reason to be ashamed of sweet love, *or* about getting your cervix pulverized into jelly by a fat drunk on wiener pills.

Nice girl, I like her. Wanted to fuck the shit out of her again tonight, but she was busy and apologized. Oh well, got workshop tomorrow, fresh chicks await! I guess for the moment I'll just fuck some kind of gourd or something, a summer squash perhaps.

SODA MODEL

It's pretty dead at the Rio. Christophe hasn't shown up yet, and I'm talking to an ex-student. This guy is out there in the field all the time, he's taking voice lessons, etc. He has a lot of dedication, which is good, because he will need it. He's got a long way to go. I know, because I had to endure the journey myself. He has a decent grasp of the tactics, but his inner game isn't there yet. His frame control leaves much to be desired. He still can't *feel* the rhythm and grab it.

He's grilling me with questions, and I oblige, but I'm in a dismal mood. It's like working at the bank and going out to the bar, and dudes are coming up asking you about mortgages and APR and shit. I just want to drink. I tell him to stop talking and start *playing*. I send him into this two set that's sitting on the stairs, a 7 and a 9 whom I had been eyeing earlier. Small chick, great ass, beautiful face. He rolls up and holds it for a while. He stalls out shortly thereafter, and the chicks leave.

Christophe sails in like Jacques Cousteau. This little Frenchman is a living GOD. But not tonight. He seems chodely, we hit up a five-set together, but his game is lukewarm and consequently we are unable to hold the attention of the group for long; they turn away.

I'm like, "Screw this, dude. YOU of all people can NOT go chode on me. Don't make me punch you, man." He agrees to shake it off. We go back inside. Lo and behold, there are the two chicks the student approached earlier. They're sitting at the end of the bar. I swallow, take a deep breath and roll up.

"Hey guys," I say as I tap them on the arms, "settle this for me and my friend . . ."

They look annoyed.

"So check it out. I just got this Louis Vuitton luggage the other day, and my friend says it's gay . . . and he's FRENCH. I know, right? But seriously, does it make me gay . . ."

They continue to look at me dubiously.

" . . . or SUPER GAY?" I snap my fingers in a "Z" in front of them.

The hot one laughs. They're cracking, but not completely. The 9 starts testing me immediately about having a leather bag and how it kills animals and how it is murder. I bust on her for being an activist. I plow with humor. Just feeling for the beat and jumping on it. It's hard going, but I keep my frame.

She brings it back to the animal rights stuff again. I say, "Are you STILL talking about that? That's so two minutes ago. Look, I'm sorry. It's just quite jarring when the defense mechanisms that protect one's fragile sense of reality are shattered. This is a whole new world for me." Plow. "Besides, the bag is FAKE anyway. It's plastic, so in actuality it's none of the above. It's not gay, it's not supergay, it's not MURDER, it's . . . GHETTO FABULOUS."

She laughs and says, "Or just ghetto. Depending on who you ask." She smirks at me. I smirk back and shake my head, ever so slightly.

The friend asks me if I'm from L.A. I ask why, and she says because I am "well put-together." I'm wearing jeans and a baby blue T-shirt with flowers and an adorable cartoon kitten, blowing its own brains out with a .45.

I improv a lot of new attract material. Chrispy enters and I throw him an accomplishment introduction: "Have you guys ever heard of Q-PLAYER? This guy wrote it."

The friend lights up and exclaims, "Oh my GOD! I use that all the time! You WROTE it?!" Wow. I've been saying this shit for three years, and this is the first time they've actually heard of it. It's fate. Chrispito engages her and we split the set. We venue-change the girls to the patio.

I start talking social dynamics. The friend tells me I'm "charismatic."

I say, "Well, I just try to feel the energy, and get a hold on it, and vibe with it and mold and shape it. It's ultimately just an expression of your inner state, conveyed by the rhythms you use to direct the energy of the interaction."

She looks at me deeply and says, "Thank you." I do this with most sets these days, delivering the same lectures I give students on program about game, as an interactive value demonstration.

I qualify them hard. "Are you a drug addict? Are you emotionally mature? If things get intimate, would you act weird?" The chick lights up a cigarette and I demonstrate that I have standards by saying, "Oh, you smoke? Gross."

She qualifies herself. "No, not all the time, only when I get drunk." They both leave to get another drink, and on their way back out, the hot one gets waylaid by some chodes doing a documentary or something. They're obviously trying to mack, but I've made the friend love me, so I tell her to go get rid of them, and she complies. I don't actually hear it, but Chrispy says, "Oh mahn, eet wahs BRUTAHL, thees chick blow them owt bettair than wee evair cood, hahaha!"

We venue change them to Bizzle. More rapport. She's quite thin, petite and very classically beautiful with dark hair. This is the kind of girl you rarely see in this part of the Mission; hell, the kind of girl you rarely see *anywhere*. I ask her if she's a Jewish-American Princess, because she seems like one. Turns out she is from Long Island. I laugh. I learn that she's the only child of wealthy parents, a Harvard graduate and a model. I ask her about the modeling, and she tells me she recently did a shoot for Pepsi Free. I start calling her "Soda Model," which seems to amuse her. For some reason, I'm feeling expansive and so I tell her all about my involvement with the pickup arts and RSD. "A *New York Times* bestselling book just came out about it," I say, beaming with pride, "I'm on page 351." She's fascinated by it. I oversell Club Jeffy to her. "Dude, I live in a PALACE. I have a fifty-gallon aquarium and a basketball court in my house. But you can only stay fifteen minutes."

We go to Club Jeffy. The aquarium DVD is playing on the plasma, and we shoot Nerf Hoops. Turns out Chrispy can't isolate the friend, however, as she's married. So they just leave after a while. I number close the Soda Model. As she's walking out, I bust out some quick push-pull to cap it.

I call her the next night. She doesn't return my call until 2 A.M., while I'm driving home from a girl's house. So the NEXT night, I call her again. She doesn't return it. I wonder if I blew it calling so much.

Whatever. I just go to the karaoke bar by myself. I send her a text message: "Your loss dork . . . karaoke night . . . I'm leaving town tomorrow see you next week!" I get called to the stage, and I sing "We Are the Champions." Suddenly she starts texting me.

> **Her:** dork? How harsh, what kind of monster are u?
>
> **Me:** oh sorry . . . nerd. Come meet me down here. We are just having a ball and a hell of a time.
>
> **Her:** where r u
>
> **Me:** Mint Lounge
>
> **Her:** is it raining? I hear noise outside
>
> **Me:** You are on drugs. It's beautiful. Now cut the shit and get your sweet ass down here
>
> **Me:** you better hurry I'm drinking rounds of the worst scotch in the bar and Budweiser

Screw this, I think, and I just call her. She doesn't answer. I hang up and immediately call again. This time, she answers. I blurt into the phone, "I'm not a needy stalker . . . I'm drunk, see the difference?"

She laughs, "Oh, right."

I say, "I just sang. Come down here. It is awesome."

"I don't know," she says, "why don't you come here?"

Uh, okay! I get the address and drive over. I am wearing a "THUG LIFE" T-shirt, fifteen pounds of obviously fake bling, a pink suit jacket with black pinstripes and bunny ears. I throw a coin at her window and she lets me in.

She's there with her roommate. As I walk in, they look at me and are taken aback. "Do you just go out like this all the time?"

"Only for karaoke," I say. They have rabbits in their house. I hop around, expecting to be accepted as one of them. The rabbits appear frightened.

I befriend the roommate. I keep having to adjust my body language, because I'm intimidated by their beauty. Both of these girls are solid 9s. Strange after all this time, this still creeps in. It is insidious, you constantly have to watch for it. Like, I catch myself crossing my arms and have to correct it.

They ask me about the pickup gig. "What do you tell the clients? How do they act?"

I say that I tell them to "act normal and don't be a chode." I then pretend to BE a chode, and emulate one. Pecking (leaning in at the waist), grabbing, qualifying myself to them, asking them approval-seeking questions. They sit there on the couch giggling at my portrayal.

After a while, I leave with Soda Model. We go to a nearby club. There's a guy dressed like a pimp out front, with a velvet rope. I'm like, "What the hell? It's WEDNESDAY." The guy eyes my bunny ears approvingly and lets us in. It is deserted inside. We get drinks and I start hardcore rapport. I talk about loneliness, sincerity, incredible connections and relaxing and enjoying the company of someone. I tell her she has a fat girl personality. She starts telling me stuff like she wants to help me run programs; she went to Harvard and she's smart, and she knows how to pull hot chicks, etc.

I say, "Do you want to kiss me?"

"I don't know . . ." Boom . . . I kiss her, then back off. I talk about romance and mention again that I hope she's not the kind of person who would act weird if things got intimate. She qualifies herself again.

I take a piss. I've covered all bases. *Solid game has been run; there's nothing else to do but pull the trigger,* I tell myself. I hope I can sack up and do it. We leave.

Back at the house, we're sitting on her couch. The roommate has gone to bed; they share a bed, so we're just sitting alone in the living room, on the couch, watching *Battlestar Galactica*. I'm stalling and I don't know why. She's pretty hot, and I'm choding out. Although I've been in this exact situation dozens upon dozens of times before, for some reason I am having trouble making the first move. Breaking the silence, she says, "So, what would you tell your students to do at this point?"

"Uh . . . yeah, right." I actually take a second to think about it. "Well, I would probably tell them to just start making out with the chick and see what happens from there." She smiles. I start making out with her, and before you know it . . .

"I wanna lick it," says Jeffy. I lick it. We pull out the rickety sofa bed and basically spend the next couple of hours destroying it. We cuddle all night, and go again in the morning. It is sweet and ruthless. I leave the house with birds singing sweetly in my soul.

Then I walk to my car and BOOM . . . there's a parking ticket stuffed under my windshield wiper. A classic forty-dollar San Francisco street cleaning violation. I hate this; it's like I paid for sex. Oh well, it doesn't matter, it can't break my state. I throw it in the glove compartment and drive off in the morning light. Looks like I have a new primary.

WEIRDNESS

I've been dating the Soda Model for almost a month now. In that time, I've learned that she's legitimately bisexual. The guys on the forum cautioned me to not try to mold the next girl I got into a relationship into "ChessClub 2.0," but the chick is straight-up asking me to make it happen. She knows what the deal is, and frankly, I think that was in large part why she got with me in the first place. So I decided, fuck it, I'm gonna do it up.

Problem is, Soda is nowhere near as naturally adept at picking up as Chessy. I was cocky; I assumed I would be able to train any chick into a cyborg hunter like ChessClub, no problem. In reality, I got extremely lucky the first time around. I'm just a dumb bastard who got some shit dropped in his lap.

Our preliminary forays into the field have revealed that Soda has poor vocal projection, poor frame control, approach anxiety and basically just lacks the *killer instinct* that Chessy had. I have come up with an idea, however. When I want to fire someone at work, I usually have them train their own replacement before I do it. Why not do the same here? Have Heather train her, from a girl's perspective, letting her know it's all right for her to step into that predatory role.

After having dogged Heather out pretty hardcore for over a month, not even speaking to her, I call her up and invite her to dinner. She accepts, and at the restaurant, I present her with a choice: she can continue to come and assist me on RSD programs, provided she trains up the new girl. She agrees.

I arrange for the girls to meet at El Rio, and they hit it off pretty well. Full disclosure between all parties. Heather works on her, then they trade numbers, and we leave.

A couple of nights later, I'm at Soda's house, and Heather comes over to get wasted with us. We all pass out in Soda's bed; no sex ensues. But the next day, Soda Model's all like, "Heather is so pretty . . ."

So. Pros and Cons of having these chicks fuck me together:

PRO: Gets the "ball rolling" on the idea of threesomes with me and the new girl (even though Soda Model has had many of them before, just not with me). Gets her excited to pull ass from cold approaches when she sees firsthand how experienced I am at threesomes.

CON: Weird fucked-up jealousy shit happens. Also, if I hold off, I could then use banging Heather as an incentive, like, "We can't fuck her until we pull off a cold approach," to motivate Soda.

Look. I know *I* won't have issues with it, and I honestly couldn't give a fuck what Heather thinks, so the only concern is with Soda Model. I brought this caveat up to her, and she said, "No, I wouldn't freak out. She doesn't threaten me at all." I'm not sure whether to take this at face value.

The bottom line is that I really don't give a fuck WHAT happens, since I'll find new chicks, just as hot, and in a relatively short period of time, should both of them bail. So I think I'm gonna bring them both over tomorrow night and fuck the shit out of them.

Went ahead and did the Chessy/Soda threesome last night. Video-taped it. The girls were both very drunk. They started dominating me, holding me down and spanking my ass and making me say shit. Then I fucked them, and one of them puked, then I got the bullwhip down and started working them over with it. Fucked them some more after this, then went to sleep.

No real weirdness to speak of. Well, actually, *I* felt weird. I was trying to pay more attention to Soda Model, to allay any potential jealousy. She called me on it today, saying that she didn't want Heather to feel left out, basically telling me to treat her equally. "I'm not threatened by her," she said, again.

The thing is . . . I think *I am*. I don't want Soda forming some "re-lationship" with Heather, and I certainly don't want some "three-way relationship" with the both of them. Those were the only problems, and we dealt with it in a very forthcoming manner this afternoon. I think it's gonna work out for the best. We'll see.

TRANSFORMING INTO A CHICK

I find myself becoming more and more like a chick every day, possibly as a side effect of studying their psyche and being surrounded by them so much. I've heard of a similar phenomenon in the medical profession, where people who clinically study the mentally insane become insane themselves.

I'm at the bar, gaming some chick that I've known for a while. Nikki.

She's twenty-one years old and absolutely beautiful. Superfit and tan Latina girl with blonde hair. I've gone on a "date" with her before, where I ended up pulling her to my pad and making out with her in bed, but didn't close because I had to work early and couldn't dismantle the last-minute resistance. She left amicably, and it seemed like it was only a matter of time before we hooked up for real. Tonight, she's telling Chrispy she loves me and shit, and it's clearly on.

Then, out of nowhere, she goes to some "alpha male" wannabe chode and starts making out with him. Okay, I know what's going on here . . . it's a jealousy plotline designed to test my reaction. The correct response is to go in and blow out the chode, something I've done many *many* times before. But instead I just get annoyed and disgusted with the chick and leave. Chrispito and I go to another bar.

She calls me. "Are you at Pops?" I am. Ten minutes later, she shows up with the chode in tow. I simply ignore her. She even tries to get my attention by touching me on the arm as she walks by, but I pay her no heed.

She goes to the other end of the bar and sits there with the chode, constantly looking at me. Again, I know she wants me to blow the guy out. It would be easy. Eclipse his fucking ass with superior game, get the girl's attention, ignore him and pull her away. Simple. He's not even a true alpha, I can tell by looking at him . . . he's just a fucking tool. But I am sickened by this shit. I refuse to fall into her frame, even though I know *this is the game and this is how it is played.* I just feel disgust, and pity for her. What the fuck makes people act like this? Fucking weak. I walk out without saying anything.

When I arrive home, I get angry at myself for not stepping up. I have a little freak-out that involves me sobbing and incoherently yelling, "I don't wanna be fucking 'Master Player Guy' all the fuckin' time!" over and over again, then throwing the television through the front window. It rips the blinds down with it and lands out in front of the house in a heap of glass, on the sidewalk. I send Nikki a text message:

Me: You're a creep. I have neither the time nor the inclination to play your stupid games. Please just leave me alone.

I delete her phone number. I need to be removing myself from this bullshit. I've already got my hot girlfriend; why do I need this shit? More insidiously, I notice I've been very emotionally reactive lately . . . this is so unlike me I don't know what the fuck is happening. What I did tonight is something a chick would do. It's like, to play this game, you have to have a condom on your heart. But CONDOMS SUCK. I don't want a heart condom. I want to go raw dog.

I'm not sure how much of this is attributable to the diet pills I've been taking lately. I'm all cracked out and I've lost ten pounds in two weeks. What's that you're saying, change my diet? PSHHH. Next thing you know, you'll be telling me to work out. What the fuck.

RAPPORT CHALLENGE

It's Soda Model. When we met, she expressed interest in tandem hunting. So I tried to teach her game. It didn't take, because she felt it was "unladylike" or some shit to be a predator like that. I thought ChessClub might be able to set her straight (so to speak), and so against most people's advice, I set up the easy threesome. I told Heather that if she started having a relationship with her behind my back, I would ostracize her for good.

Sure enough, guess what's happened? They've started going to dyke nights without me. A couple of weeks ago, they went out and picked up some chicks, went back to their house and had an all-night five-way strap-on gang bang with chicks and cocaine. I hung out with Soda a few days later. We went shopping and generally had a fun time, but when we got back to her house and I went to bang her, she was like, "No, no . . . I feel dirty because of the coke gang bang. I don't want to fuck anyone for some time."

My instinct told me, "She's lying. She's trying to chode me out. Leave." I essentially told her she was bullshit, and left.

There are probably a hundred reasons why she wants to stop being physical with me. Maybe she's trying to regain some kind of sexual control over me. Maybe she's already fucking somebody else and is lying. Regardless, I will find a way to fix this.

A week passes, I don't call her. She doesn't call me either, but then texts me "what's up." I respond immediately.

> **Me:** my threshold for BS has been exceeded.
> **Her:** you send the message my time and company is not valuable in itself.
> **Me:** Rocks and gold, fuck off princess.
> **Her:** I'm withdrawing sex from everyone to see who is my real friend and who is waiting to get in my pants.

I unleash a rapid-fire barrage of texts:

> **Me:** I feel you're using ME for my personality.
> I'm not your gay girlfriend, I have my own criteria for who I hang out with, who the fuck are you to judge me for that.
> You ain't shit. You're a selfish rich kid who has issues because she happens to look okay. Poor baby, everyone wants to fuck you.
> Look, I trust my intuition and the SECOND I feel manipulated I'm out.
> You've totally alienated me with this BS when the truth is, I would have been the best friend you had. Ho hum.

I wait two minutes, then execute my finishing move:

Me: I would fuck all of your friends just to spite you . . . if you
had any.

At this point, she gets all defensive. I'm like, "WTF do you want from
me, I don't have time for this shades of gray crap. Come over right now
or leave me be."

She makes a funny comment:

Her: The reason I want you in my life is to sell you to the
russian gov't.

I pull a rapport smacker:

Me: Please come over, I'm sorry, I'll be a good boy. I'm
scared, and I don't feel well. Come over right now.

After that, she actually calls me. Immediately, she says, "It's scary how
you can just do a 180 like that. Is that real or manipulation?"

"Both," I tell her. We talk for a while.

She's coming over.

launched some pretty ruthless attacks here, which I felt were justified
given the tests she was putting to me. While I understand that the seduction community "dogma" on this can often lead to an adversarial
mind-set that's counterproductive, at the same time, I'm not some igno-
rant rube. The intuition I've developed for this shit is based on years of
empirical evidence from time spent in the field, not some doctrine. Just
because you're paranoid doesn't mean they're not out to get you.

She's back in my sphere of influence now, after I'd written her off.
Usually I just ditch chicks like this, but for some bizarre reason I actually
care about this one a bit. Having said that, there's no way I'm gonna be
her girlfriend who she goes shopping for fucking cardigans with. In any
case, I'm banging other chicks, so this is no one-itis, just an interesting
challenge.

I think she's being genuine about feeling like a skeeved-out ho and withdrawing sex from everyone for a while. The challenge is in getting her to feel good about it again, and in particular getting her to feel good about it with ME. I feel that overtly romantic shit will probably make it WORSE. I'm at a loss; this is definitely not my forte. I feel like the student I had last month who'd never been kissed, whom I had to SHOW how to do it by moving my mouth around in the air. Time for some in-depth research into rapport and comfort building. I know if I dig deep enough into my bag of tricks, I can pull something out. Maybe devalidate her until she's so miserable that she'll have to fuck me in order to regain a small piece of her self-worth. Voilà . . . enslaved Soda Model. Just in time for Christmas. Of course, if I do that, it may be difficult to get rid of her.

Bah. What am I talking about? I can replace my car windows as quickly as they can smash 'em. Bring it on.

FIRED

I'm late for work again, as I drive south toward the airport, wearing the same clothes I wore yesterday. I hadn't gotten laid in over a month and was getting desperate, so I pulled a random off Craigslist and fucked her, which is why I'm running behind this morning. I bantered with her via email before giving her my number. She called me up at 9:30 last night, and I frame-controlled her into meeting me at the karaoke bar. She got there, and she was SUPERFAT. Holy shit. But I figured she came out, and it would break her little (!) heart if I didn't bang her. So I downed three *pint glasses* of scotch, took her home and fucked her.

Jesus. It was horrifying. Horror and soul destruction. Awkward moments in the bar, like I was trying to build rapport but sensed there was no need; the impending sex act just hung in the air, thick. No pun intended. We got home, and when she gave token resistance, I just laughed. BOOM. Awkward moments in the morning.

I look at the clock on the dashboard. It's 10:30. I'm supposed to get there at 7 A.M., but hey, it's Siberia, nobody should notice or care. For the past six months, I've been coming in at ten and leaving at three. I don't even comb my hair anymore. I just cruise around Burlingame eating Taco Bell and jacking off in my office. Half the time I don't wear a tie, or shave.

When I roll up this morning, however, there is a line of cars snaking out of the driveway and out into the street, all the way down the block.

Fuck. I forgot. There is a major trade show at the hotel this week, and today is the check-in. The *one* day I had to come in on time, and I fucked it up for some bullshit 3.

I charge onto the driveway and start yelling orders, vainly attempting to take control of the disastrous situation. The hotel's general manager, who has apparently been dealing with things in my absence, shoots me a look of pure vitriol. I'm done.

Sure enough, after everything has calmed down, I'm called into his office for a little chat. "This is the end of the line," he says, furious. "You're suspended pending further review of your file."

I know what that means, having said the very same words myself countless times to hapless employees. The suspension gives them time to have the check ready to present when they actually fire you. I sign the suspension and return to my office. Once there, I immediately draft a letter of resignation and fax it to the main office, calling the regional manager and informing him of my decision. He's taken aback, yet I get the sense he saw this coming.

"Let's be honest here, Jeff. You and I both know you've been fucking up," he says.

He's right. I thank him for all the opportunities I've been given by the company, and hang up. It's over. I feel very emotional. I'm surprised to have such a strong reaction, but after all, six years is a long time. It was like a long-term relationship that had been going badly for a while. Now I'm free.

For the first two days, I just lay in bed and smoke pot, while looking up wack shit on the internet like whether a gorilla or a bear would win in a fight. I call up Soda a couple of days later and tell her what happened. After some cajoling, she agrees to meet me for lunch. We go to an Indian buffet near her house.

"Well, you certainly look the part of the unemployed writer," she says as I sit down. I'm wearing a wifebeater and track pants, and I haven't shaved or showered since Tuesday. My beer gut hangs heavily over my elastic waistband.

"Hey, I'm free. I can do whatever the fuck I want now." I shovel some palak paneer into my gullet. "So look," I say, chewing, "I've thought a lot about what you said before, and you know, I just had a knee-jerk reaction. I care about you, and I'm willing to do whatever it takes to make you feel comfortable getting physical with me again."

Upon hearing this, she looks anything *but* comfortable. "Well, Jeff, there's something you need to know, and I thought you deserved to hear it in person, which is why I agreed to meet you today."

"Oh shit," I sneer, "is this THE TALK? Are you breaking up with me?"

"No . . . uh . . . not exactly," she says. "You know Heather and I have been hanging out a lot lately."

"And? So what else is new? What the fuck are you getting at here?"

"Well . . . she's moving in with me." I sit there with a piece of naan in my hand, frozen in place on its way up to my open mouth. "She already has, actually." Thirty seconds pass.

"Please, Jeff, just be cool about this."

"I'm cool. I'm totally . . . cool." *I most certainly am NOT.*

I'm in a daze for the remainder of the meal, speaking in generalities and basically attempting to seem as though I am unfazed by Soda's revelation. Finally, her phone rings and she answers it in front of me. "Hello? Yeah. Yeah. We're almost done. I'll meet you out front in a couple minutes." She hangs up and says, "I let Heather borrow my car. She's picking me up."

"Oh. Fantastic," I say, grimly.

She calls the waiter over and pays. After a few more tense minutes, I see her car pull up through the restaurant's front windows, Heather behind the wheel. She parks right in front and waves cheerily. *Fucking bitch.* Looks as though ChessClub wasn't dead after all; she was just biding her time until she could strike, using the very techniques I taught her, against me. *Touché. The student has become the master.*

Soda touches my hand. "Good luck, Jeff." For what it's worth, the concern in her eyes seems real enough. She walks out, gets in the car and embraces Heather before they drive off.

The waiter brings the change back and asks me, "Will there be anything else, sir?"

I shake it off as best I can and try to formulate an answer. "Uh . . . yeah," I say, looking up. "Can I get a box for this?" I'm not sure if I'm imagining it, but I sense a touch of pity from him.

"Of course, sir."

CLOSURE

Christophe and I are getting embalmed at the Rio, talking about his recent trip to Europe. As usual, I'm wearing some stupid bullshit, and people are pointing at me and whispering. I've grown accustomed to this and as such, it no longer registers as anything but background static. I'm drinking vodka tonics.

Suddenly the crowd parts and I see some chick I almost fucked . . .

two and a half years ago. And this has been haunting me the whole time, because with this girl, I came literally as close as humanly possible to fucking her as one can without actually fucking her.

I am of course referring to Alice, the young lady whose twelve-year-old gay friends stole my sunglasses, the same night that I beat my roommate with a baseball bat and my next-door neighbor held me at gunpoint. I actually had my penis inside her vagina, but just the tip. This was quite heartbreaking, the reason being I couldn't officially record it on my scorecard (for it to count as a lay, you must complete at least one full stroke, and if playing major-league rules, you must further *establish a rhythm*). I figured I'd rectify the situation sooner or later. But it didn't happen the next Monday, or the Monday after that or the Monday after that. It *never* happened. The chick disappeared, went away, gone. Oh well.

So now I'm here again with Chrispy, and I see the chick across the way. At least I think it's her; she's got different hair, and it looks like she's put on a lot of weight. Like, you've heard of the "freshman fifteen"? This looks more like "the freshman fifty." It doesn't matter. I must do this, for the record books. To tie up the loose ends. I need closure.

I ignore her completely and talk to other people. I know there's only one possible reason for her to have come here tonight: to bang me. Maybe I'm delusional, but that's irrelevant.

Finally, she approaches me. She comes up and says, "Why didn't you talk to me" or some other such inanity. She appears to be quite stupid. I ignore this and basically go cave-hog on that ass. I hug her, I sniff her like a wild pup. My dick gets hard, I put it against her. Christophe looks at her, horrified, and leaves. I decide it's time to fuck, but it's pretty early; I'll have to put in some token work. But not here. I don't want people seeing me macking a hogster and fucking up my social proof. I venue change her to a nice, dark place where nobody will see . . . the Bizzle.

Her friend tags along. They try to get me to buy them drinks. "I've got a better idea," I say. "Why don't you go fuck yourselves?" Before they can respond, I feel my phone buzzing in my pocket. I hold up a finger and take it out.

It's a text from Chrispito:

Chrispy: where did u disappear to?

Me: Bizzle with a special hog, you can occupy the cute friend.

Not much to speak of here, just killing time. Chrispy comes through and starts to occupy, but the chick dislikes him or something. Unusual. I try to mitigate it by telling her, "You ever heard of Q-PLAYER? This dude WROTE IT." She's unimpressed. But he's off and gets another girl all on his dick soon enough, so he's pleased. Alice and her friend ask me for a ride home, across town. Again I tell them to go fuck themselves.

Then I suddenly relent and say, "You know what? I changed my mind. I'm feeling like a nice guy tonight. Let's go." We get in my car and drive to their neighborhood. I drop off the friend first, then we go to Alice's house.

I basically take off my pants and get in her bed, old-school jlaix. She says, "Wow, you're really making yourself comfortable here, aren't you?"

"Shut up, come here."

She says, "No, I want to enjoy this Pinot Noir."

"BITCH, it is two-thirty A.M., and you want to enjoy 'peenoh nwar'? Shut the fuck up, put that shit down and come here. I want to show you something. Seriously. Come here and look. Look."

That's about it, token resistance, plow it out. Fucktime. This time, I get in not just a third of a stroke, but several thousand. I'm making up for lost time. Even though the chick has gone to seed, for some reason the tits remain near perfect. I attribute this to her relative youth.

I go over for seconds the following night, remembering the tits. Idiocy ensues. We're making out, butt-naked. I go to put it in and she pulls some kind of resistance bullshit. "Can we just hang out for a while?" Well, that does it. I get up without a word and start putting my clothes on, methodically. She asks, "What's up?"

I say, very evenly, "I have neither the time nor the inclination to deal with your fucked-up emotional baggage. I'm leaving." That's it. I put my shoes on, calmly walk to the front door and leave.

She starts blowing my phone up as I drive home. I don't answer. The messages, when I check them later, say, "Please come back, blah blah blah." No dice. I dislike weird games. *Don't fuck with me.*

When I get home, I park the car and just sit there for a while, in the darkness. I feel dirty and cheapened. At first, I attribute it to fatty remorse, but I know this goes somehow deeper. It's what I imagine it would feel like to meet one of your childhood heroes, only to discover that he's actually a petty asshole. After all these years, I finally get what I wanted, and it turns out it SUCKS.

Whatever. Enough. I get ahold of myself and shove the feeling down inside, all the way to the bottom, tamping it down and screwing a lid on it. I get out of the car, slam the door and go inside.

POWER EXCHANGE

It's Che's birthday and we start drinking at Cha Cha Cha at 4 p.m. End up partying on Sixth Street. At some point, pills are introduced. I'm up on some wild shit by this time, pouncing. I demand Che give me his phone; thirty minutes later, he finds me in the corner with it, laughing. "Some chick gave me her phone," I giggle. "I've been sending fucked-up emails to her mom!" He snatches it back.

The club closes. I'm so keyed up on pills and liquor that I decide it makes total sense for me to walk home. I mean, hey, it's only like three miles through SOMA and the Mission!

I walk down Mission to where it turns south and I pass the Power Exchange, an infamous "swinger's club."

"Yo," I say to myself, "I never been in here . . ." So I decide to check it out. There's some kind of protracted scene at the door, me attempting to convince the guy to let me in for a discount because "I'm an Inuit," waving my passport in front of his face, gesturing in an attempt to further explain that "the hotel sent me." God only knows why, but I am allowed to enter.

A bunch of chodes are milling about, sluggishly whacking off to some sort of activity taking place that I can't see. I shrug, say, "Fuck it," and immediately remove my clothes. I'm standing there in my boxers yelling at the air. A guy walks by with some yuck chick who appears to be the only biological woman in the place. I CLAW her in and say to the guy, "HEY! Bring that bitch over here! It's time to fuck!"

For some reason, they comply, and I prepare to bang the chick. But then I guess I said something offensive (*me?*), because they start acting funny. I whip her with my belt and attempt to apply Wite-Out to her buttocks, having taken some from Che's office earlier in the day. They leave.

Some person comes up to me and says, "Hey dude, I don't think you belong here . . . this place is not for you."

I understand. "Oh yeah . . . right." I get my shit on and go to leave.

I remember running, running, running away from, or toward, something. I get home and begin to drunk-dial everybody in my phone and relate the story. Nice, Jeff. Around the sixth call, the girl answers and I berate her into coming over. I puke at 5:30, copiously. On my cat.

I have lost my belt. Still have the Wite-Out, though.

CHODE HELL

I'm spending the New Year in Australia, on RSD business. Earlier this evening I went on a yacht cruise with the boys, sponsored by a dude we know in Sydney. The yacht was populated with other rich chodey acquaintances of the dude, millionaire power-baller guys. We were the freak-show spectacle of the fucking cruise. The "pickup guys." I really didn't care, because it was a beautiful cruise on the fucking Sydney harbor and who the fuck am I to complain, right? Right.

We go to Cargo. Hardcore direct game. We do several good sets, but nothing really materializes. Tyler leaves. So at this point it's me, Ozzie and Mike.

Boom boom boom. We decide to go to work for real. Ozzie is leaving so it looks like it's me and Big Mike. We hit a couple of sets, yadda yadda yadda, and then I see two girls sitting down. He opens; I seat myself and isolate one of them.

I start in HARD. I plow the attract shit, then I decide to move into hardcore rapport material. It hits her like a fucking bomb. She says I'm intuitive, but she shouldn't be talking about this with a stranger. I apologize; I'm staring very deeply into her eyes. The Method acting takes over; I feel it for real. She gets up, literally crying, and goes to the bathroom, then comes back. I even tell her what I do for a living, I totally open up, and the connection is solidified.

It looks as though she's still about to cry. Big Mike isn't helping things, because he's busting on the friend in a miscalibrated way, and she eventually pisses off. He overhears me running the rapport material and says, "What is this faggot shit?" as I wave him away. He leaves.

Several of the yacht chodes are there. They buy me drinks. Whatever. I continue down the path. The lights come up, and it's time to clear the club. I make my move. "Are you a good kisser? Prove it."

"I have a boyfriend."

I say, "There's nobody around. I'm on holiday, it doesn't count, let's just go to the corner." She agrees.

She tells her friends, "I have to prove something," and we roll to the other side of the club. We start making out. It is serious. She's like, "Oh my . . ." We exchange numbers; she says, "Call me." I feel a real connection, probably because of the Method acting. It is so on, it hurts. Yacht Dude's boy slaps me high-five and I don't think anything of it. Everyone leaves the bar, and I am chipper as fuck.

I see my girl walking up the street, with Yacht Dude and his crew. He signals me to follow them to the hotel across the street. We all go in, all his boys and my girl and her friend. Apparently, they all know each other. Up in the hotel, she ignores me completely, like to a ridiculous degree. If she does anything with me here, it will get back to her boyfriend. These guys are fucking me, because her friend somehow knows Yacht Dude. Small world. I finally get her aside and say, "Look, I understand the dynamic here, I'm not gonna chode you out, you don't have to ignore me." She says okay, but I sense weirdness.

We roll out with dude and his friends, basically frat boys who happen to be filthy rich. We go to "a club." Turns out it is in King's Cross, the nasty whore district. I am finally getting my chick to acknowledge me in the cab, through hardcore disinterest and secret society savvy. We get out near some strip club. Dude says, "This is gangsta, act cool." These giant steroid Tongan guys are out front and they are complimenting me on the pink suit.

We go in and it's creepy as fuck. They herd me into the bathroom and produce blow. "Do it," says this HUGE motherfucker as he shoves a sack into my hand. I snort some. We go back out and sit down. I'm alone with my target for a moment and I remark how bizarre this is; light conversation ensues. All the rapport we had is pretty much destroyed.

Next thing you know, they herd us into a small room, and this nasty-ass stripper starts dancing, to the delight of the rich chodeys and even the girls. The chick has ass acne; it looks like the Man in the Moon. I stare at my grimacing reflection in the mirror, my pocket square, teeth and T-shirt glowing in the black light, and I think to myself, *THIS IS CHODE HELL. I AM IN CHODE HELL.* I appear tortured and gripped with terror, my features drawn in a rictus of anxiety.

This is the existence of these guys. They are having the time of their lives. It is like watching some sitcom in slow-motion with guffawing antagonists in my face, raising bottles of Victoria Bitter in the air. I want to run away. I feel sick. I know the thing with the girl is ruined. I want to leave but must wait until the stripper is done with her dance. Lionel Richie is playing and Yacht Dude tries to get me to sing along. I decline, saying I don't want to upstage the stripper. "U Can't Touch This" comes on. The chick is sucking her own tits in my face; it sickens me. This is not player. Throwing money at a loathsome whore with pustules on her ass. This goes against everything I stand for.

Finally, after an interminable wait, she is done. I excuse myself under the pretense of getting cash outside at the machine. As I take a piss, some demented cockmongler is remarking on my suit. I smile and say, "Yeah man, yeah!" I run outside, dodge the prostitutes by telling them, "I have a scorching case of herpes," and get in a cab.

I have been to Chode Hell, and I feel fucked up. I never want to be like that. I get back to the hotel and I feel totally violated. I am seriously traumatized. All the guys are asleep, so I have nobody to vent to. I go in the bathroom and cry, but I can't let it out, because this would wake the guys and they will know I'm a bitch. This only makes it last longer.

This isn't just about what happened tonight. I feel like my entire world, this whole fucking identity that I've spent the last four years painstakingly constructing, is falling apart like a house of cards. I sit on the toilet, shaking, unable to sleep. Outside, the sun begins to rise.

COMA

Alone on my thirtieth birthday, crying in the darkness like a little bitch. My mojo is gone. On Christmas Eve, I went out by myself, and pulled a fucking 5 by walking up to her and saying, "I'm lonely, want to go home and fuck?" Far from a triumph, it only made me feel MORE depressed. I'm fucking useless.

I wipe at my face. On the stereo, Axl sings about a peaceful place where "there's nothing to see." This song in particular spoke to me; that calm place he describes, it seemed so appealing. I wanted to go there. That became my solution. To go numb. But guess what? It didn't work.

When I learned about pickup, that too seemed to hold an answer. A method of control over the human realm, a way to banish uncertainty, insecurity and the acknowledgment of basic nothingness. I could compartmentalize my emotions. If there were rules that governed human interaction, then I could learn them, I could protect myself. By dehumanizing people and learning to control them, I could restore some measure of *order* to things.

But it DIDN'T FUCKING WORK.

I've felt helpless for as long as I can remember. That manifested in my desire to be this awesome, cool dude, and I definitely succeeded at that. But when it comes to any sort of deeper relationship, people can see me for who I truly am on the inside, and then POOF . . . everything spins out of control again. Heather felt helpless too, which is likely why she found me so attractive and felt the desire to learn my "ways." But ultimately, she found that she couldn't shut off that side of herself, and grew to resent me because I could. On some level I knew that.

Except that I can't. It was just a lie that I told myself, one that I ended up believing. In actuality, I have NO control over my emotions. Everything I do, in fact, is usually some kind of emotional reaction. The only difference is that now I'm disconnected from them, while still being controlled by them.

Realizing all of this, however, does nothing to change where I'm at. The fact that I have chosen this doesn't make it hurt any less. Salvation through sin? There is no salvation here. Just another bullshit illusion I created to delude myself into thinking that the universe is somehow "fair." Another way to avoid the issue. I thought if I could become somebody else, then it would all be okay, and everything was geared toward achieving that end: the hair, the clothes, the routines. I've spent all my time trying to craft the *image* of the "awesome, cool guy" instead of actually BEING him and letting the chips fall where they may.

The phone rings from across the room. For a second, I think it's my father, but when I look at it the caller ID says "TylerDurden." I answer it.

"Eeehhh man, you awake?"

"Of course . . . I'm always awake at two A.M. on a Monday morning."

"Happy motherfuckin' birthdaaaay, man! You celebrating it up?! What are you doing?"

"Uh . . . nothing."

"Cool, cool. Well here's the deal, I just wanted to pose something to you. I'm over here in Barcelona with Papa, and we've just decided to bring Ozzie on as an instructor." I met Ozzie over in Australia last month when the guys were first scouting him out; they'd flown him out there to guest instruct on program to see if he was up to snuff. Apparently, he made the cut.

"Awesome."

"Yup, yup. Now this means that somebody is going to have to train him, and I thought you would be the best person for the job. Which would mean you're going to have to move to Barcelona for a couple of months." Reflexively, my mind instantaneously comes up with at least twelve rationalizations for why I shouldn't go. Why I *can't* go. My head is swimming. *But this . . . but that . . .*

. . . Fuck it. There's nothing left for me here anyway. I wait a couple more seconds before I answer him. "Yeah, I'll do it."

"Aaaawwwwwesome bro, I knew you'd do it, eh? Cool. Make all the necessary preparations. You're leaving next week."

CLIFF DIVING

I leave for Spain the day after tomorrow. I will be gone for two months. It feels like I am standing on a tall ledge or cliff and I'm about to jump off. I will be in a completely alien environment, working seven days a week, night and day, commuting back and forth to London every weekend. This will either break me or make me better. Either sounds fine at this point.

Chrispy and I are at the Rio and it sucks (as usual) so we go to the Mint. We get fucked up there. I get cockblocked by a fat lesbian when I hit on her girlfriend. I start referring to Chrispy as "the French midget," which seems to irritate him. I sing "Juke Box Hero" in a very impassioned manner; during the bridge I grab a large handful of condoms out of the bowl they have there, scream out, "ROCK!!!" and throw them over the crowd, which causes them to shriek and cheer in delight. This bores us and we go to the Bizzle. It sucks as well. For some reason, we decide it would be a good idea to go to Chrispy's house and smoke the *Salvia divinorum* that our buddy LD brought up when he visited a while ago.

We head over and throw it in a bong, and I promptly take two FAT rips of it without a second thought. Ho hum. "I have a hard time believing this is going to do anything," I say. Within thirty seconds, however, shit gets out of control. I start falling backward through reality, and at the same time reality starts moving forward, like a tunnel. I can't stop it. Everything goes flat, and I become part of it, I become two-dimensional, I'm no longer distinct from anything else. I try to keep myself separate from it, but I'm trapped, I'm part of it. All of reality is just one thing, one flat-panel picture on a wall or some shit. I can SEE the fourth dimension, time moving, it's like a worm *I'm FUCKED I know I am FUCKING FUCKED* layers keep ripping off reality, like ripping off wrapping paper, and underneath it, it's the same wrapping paper, the layers keep flying off at incredible speed, and there are endless layers, the same thing underneath each one like standing in a roomful of mirrors like one of those computer-generated pictures you see of people where it's made up of little pictures, but imagine the little pictures are all the same image: the big picture and this goes on for infinity, or you pull back from the scene and you keep going, and eventually you see the universe is just an atom in a bigger universe, and when you pull back enough, it's the SAME FUCKING SCENE of me sitting there in Chrispy's loft, and THAT universe is an atom in a bigger one that's THE SAME FUCKING THING, over and over again for infinity, I am it and I'm a zipper made out of crayons and I'm being unzipped . . .

I'm not even in the room anymore, it's all gone, it's all flattened out and smeared, all I can see is Chrispy standing there, that's the only thing I can actually discern. Now, I realize, I'm fucking done. My life as I know it is over. I smoked that shit, and it's irrevocably changed everything forever, peeled off the veneer of my life, which was, in fact, not "real" at all. THIS is real. This is it, I'm fucking gone and I'm not coming back. I am incredibly SCARED. My life is OVER. Am I high? I don't remember having taken any drugs. This is REAL and I KNOW I am DONE. My life was all a lie, but it meant something. My whole life was an elaborate joke, or a game. The music on the stereo starts saying shit to me, like literally, it's Creed or Seven Mary Three or something (God knows why he has that shit on) and he starts singing, "You are gone now, dude . . . you are done, it's rotating, you're on the other side . . ." in his Creed voice, which I manage to find somewhat amusing, in spite of everything.

Chrispy isn't Chrispy, he's a construct of the godhead that I can communicate with, like an angel or a demon or a guide from the other side . . . like a fucking David Lynch movie with a supernatural *French midget*. My life has been an illusion that led up to this point where the truth is now revealed, everything that has ever happened in the universe, my childhood, moving here eleven years ago, meeting Chrispy, EVERYTHING, it was all elaborately orchestrated to bring me to this moment. He says, "It's okay, just let it happen," and I'm like, *Fuck, he's known this the entire time I've known him and he never said anything. Now it's over.* It's the creepiest feeling, that everyone was in on the joke but me. They were in on it the whole time, they're just cardboard PROPS in the game. Figments of my imagination. All my friends, my job, all the girls, my whole fucking life was a GAME or maybe a test to train me for the next level, and now it's game over, and I'm transcending to a higher reality. Complexifying into the supercontext. It is immediately made clear that my life was like a TV show. It hasn't been real and now I'm being shown that everything that I've loved, and everything I've done never really happened. I am terrified and desperate to have my life back, but how can you have something that isn't real? The feeling of loss is so deep and maddening. Literally, I know my life is over and I am dying. So this is what it feels like to die . . . at first I'm struggling and upset that it's all over, thinking about regrets and things I am embarrassed at having done, because God knows I did all that shit, but then, finally, I think, *Fuck it, there's nothing you can do, let's just accept it.* And I just wait for whatever comes next.

"Chrispy," I say.

"Jeffy." I can hear his voice but I'm not sure where it's coming from anymore.

"So," I say, tentatively, "what are we gonna do about this?"

"I don't know."

Slowly, however, I start to get an inkling that I can come back, like if I turn a little, I can become 3-D again. I become aware of the bong in my hand, and I start rotating it . . . it's making the ripping of the layers kind of slow down, and I start to grab on to the 3-D world, and slowly, I come back. It is very surprising when I actually return, more surprising even than when I first went "away," in fact.

The whole thing has taken maybe five minutes. Once I'm finally able to make sense of what's just happened, I can't stop laughing. "That's the funniest thing I've ever heard in my life!" I exclaim to Chrispy. "Man, I thought I was fucked. I thought I was done. This stuff is LEGAL? That's insane. Somebody should do something."

"Haha, yeah I guess."

After about thirty minutes, I feel completely normal. I get up to go, and say goodbye to Chrispy.

"So, thees is eet, hah?"

"Yeah, it looks that way."

He slaps me five. "*Bon voyage.* See you on ze othair side."

IV

TAPAS Y DISCOTECAS

My first week in Spain. Ozzie and I have an apartment just off La Rambla. It seems like everybody has a fucking motorcycle; you drive around and they buzz around your car like mosquitoes. It's terrifying, even by San Francisco standards. Trying to find my way back from the bar drunk at night is like wandering around in a labyrinth in a mystical hobbit village.

The language barrier isn't as bad as I expected it to be. My Spanish, while limited, is decent enough to get me by. The cultural differences are immense, however. People don't go out until midnight at the earliest, and you might not get home until 5, 6 A.M., or even 9 A.M. on the weekends.

We don't know anybody here, as Ozzie moved to Barcelona from a rural area in northern Spain, specifically for the training. It's like I'm starting at ground zero, a complete reset. I'm going back to basics. Here I'm a fucking chode, I'm just some guy. What I mean by this is a return to the fundamentals. Doing my warm-up sets like any fucking dode. Going up to the worst imaginable scenarios, swallowing it and expecting to get blown out, so I can laugh at what a dork I am. Enough with all this self-aggrandizement wankery bullshit. The ideal is to be *in* the game, not of the game.

Anyway, I'm working extremely hard here, so I can destroy my enemies. They will be annihilated. Ozzie is deeply into health and fitness, and I've started tagging along with him to the local gym. I am focusing all my energy. Every time I work out, as I feel the pain, I imagine smashing in the faces of haters.

That is all for now. I must take a nap; my internal clock is all fucked up.

SEX

Just got back from this trashy neighborhood thug dive bar called Jamboree. It pretty much sucked, but Ozzie's training requires us to go out every night, and Jamboree happens to be in the neighborhood.

There's some chick on our block who is getting pounded with regularity. I know this because she yells, "AWK...AWK...AWK...AWK...AWK...AWK..." at top volume whenever the pounding is taking place, usually around noon. Right now, however, it's 4 A.M. and I can hear her squawking away.

Welcome to Spain.

I flip open my laptop and check my email. There's one message waiting for me, from "Me." I open it, puzzled.

> Feb 2006 05:00:03
>
> Subject: 3LR @ Jack in the Bozzie
>
> (The following is an email from the past, composed on Tuesday, February 15, 2005, and sent via FutureMe.org)
>
> —
>
> Dear FutureMe,
>
> You fucked two girls last night. One of them passed out in your car at Jack in the Box. The other freaked out when she couldn't find her wallet and you dragged her out of the room by her hair.
>
> Don't drag bitches by the hair. Unless they piss you off.

Jesus. I remember composing this, a year ago today. At the time I thought it was hilarious. It's only been a short while, but being here has already given me a new perspective on my life back home, one I couldn't get while I was there, caught up in it. I thought I was so fucking cool, and most casual observers would probably have agreed. But there wasn't any substance to it; it was simply a veneer of game laid over an empty core. Yes, I could pull girls. But after my ten hours of material was exhausted, the curtain was pulled back to reveal the needy, angry little man behind it, furiously working the levers.

This is how I fucked up with the Soda Model. I'd fucked some stupidly hot girls before, but for the most part, those had been one-night stands. If I pulled some trashy stripper or googly-eyed bar slut, she knew the score; my complete lack of humanity was almost *required* in those instances. No harm, no foul. With Soda, I was attempting to forge a relationship, however . . . and I wasn't up to the task.

They say there are two ways to get an amazing woman: you can become an amazing manipulator, or an amazing man. I haven't actually been improving myself over the last four years; I've simply become a more potent, tactical version of the same old guy that women like Soda ignored. Deep down, I felt she was out of my league, and that I'd merely fooled her into liking me by means of trickery. After she had the cokewhore gang bang with ChessClub (a skilled manipulator in her own right who got her to go way past her comfort zone), she felt like a slut and began to question if anybody really wanted her for anything beyond her looks. The fact that I felt she was of higher value than me exaggerated this effect. On one hand, I had "sick game," but at the same time, I was also a desperate loser.

When she told me she was taking a break from sex, it wasn't "how can I let my girlfriend know that I love and care for her," it was a "rapport challenge." Like she was a kitchen appliance that wasn't working properly, as opposed to a girl who genuinely liked me and was having a crisis. It never occurred to me that there might be something wrong with trying to manipulate her head right to fucking pieces just to fill some sad hole of insecurity.

It's a lesson I should have learned over a year earlier, the night I pulled Lisa off the alpha dude at Phone Bizzle: "you are enough." That guy was cooler than me only because I *thought* he was. It's been staring me right in the face ever since, but I haven't been able to see it until now. Soda too was only "out of my league" because I believed her to be. It made sense, because at my core I knew I wasn't living up to my own standards. So I grasped at tactics. Attributed the success to those. But when the tactics finally ran out, the truth was revealed: I was just a fat, boring drunk, devoid of passion, with nothing going on in his life. I didn't deserve a quality girl. And in spite of my best efforts to conceal it, that dynamic inevitably began to seep into the relationship and erode it from the foundation.

"AWWK . . . AAWWWK . . . AWWWK . . ." The neighbor's still squawking. This dude's a real marathon man; he's been pounding away consistently for the past hour. Personally, I'm so out of shape that I typically last around three minutes, a fat fuck sweating and shaking on top of the girl. Then again, I haven't been doing *any* pounding lately. Nor do I intend to. I have decided to observe a period of celibacy. Once getting laid became so easy that it was literally as tough as going to the kitchen and making myself a sandwich, my ego started playing tricks on me. Somewhere along the way, the game stopped being an enjoyable hobby and mutated into a ball-racking referendum on my value as a human being, a source of validation. "I can get a stranger to fuck in under an hour. That means I must be worthy."

In reality, it means nothing. It means that you learned how to play the game; that's it. The validation I got from it was a cheap and dirty high; it didn't last, and inevitably, I found myself needing another hit. And another, and another, until I was basically a strung-out junkie, "chasing the dragon," trying to re-create the original euphoria of the first hit, but needing more every time to even come close. It was like trying to fill a bucket with a hole in it. No matter how many girls I fucked, how many ridiculous stunts I pulled off, how many fanboys I had online stroking my e-peen, it would *never* be enough.

Eventually, that desperation became palpable. Girls could sense it. I was desperate to pour more fuel on the whole "jlaix badass pickup guru" identity, so much that I became paralyzed by my own game. Suddenly it was simply not worth it for me to approach a girl unless it was assured to result in perfection. After all, "jlaix" is perfect.

FUCK jlaix.

It was just a persona, albeit a very useful one, one that allowed me to navigate the alien landscape of the game. There are lessons and aspects of that personality to be valued and retained, absolutely: the ability to man up and remain cool in the face of overwhelming odds, the embrace of unbridled sexuality and the power it brings, the capacity to see the absurd in the most dire situations. The sheer *audacity*.

But it's time to move on. I need to get to the core, to figure out how to get my validation internally, which is why I'm going cold turkey. No sex at all for the foreseeable future. I haven't thought about how long this is going to last, but I figure when it's time, I'll know.

Going to London in nine hours. I put in my earplugs and turn out the light.

BARRIO GOTICO

Shit man. I still can't believe I fucking live here.

The neighborhood is called Barrio Gotico, the "Gothic quarter." It's a sunny afternoon, and I step out for a walk through the neighborhood. Many of the buildings date from the medieval period. It's like living in a city five hundred years ago, but with modern technology. Tiny narrow cobbled streets so small you have to press against the wall when a car drives through so you don't get hit by the mirrors, swarming with hardcore hipsters speaking every language, hippies, drug dealers, yuppies in Prada suits, psychotic football fans, dogs and cats running around. Little couture boutiques bumping 2Pac, tattoo parlors, bakeries the size of a closet, Pakistani convenience stores, tapas bars tucked into literal holes in the wall. I wake up to cathedral bells, kids yelling in Spanish and buzzing motor scooters out my window.

I go to the butcher and get some chicken, go to Vodaphone and they're closed from two to four for siesta. All businesses do this. Shit is so laid-back here, nobody gives a FUCK. For example, we'll walk into a restaurant and the guy will say, "Uh, now's not a good time for us, come back later." As an American, I find this disconcerting. I'm used to GO GO GO, and that just doesn't work here.

I walk into some tiny *cerveceria* bar with like two seats in it (there are tons of these everywhere), have my one beer for the day and read a book while, oddly enough, they play dick-washing music like Bryan Adams and Extreme, interspersed with Spanish hip-hop. Afterward, I get my cell credits, pick up the laundry and go home, where I make some chicken salad.

My Spanish is getting better as I interact with the local chodes while running errands. It's taken a while to get used to the customs and the way things work. Ozzie and I have a regular routine. Wake up at around 2 P.M., hit the gym, chores, read various self-actualization books, siesta time, write write write, then hit the local chode bars at midnight. From there, we pick up girls to pull to the *discotecas*, run Ozzie's training module and get home at 6 A.M. On Friday mornings, we take the plane to London, run Bootcamp all weekend, then rest on Sunday night. It's the only rest we get all week.

I find myself asking if "game" as I know it is relatively useless. I know that I have reached the limit of what can be achieved with simple tactics and routines. Obviously a certain level of outer game is a prerequisite. But once you've got the nuts-and-bolts mechanics down, "more game" is not going to increase your odds. What outer game does is give you the ability to consistently approach groups and not look like an idiot. It also allows you to avoid making stupid errors, to move the set forward in the proper way and to deal with logistics.

Put another way, I might ask, "Is driving skill useless?" I mean, what the fuck . . . all driving skill does is prevent you from crashing your car. In reality, it's composed of many facets, from gear shifting, to steering, to braking, etc. But since you've been doing it for decades, it becomes invisible to you. Now, if you were to go to *racing* school and try to learn a whole new level of driving, then you'd see that driving skill is not useless at all; in fact there's a whole new world of it you never knew about. So that's what I have to do: find the next level. That means further developing my emotional intelligence, so I can become highly attuned to others' subjective experiences. Learning advanced sexual techniques. Stepping up to the hardest sets every night. Hitting more exclusive venues. Rounding out the rest of my life to bring to the table as much value as possible (inner game, physical, having awesome shit going on, getting my finances straight).

Really, that's the only thing I'm consciously thinking when approaching women these days: "bring value to the interaction." Being the party, as opposed to trying to weasel my way into theirs. I think this frame of bringing value, unconditionally, even if it means you don't get laid, is the final piece of the puzzle. Done correctly, it sets off a chain reaction that gets your "inner game" spiraling upward off the charts. In many ways, the abstinence has been a blessing, because it's removed the pressure. There is no outcome dependence, so I'm free to express myself congruently and in a completely nonreactive way. Whereas before, I was merely pretending not to care about the outcome, now it's genuine. Before, I was actively trying to control everything in order to give the illusion of certain internal attributes, which actually served to subconsciously *increase* my neediness in the long term.

Now I just dutifully execute what I know to be solid game, without caring about what happens. I'm not trying to "establish" a strong frame anymore; it just sort of happens of its own accord. After having done a few thousand approaches, I've built up so many positive reference experiences that when I do an approach, I don't NEED it to work, because I know it probably WILL. Experience breeds competence, which breeds confidence. The girl sees that confidence and finds it attractive, and that has served me very well thus far. But again, up until now it's been like a skyscraper erected on sand. An amazing structure, built on a weak foundation. It's time to go deeper, to solidify that foundation. That means really establishing how I want to live my life and then striving every day to make that a reality. Working on myself to get to a point where I can pass by the girls I know I can have, and attract the ones I actually want. In order to do this, I'm going to have to sort out who I really am, under it all, and furthermore, to learn to accept and love this person. Not in a narcissistic way, but openly and without reservations.

In other news, the way the boys are running the London program floored me. I don't give compliments lightly, but they have this shit sewn the fuck up. This is the next generation of our program, and it's amazing. One dude was fucking CRYING at the end of it this past weekend, saying, "I read the testimonials and I thought it was fake, but it's not; I'm sorry man, my life is changed forever!" Fuck, *I* feel changed by it. Mad props. This new style adds so much value to our program it's insane. My program's definitely getting an overhaul when I return to San Francisco.

Gonna take a quick disco nap, then Ozzie and I are off to check out our local karaoke bar. Some things never change.

BUTANO

There's some guy that roams around the neighborhood screaming what sounds like "Cubanoooooh!!!!" at the top of his lungs on a daily basis, at random times. This irritated me a great deal at first, as I thought it was some drunken asshole being stupid. Then Ozzie told me the guy is actually saying, "Butanoohhh!" and he goes around selling butane for people to heat their homes with. Now I think he is cool and admire his vocal projection, although I still like to imagine he is saying "CUBANOOOOH!!" If this RSD thing ever falls through, I can always move back to Spain and get a job selling butane.

BUTANOOOHH!!

Ozzie's a funny guy. When we moved into the furnished apartment, we discovered a DVD of *Hedwig and the Angry Inch* with Spanish subtitles, sitting alone on the bookshelf. "Oh shit," I said, "this film is awesome." I threw it on the thirteen-inch television and watched in amusement as Ozzie tried to figure out what the hell was going on.

"This person ees soo INTENZE," says Ozzie, in his trademark Spanish accent.

I'm starting to think the decision to come here was a very wise one. The move has served as a massive pattern interrupt for my bad habits. I've essentially stopped drinking: I allow myself one beer per night, tonic and lime afterward. My diet, which back home was total gastronomic mayhem with gourmet sauces and burritos, is now hardcore health-oriented. We eat only fresh chicken, fruits and vegetables, whole carbs like yams, no bread, nothing white, small portions throughout the day. Ozzie stays on my ass about the health shit; I stay on his ass about the game and the administration of a program.

It's weird . . . giving up the booze and the sedentary lifestyle has been remarkably easy. I think I just hit the breaking point. It was hard to let it go before because it was inextricably intertwined with my identity. For better or worse, we are predisposed to cling to our identity, even if it's a disempowering one. People liked the character of "jlaix the hard-drinking sonofabitch maniac" and gave me accolades for all of my demented and wacky shenanigans, and I fed off that. What I've come to realize is that that way of living is not serving me anymore.

Neither is the anger. It was an effective coping mechanism; being belligerent seemed more proactive than being sad and meek. I took refuge in it. It was like a protective carapace over my wounded slug soul. No more. It's time to let be what is.

Rather than trying to stuff my emotions, from now on I am going to allow myself to experience them fully, recognizing them for what they are: signals, designed to support and guide me. Before, any time a strong emotion came on, it felt like I was spinning out of control. I'd be gripped by a sense of panic and the emotion would be immediately rammed sideways into some obscure corner of my mind. Now I accept what's happening, then say, *Okay, let's turn the volume down from a 10 to a 2. I've faced this before and I can face it again.* Instead of ignoring my emotions, I will act upon them to make my life and the lives of those around me better.

Anyway, all this time in the gym, the sobriety, and the extremely clean diet . . . it's all beginning to pay off. I no longer have the build of a Chicken McNugget with tits. I've lost fifteen pounds. My beer gut is going to the land of the lost dryer socks and blown-out chodes. My face is thinner. I wake up alert and ready to fuck and kill. I don't slur my speech and make miscalibrated comments, unless I want to.

I'm over the initial hurdle: the habits have been formed. The challenge will be transferring them to my life back home. I don't envision this as being too difficult. Desired outcome is ripped fucking abs by the end of summer. Purpose is vitality and health. Action is training and diet.

No London program this weekend, a freak anomaly. That means we actually get to spend a weekend in Barcelona for once. Mansion party in the hills tomorrow night. Whatever. Going to bed. I'm sore as fuck. It feels great.

DOMINGO PEREZOSO

Today has been relaxing, which is something I haven't been able to say since I got here.

I woke up at the usual time, around 2 P.M., ate an orange and then meandered down to the gym. When I got there, it was closed. Oh well. But there happened to be a fucking *cat show* being held in the actual gymnasium there. I paid six euros and went inside. After this, I walked around the neighborhood. It was like a ghost town, very quiet. Only one Moroccan tried to sell me hash. It was so idyllic. Right then it struck me how much I'm going to miss this place.

I go into the vegetarian restaurant in George Orwell Plaza and they make me a *cafe cortado* before I can even ask. I drink that shit down and pick up some red and green peppers at the Chinese market, then go home and scramble up an egg with the peppers, some mushrooms, avocado and jalapeños.

Today's assignment from headquarters was to locate daytime venues.

I wake Ozzie up and we're headed to Castelldefels, where we've heard there are beach parties in the summer. But his car won't start, and the chode at the garage flat-out refuses to help us. "Welcome to Spain," I mutter.

Instead we check out the major tourist shit. We go to Sagrada Familia, the famous Gothic cathedral designed by Antoni Gaudí. Amazing. This is absolutely ridiculous. It's like a nightmare come to life: every surface of the building is ornately carved with bizarre iconography, and it is enormous. This guy must have been insane. Just looking at this building inspires the fuck out of me. To imagine the sheer willpower and dedication it must have taken to not only envision this project, but to also actually execute it, boggles the mind. And here I am trying to get my little bullshit together. It really puts things into perspective.

This Gaudi character designed most of the famous buildings in Barcelona. He was a visionary. As such, I'm sure he had to fight hard against opposition. All of the greatest minds throughout history probably were considered "weirdos" by their peers. I'm starting to realize exactly how much time I waste focusing on things that fall outside my sphere of control and influence, from bad reactions from girls to unwarranted and unconstructive criticism from haters, competitors and the like. I thought I had it licked, but I need to get down and dirty and LASER that shit out; by doing so I could easily gain several hours a week to take more classes, get more work done, make myself better.

I've been doing a ten-day "positivity challenge," where I am not allowed to dwell on *any* negative thoughts for longer than two minutes. If I do, I have to start over again. I've already failed once. You'd be surprised how frequently negative shit enters your head once you start looking for it. Like, I'll hear that song "My Humps" and start to get annoyed, but then I cut it off and say, "Hmm. I would PREFER not to hear this." Or I'll be in line and getting pissed off that I have to wait, and I say to myself, "This is beyond your control, it is useless to get upset." Ozzie is constantly testing me as an ongoing joke. We got stuck in Geneva on a layover last week and he kept saying, "We're late? Aren't you PISSED?" I just had to smile. The bastard. Another time, he busted in on me while I was asleep and threw some water on my head. "Time to wake up!"

"WHAT THE FU . . . er . . . I mean, cool, bro. Thanks! Yup, time to get up!"

I'm beginning to understand that a lot of the bad things that have manifested in my life were my own fault. Not all of them, sure, but a lot of them. By harboring all of this negative energy, I was only bringing more of it upon myself. The old maxim, "You reap what you sow." Karma is physics, pure and simple. There are consequences to your thoughts and actions.

They say you hate and fear that which you dislike most about yourself. I was constantly bitching about being surrounded by drug-addled whores, yet at the same time I was a deranged maniac with no self-respect of my own. I hated liars and disloyal people because I was constantly lying to myself. Saying, "I'll stop drinking. I'll do this, etc.," and never following through. I would go berserk if I heard someone hating on me, and in the same breath I would turn my criticism and judgment right back at them. Fighting against all of this hasn't worked; it's been like slamming my head against a brick wall. Whatever you resist, persists.

As I look up at the massive church in front of me, it dawns on me what I have to do to break the cycle. I have to let go of all the hate and pain I've been carrying around; I have to forgive everyone who's hurt me and whom I in turn have hurt.

I've always thought it was weak to forgive. But in actuality, it was weak *not* to. I was just creating an identity around the pain, allowing it to survive and continue, endlessly. This is not about them; it's about me. It's time to leave all of it behind and start living for myself.

"Ey man, are you all right?" Ozzie appears at my side. I must have been staring up at the church façade for a while.

I blink the red out of my eyes. I turn to him and say, "Yeah man. Never better. Let's go." I buy a bunch of souvenirs for everybody back home, and we head back to the apartment. Tourist time is over. I'm gonna chill out tonight, then it's back on the chain gang starting tomorrow.

MILE-HIGH CHAV LOVIN'

I've been living with Ozzie in Spain for over a month now, and have had many exciting and boisterous adventures involving girls with funny accents. Each weekend it's off to London for Bootcamp. Every time I go to London, I get sick, due to the weather and the germs. I've tried everything: vitamins, echinacea, etc., but nothing's worked. However, I think I have found a solution . . . my magic euro.

A few nights ago, I put a euro on the bar in some dive in Barrio Gotico, and the bartender watched quizzically as I sprinkled it with salt. I asked her for a lemon wedge, which she gave me and I proceeded to squeeze all over the coin. Then, standing bolt upright, I waved my hands over it and intoned the magic words:

"In nomine Dei nostri Satanas Luciferi excelsi! Wokka wokka wokka! Chaka khan, chaka khan, it's all I wanna do! Tu madre esta desnuda en el bano con el pollo! EVERYBODY DANCE NOW! BASS!"

Shaking the juice and salt off it, I placed it in my breast pocket. Now I am impervious to sickness of all kinds. MAGIC EURO. This shit works!

I have also become obsessed with "chavs," a particular kind of violent urchin that is basically the British equivalent of "white trash." Sporting counterfeit Burberry clothing, tracksuits and gaudy, fake bling, chavs are both a laughingstock and a scourge to the United Kingdom. I've gone and made this into my default London opener. I roll up on the girls, and with my best American accent, blink my eyes and say, "Hey, guys . . . are you English? Oh . . . what's a CHAV?"

They for some reason find this hilarious, and proceed to explain it to me. I then ask them whether they would date a chav, and tell them how I want to become the first American Chav. Upon seeing my bling they concur I am well on the way to doing so, whereupon I say, "Oh, great. Hey, so who's this dude on your money?"

"That's the queen!"

Further, I have begun to dress like a chav. I went to Burberry on

Regent Street and bought a scarf in the traditional check pattern. I roll around in a tracksuit and running shoes with the goddamn scarf on, carrying a Louis Vuitton bag. American Chav yo! The reasons for this are twofold. One, I think it's funny. Two, traveling is much more comfortable in these clothes.

O zzie and I proceed to the airport to go to London, and I'm bedecked in the full American Chav regalia. We get to the gate and the goddamn flight is delayed. They don't even announce it. There's no plane, nothing. That's what you get for flying Iberia. These fuckers are shameless and couldn't give half a fuck less about business if they tried. "Welcome to Spain," I mutter as I sit down and throw my bag to the floor.

Some chick about four seats to my left makes an indistinct comment. I look over and she's pretty cute. I'm debating whether to open her. I look over at Ozzie. He's sleeping, because he was up all night fucking some French chick he pulled from Fellini on La Rambla. I heard it, because I was up watching the first season of *Miami Vice* (the only English-language DVD I could find at El Corte Inglés, the department store). Now he's out. Looks like I've got nobody else to talk to. *Fuck it, let's open her.* I've always wanted to game at the airport, but I'm usually tired or sick. Not now. I feel like a million quid.

When I turn back to her, however, she's put her headphones on. Grrrr. Time waits for no man. I talk loudly at Ozzie, hoping she'll take them off and listen in again. No dice. Then an announcement comes on about the flight, and she removes them for a moment. I strike . . .

"Hey . . . are you English?"

She turns to me and says, "No, I'm Australian." Fuck, there goes my opener. Whatever, I roll into some Australian banter, about how I met Ozzie there, and he's my nutritionist, and we're roommates in Barcelona. She responds and it's on. "I'm Sharon," she says, extending her hand. I take it.

"HELLO, SHAZZY. I'm Jeff."

I don't even know what I'm saying, straight vibe, but I'm being funny, she's laughing. My eyes go bright. I know this feeling. It means I'm fucking UNSTOPPABLE.

I move over toward her; there's still one seat between us, though. Day game shit: cautious . . . don't want to spook her. My calibration is amped to a supernatural level after thirty days straight in the field. I'm wound the fuck up and have no time to waste.

Thirty minutes pass. I'm qualifying her. Loves cats? Check. Doesn't smoke? Check. No drugs? Check. Time for identity grounding. I tell her why we're going to London: we're "motivational speakers." I start telling her about bringing value, and all my current self-development goals.

I look at her again. She's hot. Tight body. She's mirroring me. She's my age. We have a lot in common. She quit her job to go traveling for a year, just flew in from Brazil. She does an American accent for me, which I love. I dunno why, I love it when English or Australian women imitate an American accent; it makes me fall in love.

The gate for the flight is changed. We walk over there. This time we sit next to each other. I find myself layering in physical escalation and the slightest touch of material to lock it down. Little Sister. Too Similar. Just sprinkling it in, not even consciously thinking about it. I do some self-deprecation/vulnerability shit; I talk about how I'm "bothering her" and how I'm "ugly as fuck and stupid," in a humorous way. She decides there's time to go shopping for a coat since the flight is delayed. I tell her I'll watch her items. She leaves.

I turn to Ozzie and say, "Dude, wake up. I'm gonna fuck this chick on the plane."

"How?" he rubs his eyes.

"Easily," I say. "I'll just swap seats with the person sitting next to her." It's a tactic I read long ago. When you check in, you game the desk person into giving you a seat in the exit row, which has extra leg room. Now, you go to the gate and game up your chick. When you get on the plane, you can easily switch seats with the guy next to your chick, because the exit row is a commodity. I've been getting exit row on every flight I've ever taken since reading that, and this day is no exception. "This shit is fucking ON yo. I'll switch seats, game her up and fuck her in the bathroom.

Mile-High Chav, INNIT!!! INNIT!! HAHAHAHAHAAA!" The dude to my right looks at me sideways. Irrelevant.

The plane starts boarding, and my girl hasn't come back yet. *Fuck . . . fuck . . .*

At the last moment, she comes running up, and we get on the plane. Everything goes according to plan and I end up sitting next to her. Now, I have two hours to get her into the bathroom. I go in there and examine it, and work out how I will position for the fuck. Hmm. Not as cramped as I thought it would be.

Back at the seat, I do more identity grounding. Trust Test. Eskimo Kiss. "Look," I say, "I want to take you on a ROMANTIC DATE . . . to Burger King. Anything you want. ANYTHING. I know the maître d'; we'll get the best table in the place, right up front. See and be seen. Then we'll go to the park, and hold hands (grab her hand and gently hold and caress), and run through the meadow, and gaze at the doves when they cry. Then we'll buy balloons and let them go . . . they fly away so free, like our hearts. Then we'll go to the beach, at sunset, hold hands more, and take off our shoes, and write each other's names in the sand."

I wait three seconds, then say, "Or, we could just go fuck in the bathroom."

She giggles.

"I'm fucking serious. Let's go. Come on."

She nervously looks back toward the "loo." There's two airchodes standing by it. She's like, "I dunno . . . we might get caught . . ."

Holy fuck . . . she's considering it! Yes.

"Come on," I say, "it's simple . . . I'll go, and you come knock a couple minutes later. We'll wait till they serve the bullshit food."

She's like, "Uhhh, I dunno . . ." It's getting strange.

I change the subject immediately and revert to vibe banter with some light material interspersed. After a while, I try again. I'm talking about how people assume because I'm American I'm vulgar, and how I'm falling in line with that. "For example," I say, "at any moment I'm liable to say some fucked-up shit. Like, I'll talk about how I want to fuck you up the ass in the bathroom right now." Hard stare, smirk. "Come on, let's go. How many people can say they got fucked up the ass on the airplane?"

She laughs and looks back again. I can see it, she wants to, but doesn't have the balls. "If I had a skirt on it would be easy," she says.

Fuck. It looks like this isn't happening. I don't want to push it too much more and fuck the pickup, so I drop it. But to my surprise, she asks me what I'm doing tonight. I tell her I'm working until 2 A.M.

"Well, come by my hotel after you get off. Here it is . . ." She writes the name and address of the hotel on a paper. We exchange numbers, and after landing we go our separate ways.

I'm feeling chipper as fuck and give a killer program. After debrief, I walk outside On Anon and call her up. "Hey, kiddo what's up? I'm downstairs."

She seems unsurprised. "Okay, come up, I'm in room 401. I'm in bed." What the fuck. I'm too good at this.

"Haa, well, I'm actually on the way there. I'll be there soon."

She goes, "Okay, well I'll let Robert at reception know you're coming."

I take the taxi to Paddington and go up to the hotel. Sure enough, "Robert" is waiting for me, and he's laughing. "Going to see your friend?" That's right buddy.

Boom. I go up, walk in, take off my pants. "I wanna lick it." Fade to black.

I really like this girl. I'm going to miss her when I go back to the States. But for now, she's my London girlfriend. We hung out again on Sunday. I even bought her dinner. I asked her why she wouldn't fuck me on the plane, since she knew we were gonna bang anyway. My suspicions were correct: she was just too scared of getting caught. It was broad daylight, the attendants were there, etc. Maybe next time, intercontinental flight overnight while everyone's asleep.

In retrospect, I shouldn't have done so much "convincing" on the plane. I should have just said, "Okay, I'm going now, come back in two minutes," and just DONE IT. Oh well, there's always next time.

Looks like my celibacy is over. I'm back.

SUPERSTAR

My time here is almost up. I'm making sure that my last week in Barcelona is unforgettable. Sharon flew in from London to spend it with me. Tonight we all went to ANTI-KARAOKE and it was the most intense karaoke experience I've ever had in my fucking life (which is saying a *lot*). These guys got up and sang Motorhead's "Ace of Spades," which caused a full-blown MOSH PIT to erupt, and at the end, the guy jumps off the stage and the crowd carries him. It was the only time in my entire fucking life I've seen a successful karaoke *stage dive*. I am still in awe.

We head to Nasty Mondays at Fellini, the local version of El Rio Dollar Drink Night, with suitably "nasty" rock/electronica. Once there, I start emulating this guy we saw in On Anon last week, whom I called "SuperStar."

Let me elaborate. Here is the scene: a crowded dance club in London, the place is packed, the music pumping.

All of a sudden, I see him. There he is, on the periphery of the dance floor. Everyone is giving him a wide berth as he does his magical dance. He is . . . SUPERSTAR.

This guy, at first I thought he was playing around, it was so bizarre. He's an Indian guy with nondescript clothes. Tight jeans and a button-down shirt. He has this incredibly intense expression on his face. The brows are furrowed, and he is gazing off into the distance at . . . something nobody else can see. His mouth is open, in an O as though he is in ecstasy.

His arms slowly raise up to his head in a ridiculously exaggerated manner, with the fingers spread out. He walks slowly across the floor in slow, long strides, kicking his feet out. He then WHIRLS around like fucking Baryshnikov and LEAPS in the air, with the bizarre expression on his face.

Again, I'm like, "Is this guy for real?"

Oh yes. He's VERY real. He rocks his pelvis about in a leering fashion, like he's sexy as FUCK. He *knows*. He continues to do this indefinitely, completely oblivious to anything and everything else. People are literally getting out of his way, or openly mocking him. He does not care.

I'm thinking, *Dude, this guy is AWESOME!*

I asked Ozzie about it later, and he said that he'd seen the guy before at the same club while on a previous Bootcamp. At the time, he took his students around the guy and started cheering him on. This caused Super-Star to get even MORE crazy and intense. The frame control on this guy is amazing. I imagine he could get tons of girls if he wanted to. But girls do not interest SuperStar. He must *dance*!

I got a video of him, but in the low light of the club, you can't really see what the hell is going on . . . it's like those films of Bigfoot or the Loch Ness Monster, where it could be anything.

I must capture him on film.

But I have captured his spirit, because it now resides within me.

So back to Nasty Monday. Without warning, I am overcome with a strange sensation. I feel as though I am possessed . . . by SuperStar.

It starts out as a joke, as I begin imitating his facial expressions and movements, right here in Fellini. But soon I'm really getting into it. Ozzie is actually getting freaked out. I roll up while he's speaking to girls, and begin doing it. When the girls start laughing, I leap away in typical Super-Star fashion. One group of girls, however, pulls me back. They speak Catalan, so Ozzie has to translate. He says, "They think you are cool, and they want to know how to do it."

I teach them the SuperStar maneuvers. The fingers, the facial expression, everything. Soon we convince them to go out to the dance floor and do it with us. There is a large stage area overlooking the club, and we all climb up on it and start doing it, in synchronization.

A few people become interested in this strange phenomenon. Ozzie leaps off the stage and grabs more girls. They come up and start doing it. He jumps down again, finds more girls and brings them up to join the dance.

At this point, the entire club is watching us do this insane freakdance onstage with a huge group of girls, cheering us on. Such is the power of SuperStar. Good times. Thank you SuperStar, wherever you are . . . I'll capture you yet, you wily bastard.

The next evening, I go with Sharon to one of the more upscale tapas restaurants in town, Cerveseria Catalana, and enjoy a fine meal. As we walk home afterward, I feel just too pleased for words. When I was a kid, I always dreamed of going to Spain. Now I'm actually here, and I feel so fucking grateful I can't begin to express it. I'm strolling down La Rambla in the cool Mediterranean air, with an incredible girl on my arm, and I literally could not be more content.

My life is totally repurposed. I see now where I was completely misguided and where I need to go. I apologize to everyone I hurt with my callousness; whether they forgive me is out of my hands. It's time to move forward. My entire way of living is transformed. What I eat, my patterns of behavior, how I perceive things, how I react. It's all realigned to reflect my core values and beliefs.

That is where the internal validation comes from. Living up to my standards, not somebody else's. There's no point in being overly concerned with what others might think or how they might respond to me, which was the foundation of my old "game." No more self-seeking in other's reactions or trying to micromanage their perceptions of me. I'm done with all that.

I'm not advocating a solipsistic outlook. In fact, it's quite the opposite. The thing is, it's not about what they think, it's about how they FEEL. More accurately, the feeling I'm creating in other people as they interact with me, from moment to moment. Instead of looking to their reactions to dictate my state, I put myself into a fun, confident, sexual state, draw them into my reality, then move things forward from there. Now I'm not running around trying to fill up the validation cup from some external source. Instead I have an infinite well of validation inside myself that I can draw from, and even share with others.

I was initially attracted to the game because it appealed to my sense of logic: I thought it was a cute little puzzle I could think my way out of. I could use my intellect to solve it and then I would never have to feel bad again. In the end, however, to gain true mastery I had to let go of logic and embrace emotions fully. Learning the game is not learning to be emotionless, but learning not to feel emotions toward silly shit that in the big picture is fairly trivial. Feelings exist, and nothing will change that. Learning the game simply conditions you to be emotionless toward the pointless stuff, so that you can point your attention toward the things that you really care about and that are really important.

We get back to the apartment and Shazzy hops straight into the bed. This girl is frisky as hell. I strip down to my shorts and go to the bathroom. As I pass Ozzie's room, I hear music: "Midnight Radio" from the *Hedwig* soundtrack. I look in and he's asleep. He must have passed out while watching the DVD for, like, the tenth time. I chuckle and continue down the hall.

Our bathroom is no bigger than the one I almost banged Shazzy in on the airplane. I brush my teeth and splash some water on my face. Looking in the mirror, I notice the upside-down star on my arm, still thick and defined after almost ten years. I run my fingers over it. Way back when I carved this shit in for the first time, the idea was, "Better to reign in Hell than to serve in Heaven." My version of reigning in Hell was attempting to exert control over everything, yet remaining fucked internally. I get that now. The five-pointed star really comes from the Pythagoreans, a mathematical symbol of organic perfection. Lust is integral to that perfection; it's what keeps us alive, generation after generation. It is hardwired into us, yet we get in its way with our guilt and our conditioning and our insecurities, instead of letting it just work. To "serve in Heaven" is to let go of that obsessive need for control, and be at peace with what is. There is only one thing that you can truly "control," and that is yourself. The only real control comes from within. It's so counterintuitive: I had to give up the thing I valued most in order to actually gain a semblance of it.

I always said that eventually, everybody leaves and ultimately, we are alone. In reality, *nobody* leaves, *ever*. Nobody is alone. We are together in our aloneness. My fear of abandonment came from knowing that I wasn't self-sufficient. I was terrified of being alone with myself, because I didn't like the person who I had become. That changes now. I'm still the same Jeff, I still have the same fundamental personality, yet I know with utter certainty that I'll never go back to living like that.

I'm filled with a sense of pride, not in an egoic sense, but pride in who we are as human beings, without fear or shame. I am finally aware of the mistakes I've been making. My "game" isn't just a veneer anymore; it finally permeates all the way to my core.

That's not to say I won't be tested. There's an old saying: "After enlightenment, the laundry." I know this new level of emotional fitness is something that's going to have to be maintained. You don't just go to the gym until you get in shape, then say, "Okay, that's enough!" and stop going. Once I get home, I'm going to have to get back down into the messy business of life, and do my best to integrate what I've learned. It's not like all of a sudden I've become some saint here. I may relapse and indulge in those old behaviors from time to time, despite my best efforts. But you know what? *Fuck it.* I accept and honor that too. My focus will be consistency, not perfection. If I keep heading in the right direction I'll get it. On a certain, intrinsic level, I have *won*.

Truth be told, I'm not really looking forward to leaving. I've made a good friend in Ozzie. Me and this dude have been through it in the past two months. But it's time to get back to the "real world." Got an Australian girl waiting in my bed to cuddle me.

This is the best week of my life.

ADIOS

Leaving Barcelona in a few hours. Ozzie drives me to the airport. When I get up to the counter, the guy next to me is having some kind of fit, yelling at the agent in Spanish.

"Whoa," I say, "trouble in paradise." The agent grimaces at me as I present my passport.

"Ah yes, sir, this flight was canceled." She braces for my response.

"Oh, well, that's . . . unfortunate. When's the next one?"

"I am afraid there is not another flight until ten P.M."

I look at my watch. That's in eleven hours. I laugh. I'm not even pissed. There's no point. I'm going to get where I'm going eventually. In the meantime, I can get some reading done. "Okay, that's cool. How's your day going?"

She seems surprised that I'm not blowing up at her, and that I'm actually taking some kind of personal interest. A smile crosses her face, and this time it's genuine. She sighs and says, "Ah, not so good."

"What are you gonna do, huh?"

She takes my bags and then starts typing into her computer. "Here you go, sir. I apologize for the delay. However, I was able to upgrade you to first class." I thank her and walk off, leaving the other guy at the desk, still screaming impotently. I smirk to myself as I stroll through the terminal, sunlight beaming in through the floor-to-ceiling windows.

I find a nice place to settle in for the next eleven hours, and reflect on the past two months. This experience was exactly what I needed at this particular time. I feel at peace. Optimistic. It's a strange feeling. I'm excited to get back home and start applying everything I've learned. I think for me, the ultimate message is to go out and bring value by expressing myself freely and harmoniously and not be attached in any way to the outcome. Living my life entirely on purpose and not being concerned with getting the "credit" for my actions, which is basically in direct opposition to the way I've been living for the better part of my life. All I've ever cared about was getting mine, and getting over on people, and I'm not proud of that. Yet in some ways, it was that suffering, that anger, that allowed me to get where I am today. When you're in the darkness, it's often *defiance* that spurs you on . . . you say to yourself, "If I break, it will be AFTER I defeat this BULLSHIT." And if you do go down, you're going to go down with your hands locked around its fucking throat, white-knuckled. The moments that define you are not those when you're lording it up in the club, but rather those times when you are on your knees, broken, your mouth filled with blood, and you want to give up. When all your beliefs, and all of the things you treasure are bullshit, and they mean *nothing*.

That is when you decide.

That emotional leverage is what allowed me to excel at pickup. Even though my motivations were fucked, it was all a necessary part of the growth process. Like the seed of a rose: it's not considered somehow "imperfect" because it's not fully formed yet. At the time, it was exactly what I needed, even though I couldn't fathom why.

I kick my feet up on my bag, crack open my book, a collection of letters written by the German poet Rilke, and begin reading where I left off:

> *Don't search for the answers, which could not be given to you*
> *now, because you would not be able to live them. And the point*
> *is to live everything. Live the questions now. Perhaps then,*
> *someday far in the future, you will gradually, without even*
> *noticing it, live your way into the answer.*

CABANAS COPAL

A hut in the middle of the jungle in Mexico. I've flown down for the week to attend the wedding of a friend from high school, Taffy, Hudson's date to the senior prom. Miraculously, she was able to corral nearly 120 people into coming, and we're all ensconced in this eco-resort about two hours south of Cancun. It's extremely Spartan: there's no electricity, and the lodging consists of log cabanas with thatched roofs, concrete floors and padlocks on the doors. There is, however, an abundance of natural beauty and serenity, which is exactly what I've been wanting lately.

It's been an interesting trip. About half of the attendees are people I've known since high school and haven't seen in several years. Many of them were shocked at the dramatic transformation I've made in the past six months. Over the course of the week, several of them have approached me, drunkenly gushing that they were "inspired" and vowing to effect a similar change in their own lives. I wasn't sure how to take this, but I told them each in turn that I'd be checking up on their asses.

I saw my old high school crush Anna Becker and her husband last night at the reception after the ceremony. I had mixed feelings as I approached them. Over the years, I guess I'd built her up to be this idealized phenomenon. And yeah, she looked just as radiant as I remembered her . . . better, even. This time, however, I didn't feel that yawning chasm between us, that sense of unattainability about her that I felt back in high school. Instead I just felt a certain presence. When I looked in her eyes it was like I was recognizing myself; that same consciousness manifesting itself. It's akin to a light shining behind a board with holes punched in it; while each hole may *appear* to be an individual source of light, in reality it's all the same. "Presence" is recognizing that and connecting with the other person in a way that transcends the actions being taken in the physical world. It's drawing people into your reality and saying, *Come here, shine through my pinhole, we are the same.* I wished them both well and went off to join the others on the beach.

There's a knock at the door and Hudson enters. "Oi," I say, "how'd it feel seeing your prom date get married last night?"

"I'm heartbroken." He feigns angst, bringing his hand to his chest as he sits down across from me. "There was an interesting conversation about you at breakfast this morning."

I'm intrigued. "Oh really?"

"Oh yeah. Half of these people are just trying to figure you out." I've been strolling about shirtless for most of the week with my ripped fucking abs rippling in the breeze, THUG LIFE emblazoned across them in a very realistic-looking fake tattoo. Not to mention the scars. "So," continues Hudson, "do you know that guy Paul? The little dude with the goatee?"

"Yeah. We spoke briefly the other day."

He says, "Yeah, well we're at the table and he goes, 'So what's up with that guy with the pentagram? Someone told me he teaches guys how to pick up girls?'"

I sigh. "Ahh here we go."

"Right. So I was like, yeah, and then he goes, 'Has that guy even gotten laid since we've been here?' And your girl was sitting right there, and she turns bright red and sort of sheepishly raises her hand. OOPS!"

I laugh, "Ohhh, haha, that's great." When I flew in, I had to take a shuttle from the airport with several other people, and randomly struck up a conversation with a nice lady who happened to be attending the wedding as well. Within two hours of arriving at the resort, she was back in my hut, sucking my dick while a lizard watched us from the ceiling. "YUP. I kind of hate to disappoint the guy, but you know," I say.

"Yeah, he shut up real quick."

"Ahh, she's a nice girl though."

"Yes, she is." We're both quiet for a minute, enjoying the moment. Hudson takes a hard look at me, then says, "Man. I gotta say . . . what the fuck happened to you in Spain?"

"Dude, just a lot of hard work, watching the diet, hitting the gym, riding the bike."

"Well yeah," he says, "but beyond the physical change. You're . . . different."

"How so?"

"Well . . . you smile now."

I laugh again. "Yeah, I guess I do. Weird, huh."

"Seriously. It's amazing. Look . . . I'm going to do it. I swear to you right now. I've been fucking up, dude. I'm gonna quit drinking; I'm gonna get my shit together. You're my witness. It starts here."

I nod. "All right. Shit, if I could do it, then anybody can. Congratulations." I extend my hand and he shakes it. "What time are you flying out?"

"Pretty soon. In fact, I better get going. Just wanted to say goodbye." He gets up. "Keep in touch, okay?"

I reply, "Absolutely. I'll see you soon." He walks out of the hut.

I lie back, under the mosquito netting. Time passes.

I'm staring at the lizard on the ceiling. He knows and now I finally see him move. I feel content. I contemplate a life like this and say out loud, "Why not?"

Why not?

Because I need to contribute. I need significance. I need variety and uncertainty. Rest has been necessary after the last six months of intense work. I feel my tendons and my muscles, hell, even my bones, RELAX-ING. I take a deep breath. I know I will come back stronger. It's time to go.

A couple of hours later, I'm in the airport, nursing a margarita in the bar as I wait for my flight to board. I think about this past week, and a strange feeling wells up in my chest. I think about what Hudson said in the hut, what the others said earlier in the week. I actually start to mist up, and I put my sunglasses on. I really inspired them. I've never felt like this. It's amazing. I will follow up on these guys, on all of them, and share in their success. Sounds like a new goal. As I sit and ponder this, I'm overcome with a certain tranquility. It occurs to me that I am, for the first time in my life, actually *living* in alignment with my purpose and working to fulfill the roles I've been neglecting; being a better lover, a better friend, a better coach, a better son and brother.

This experience has been truly strange. All of the things I thought were so important, the adulation, the lay score, none of that matters to me anymore; oddly enough, however, I find those things coming to me more and more, often through some strange convergence of circumstance. The difference, however, is that now they're simply the icing on the cake. I understand now that the true reward comes from the *playing of the game*: from getting out there and meeting people, from going in fearlessly and bringing the party. There is no reason for the interaction but the interaction itself. The interaction IS the reward. Channeling that awesome "nimbus" feeling in myself and sharing it with other people, shining it brightly to the world, that's the best high there is.

ORANGE COUNTY

I'm sitting in the living room in my mother's house in Orange County, next to the Christmas tree festooned with ornaments, some of which I made myself when I was in first grade. It's the middle of the afternoon, and I'm the only one here. I'm working on some stuff for RSD. Tyler has commissioned me to prepare a six-hour seminar based on my experiences in the game, and I've been hacking away at it diligently for the past couple of months. It's coming together nicely, and it should be ready to present at the next conference.

I decide to take a break, and open up my web browser to check my email. There's one message in my inbox. It's from a former student, a guy I had on program a few months back. If I remember correctly, he actually got laid during the Bootcamp, something that's been happening more and more as we continue to refine the program. When our teaching focus was solely on tactics and routines, a student actually getting laid on program was a rare occurrence. Novice students on average took two years to get "good." Now we teach a "natural" game: the focus has shifted more toward letting the student learn from his own experience, helping him tap into the charismatic part of himself that already exists and helping him get out of his own way. Getting him to experience the flow state and letting his biological imperatives do the rest. Bringing to his attention the most obvious, easily correctable errors, and guiding him in the right direction so that the more difficult ones self-correct over the long term. Novice students (many of whom have never heard of "opinion openers," "negs," "AMOGs" or any of this shit) are getting laid on the program roughly 65 percent of the time, and it takes a guy on average two to six months to attain a level of competence that most would describe as good.

Occasionally I'll get a student who asks, "Well, you learned routines first, isn't that a necessary phase?" I'll patiently explain to him that in light of the above statistics, the "routines phase" isn't necessary at all, and may in fact be *detrimental* to their development. In any case, I'm a firm believer in Bruce Lee's *Jeet Kune Do* philosophy: "Take what is useful and discard what is useless." There is a time and a place for "canned material." However, it is employed much more sparingly now. The focus is on developing core confidence, bringing value to the table, leading and escalating, and remaining untouchably positive.

The proof is in the pudding, and the results speak for themselves. I'm very pleased with the program these days, yet I'm still striving to improve it even more; it can always get better. I pop open the email and start reading:

> Four Months Post-Bootcamp.
> Hey guys, so this just happened last night. I was at a bar in Venice. Hitting on this rather stunning blonde bartender dressed in a nurse's uniform, it's the theme of that place.
> I turned to chat to the girl next to me and noticed a pair of

big brown eyes watching me. Timid smile and shy giggle. I opened this amazing young angel who I found out later had broken wings. This girl was an artist, a kindred spirit and she was hurting.

We started flirting and bonding and I could just tell it was on. She slipped away to the bathroom and while she was there the Nurse Bartender leaned over and told me the story. This girl I was with had been sexually attacked three weeks ago by some dirty random bastard in a bathroom at a restaurant. It had broken her world in two and she was in bad shape.

She came back and we started joking around again. Heavy eye contact, deep connection and later she told me what had happened to her, and that she didn't expect to meet someone like me that night. When she told me I didn't flinch. Later I made her laugh, I made her smile, we talked in gibberish and giggled at nothing. Everything I said connected. Not even with words.

She took me home, she said I just understood her and that she needed to be reminded why men are beautiful. She cried during the sex, just needing that release of energy. I reminded her that she was a goddess, that she was special and she was a woman.

After we'd slept together she played me her CD. Guys, she has the most amazing voice I have heard in a long time and was a very spiritual soul. Her whole life has been turned upside down by this tragic event. She felt guilty about it. Because of some scumbag. He had tried to take sex away from her, make it dirty, make her dirty. Around her bed were printed statements of affirmation. Attempts to rebuild her soul.

I helped ground her later, a rock to hold on to in the storm. This morning I sent her to the police station to finish giving them her story. She didn't want to go. Wanted to put it off again. She called the detective to try and procrastinate. I gave her a gentle push and she went. They have the guy, now they just need her to tell her story again. They have enough to convict the guy, yet SHE still feels guilty.

I left her my number. Maybe I'll see her again, maybe I won't.

It's times like this I'm glad I know what I know and that I can bring the world back into alignment a little bit. The Game can be beautiful sometimes. It's not just about banging 9s and 10s, it's about reminding the world what real men are.

Best wishes to you all, James. Bootcamp Aug 2006

LOVE

I am at a point where I truly don't give a FUCK anymore. I've said that before, but this time it's in a *good* way. I go out, and I blast game on autopilot because it's my personality now. I rarely take numbers, preferring instead to give mine out. If thcy call, they call.

I'm not a player, and I'm not a boyfriend.

Sex comes to me if I want it. I lay back and they show up. Once you understand that game is not about individual wins and losses, but about the "snowball effect," that's when a true abundance mentality takes hold. And it's real. "Last-minute resistance" is no longer an issue because I'm no longer trying to *entertain* her into the bedroom. If she's down, the switch has been flipped long before that. If she's not, then that's fine too. Shit like that doesn't bother me anymore. Come to think of it, almost nothing bothers me anymore.

My view is this: I've been to the moon, man. Porn stars, threesomes, strippers, etc. What more is there? I'm not trying to prove anything anymore, not to myself or anyone else. It's just self-evident. It is what it is, and I just am what I am now: a guy with some pretty tight game. Being able to pick up doesn't make you superior. It doesn't save your soul. At the end of the day, it's just about as cool as knowing how to do kung fu.

And kung fu is very cool indeed.

Thing is, just because you know karate, that doesn't mean you have to go around kicking everybody's ass. I don't have to pick up every girl I see because, let's be honest, I know that I probably could. The struggle of the initial learning curve is over. Now all that remains is to just refine refine refine, and more importantly, enjoy the fruits of all the work I've put in thus far.

I didn't do this just to fuck a shit-ton of hot chicks (although that has been, admittedly, AWESOME). I did it so that when I do finally happen upon a woman I'd actually want to have a real relationship with, I have the ability to step up, execute and *not fuck it up*. I can bring her into my world, and explore hers. I can make her my girl. Not to fill some void, not as some object to possess, but as an individual and a gift. To be kind, not "right." Love, like control, comes from within. I'm ready to share it now, unconditionally.

In a way, the game was my therapy. When you go out and interact with thousands upon thousands of strangers, it's like having a decade's worth of emotional experiences shoved into a couple of years. After all of this, I simply feel as though I am impervious to bullshit. This allows me to be more "present" in my relationships. I feel completely aligned with that masculine polarity, the rock in the storm. I'm finally prepared to show vulnerability. If I get hurt, oh well. I'm willing to accept that. You can't control others, you can only control yourself. I know that if my woman were to violate any of my serious boundaries, I'd be GAAHHHN. Boom, field time again, and I'd enjoy that equally as much as being in the relationship. Not that I'd be entertaining negative outcome scenarios, but were it to happen, I'd have no problem getting back out there and letting the warrior loose. None. The game will always be a home for me.

Most guys just "settle down" with the first girl they're semi-attracted to who will agree to fuck them, and then when the relationship goes to shit, they scratch their heads, wonder why and repeat ad nauseam. You can't change people; you can only preselect to the best of your ability and see what happens. My experience has allowed me to really home in on the qualities that I absolutely will not accept, and the ones I actively want in a relationship. The kind of stuff that literally would never have crossed my mind prior to getting out there and experiencing it firsthand. Further, I've learned that we don't attract what we want, we attract what we are. Since I've started to embody the characteristics I want, the quality of girl I've been hooking up with lately has gone through the roof. Right now I'm seeing a successful photographer, a lawyer, a sportscaster and a political consultant. These are all intelligent, athletic, well-adjusted and ambitious women. It's awesome. Fantastic.

There's no longer this compulsion to rack up some massive lay score. I'm on the lookout for a girlfriend, but that's not born of some compulsive need either. When she comes along, I'll know. If you keep the window closed, then the wind won't blow in; but even if you open it, it might or it might not. All you can do is open the window. Or you can open three or four, and maybe try and get a draft going. Heheh.

It's 7 P.M., and I roll to Nihon Whisky Lounge.

I'm meeting the High-Powered Political Consultant (HPPC) and some of her friends here. I stop at the bar to order a drink and take a look around. Interesting atmosphere . . . old-school Japanese meets industrial chic, wooden beams and iron, low couches, candlelight. The wall behind the bar is covered in bottles of scotch, all the way up to the twenty-five-foot ceiling. I'm wondering how they get at those bottles up at the very top, when I get a text message: "We're upstairs."

I go up . . . seems this is where the dining takes place. As I approach the table, I recognize several of her "friends" as high-level elected officials and prominent figures in local politics. I sit down. I didn't realize she was this connected.

"So," says one of them between bites of mediocre and overpriced food, "YOU'RE Jeff Allen." It appears that everyone in this group refers to one another by their full name, first and last. "The motivational speaker, right?"

"Yeah, that's me." All eyes are on me as they start grilling me to see if I'm good enough for their beloved girl, HPPC. I can feel the pressure.

A round of shots is ordered and brought to the table. Before the toast, however, my glass is removed. "You can have it after you give us a one-minute motivational speech," says Elected Official #1. Jesus, I just woke up.

They stare.

I clear my throat and launch a little bit into disempowering identity frames, ending with a quote from James Allen: " 'Circumstances do not make a man; they reveal him.' The sobering aspect of this is that we have no one to blame for our problems but ourselves. On the other hand, this means our possibilities are limitless."

"To limitless possibilities," says Elected Official #1, as we all take the shots.

RED RACER

So I'm on a goddamn roll these past few weeks. It's been nice. Bang bang bang. Every day I'm banging, usually multiple women. The overall effect of this has oddly enough been to make me hornier. I feel like a shark with a boner. They can pick up on this. Add a professional level of smoothness, game and value, and all doors are opened for you. Girls just wanna have fun.

I'm meeting Chrispy tonight, at what used to be the Odeon. It's since changed ownership and they've instituted something called "Gong Show Karaoke." It's a bit like *American Idol*: three "celebrity" judges watch the performances and have the ability to gong your ass offstage. If you manage to get through the whole song, each judge scores you from 1 to 10 and the singer with the highest score wins the grand prize of $23.50. Invariably, by the end of the night, it deteriorates into an alcohol-soaked nightmare.

I roll up on my red Schwinn. As I'm locking it up out front, a homeless person approaches me, trying to sell me a copy of the *Street Sheet*. "Hold on," I say. I stand up and dig in my back pocket, bringing out about a buck's worth of change and some pills. "Here dude." I hand him the change. "You want some dietary supplements too? These are digestive enzymes, here's some branched-chain amino acids, and uh . . . milk thistle, it's for the liver."

"Fo da livah?! Give ME dat one!"

I go inside and post up at the bar, reading the *Street Sheet* as I wait for Christophe. I wonder whatever happened to the homeless guy who punched me in the mouth on Christmas Eve all those years ago. Heh, he's probably still standing there on Fourth Street. I remember how I felt when I saw the "bruise" on my mouth after being hit, not realizing that it was just dirt: violated, powerless. In actuality, I wasn't hurt at all. It's funny . . . that's sort of a metaphor for my life. I thought there was this giant bruise on it, but the whole time, all I had to do was wipe it away. I order a Johnnie Walker Black, neat, and cheers to the air, sipping on it.

Before long, a cute girl takes the seat next to me at the bar. I turn to her and say, "Excuse me . . . you appear to be quite a classy lady."

She smiles and says, "Oh, do I?"

"Yeah. You know, I would LOVE the opportunity to purchase for you a bottle of *fine red wine* . . . PERHAPS OVER CHEESE?"

She laughs, and I'm in. I introduce myself and we start talking. Boom. I open the valve and unleash the flow. It's good. About fifteen minutes into the conversation, she says something and curses ("motherfucker") and I chastise her: "Do you kiss your mother with that mouth?"

"Yes," she replies, "every day."

I say, "Yeah . . . SO DO I." She sits there shocked, and I go, "IN THE ASS. Damn, girl your teeth look white, do you bleach them?"

"Uhhh, no." She's confused, but still sort of smiling at the compliment. I lean closer.

"I want to see . . . what they taste . . . like . . ." Cue makeout. I pull away. She's breathing heavily. Her friends come to take her home, but before she leaves, she gets my number. This shit is on for sure.

By this time, Chrispy has shown up. I go outside with him while he has a smoke. While we're out there, who shows up but the leader of the old "Anti-Jeffy Conspiracy Group." Lauren. As she walks past, I say, "Hey." She looks at me but doesn't recognize me, which is understandable, given that I've shaved my head, grown a beard and put on ten pounds of muscle. She does a double take and walks into the bar.

Later, she approaches me as I'm telling some story to Chrispy near the photo booth. "So," she says, "thought I didn't recognize you?"

"Hey, Lauren," I say. She stands there with her arms crossed, glaring. "It's really good to see you."

She doesn't know what to do with it. She says, "What is this, some kind of trick?"

The energy I'm giving off is entirely nonconfrontational. I know I was wrong and I deserve whatever she's going to say here. "No trick. Look . . . since you're here, I just wanted to apologize, for, you know . . . being a douchebag." I laugh.

She looks to Christophe, who says, "Yeah that's true, he wahz a beet of a doojzhbahhg."

She stammers for a bit, then says, "Well . . . yeah, you were. I guess I was too. I'm glad to see you've grown."

"Yeah, so am I . . . so am I." I look her up and down and say, "Wow. You look really good." It's true, she does. "Damn, girl . . ."

"Uh . . . thanks?"

I say, "I just want to give you a hug," and go for it. She stands there, slightly weirded out, with a look on her face that borders between amused and disturbed.

"Um," she says, "okay." Her buddy stands off to the side, shocked. "I guess this means we're friends again?"

"Yeah, I guess so."

"All right then. Try not to fuck it up this time."

"Hey, I can't promise anything. I'm still kind of a dick. I'm just not a COMPLETE dick anymore."

"Okay Jeff," she laughs, shaking her head as she walks off.

The night continues. After a devastating Journey performance that sees me ripping off my shirt, beating my chest with the mic, having an epileptic fit on the floor and slapping duct tape on my mouth, the female judge gives me a 10 for the second time in a row and that's when I know it's on. I can see it in her eyes.

My final score is a 28 out of 30. I'm in the lead, but I'm edged out by a guy who does "Purple Rain" at the very end of the night. A classic trump move . . . shrewd. I know they're going to award him a perfect score, but I don't even care. As he goes through the song, I'm right there with him, hands in the air, waving them back and forth, cheering louder than anyone. I'll win it next week, assholes. I came to ROCK.

The judge chick comes out as I'm unlocking my bicycle. I go, "Hey."

She goes, "Hey."

I say, "Look, you wanna smoke some chronic with me?"

She says, "Yeah."

I pull my bike into the street. "Get on the pegs."

She gets on the pegs, and I pedal off; on the back, she feels weightless.

ABOUT REAL SOCIAL DYNAMICS

www.realsocialdynamics.com

www.rsdnation.com

1(888) 546-7286

MY COMPANY REAL SOCIAL DYNAMICS (RSD) is the world's largest international dating coaching company. With coaches based in Los Angeles, New York, London, Sydney, and San Francisco, programs are conducted in major metropolitan cities throughout the world.

Through its LIVE world tours, Real Social Dynamics conducts Bootcamps and conferences that have trained over 20,000 clients, including a diverse variety of individuals ranging from Fortune 100 executives, royalty, celebrities, college students, and professionals in over 200 cities and 60 different countries.

RSD specializes in dating advice, image consultation, public representation, and integrating clients into social scenes. Initially, live programs were offered solely through word of mouth via private clients. However, now, top-tier dating coaching is made available for the public via the internet and direct phone contact with the RSD Headquarters in Los Angeles, making available a variety of products aside from the signature Bootcamps and conferences, including DVD programs, live teleconferences, and monthly "mastermind" seminars.

RSD's dating coaching branch is a top-tier operation, run by the firm's best instructors, who invested thousands of hours of field research over the years meeting attractive women, and interviewing the world's most popular dating book authors, image consultants, and executive coaches.

RSD's Live Programs provide clients a unique opportunity to meet its dating coaches, become their wingmen, learn from countless hours of field research, witness dating coaches attract beautiful women in live demonstrations in real-world scenarios, and have them as their personal coach and image consultant.

THE JEFFY SHOW: If you're interested in a more detailed explanation of the tactics and principles I've alluded to throughout this book, check out *The Jeffy Show,* a six-DVD program produced by RSD and featuring Jeffy himself.

The Jeffy Show will give you a soup-to-nuts tactical breakdown of every stage of the game. Lines, gambits, stories—he lays his entire toolbox bare.

He's holding nothing back. This is the distilled wisdom from five years of Jeffy's one relentless obsession—attracting women.

If you want a program that will give you everything you need to get off the ground, this is it. *The Jeffy Show* WILL deliver you to the "promised land." So prepare to have your mind blown . . . and your entire way you approach the game changed forever. Get your dating life handled now, Jeffy style: http://www.jeffyshow.com

"The biggest thing that I've learned from *The Jeffy Show* is that you can do absolutely anything you want. It all comes from your core. You can do anything—there's limitless possibilities. Listening to Jeffy speak, it was so inspiring, like to the point where . . . wow I feel like I could take over the world if I just put my mind to it like he did. It was absolutely phenomenal.

"This will change you! From the core of your being. This will help you overcome <u>every single sticking point and problem</u> that you've had in the field, that you've had in pick up with women, and basically your entire life. Do it!"

—Adam L., Connecticut

"*The Jeffy Show* had a real experience to tell me. It told me about all this stuff that I couldn't even imagine if I didn't hear it from a real person.

Seeing is believing. Jeff gives his life story, and not only that, but his secrets of pickup. Without his speech I don't know if I would have had the vision to succeed that I have now."

—Dan B., Kentucky

"*The Jeffy Show* was just unbelievable. He really addresses every issue to what you're looking at for having game, not only from the outside. It starts from the inside out.

"The program is worth every penny and you're not going to be disappointed. It'll address everything that you're thinking about, you know? It's worth it . . . buy it!"

—James S., Los Angeles

"I watched through *The Jeffy Show*, and in less than a week it's made a dramatic difference in my game. This last Friday night I had my first 'one night stand.' I'm 19 and I'm glad I got ahold of this as early as I did."

—"Noodle" (taken from RSD Nation forum)

"I attended the recording of *The Jeffy Show* and just had the best day of my life learning all kinds of great stuff: how to create opportunities in the bar scene, how to just get and command respect with women and with men in all situations. It's like I have a map and a plan to follow, I feel like I'm not trapped in the maze . . . I would've never dreamed that I could have this much fun.

"Jeff just kinda showing his soul, where he started from a low point and not covering that up and just saying, 'Hey I was way down here,' and then giving all of his heart and putting himself on the line just shows anybody can do it.

"He stuck with it, and it's like any of us could be that guy, just takes a little bit of work, that's the main thing to remember. It's not looks, it's not smarts, it's just doing. I'd say it's comprehensive, it's from the ground up . . . He covered everything, from meeting the girl in the bar, to how to get her home. There's nothing missing, it's complete."

—Eric, Los Angeles

"It's a phenomenal program, well rounded start to finish, gives you just about everything you need to know with pickup, with developing your game, fundamentals, you name it. It's a true inspiration for the average guy, for sure.

"It taught me to reach out and pull out my inner uniqueness, to grab on to it, go with it, go with what you know inside, develop it, and it will come out. And to pretty much break free and make your own life.

"Yes, it taught me to go out there and focus on what your intent is, go out there and focus on what you need to get accomplished, and just do it. I would say that it's a definite, credible, well thought out program and I highly recommend it."

—John, Phoenix

"I just watched *The Jeffy Show* and I must say Jeffy is the man! He goes down in detail to get you through the whole pickup: from the approach, to on the phone, to the Day 2, I mean anything you want to know about pickup basically . . . it's here. In detail. In depth. Everything you need to know . . .

"I mean whether you're old, bald, ugly, whether you think you're ugly . . . doesn't matter. Come check this out because he will teach you how to live the life of like a rock star. I learned from Jeffy the phone game, how to get rid of all these nervous little body ticks . . . just what lines to use. He just has so much there it's just like . . . I mean everything is there. It's all encompassing, I'm just blown away at this point. If you're on the edge about buying the program, just buy it!"

—Kevin, Los Angeles

RSD BOOTCAMP: An astonishing three-day "mega-intense" live-in-field training program that obliterates all obstacles thwarting your success with women, the RSD Bootcamp has been meticulously honed since 2002 to guarantee nothing but undeniable, hard-hitting and instantly noticeable results.

Taught by some of the most extraordinary men on the planet . . . each executive coach is "hand-picked" personally by Executive Producer and RSD Co-Founder Owen Cook (aka "Tyler Durden") from among thousands of the world's most successful and qualified men who've applied.

With a hyperstrict student/instructor ratio of 3 to 1, nothing can compare to the riveting rush of challenging yourself to the core . . . blasting through success barriers and likely getting what most men would consider "lucky." We promise you will sharpen your pickup skills to a razor's edge and instill a breakthrough "sexually abundant" paradigm in your reality or your money back . . . with our full "ironclad" 100 percent money back guarantee.

When you've mustered up the guts to man up and finally take immediate control of your love life, know that your Executive Coach is patiently waiting to launch you on the "fast track" to your new (and deserved) lifestyle of sexual abundance and dating success.

Absolutely open to all skill levels (as this program is tailored to you personally) and guaranteed, no matter who you are, to change your life forever.

http://realsocialdynamics.com/bootcamps.asp

Glory and Destruction:
Jeffy Bootcamp—August 23–25, 2008

"Jeffy leaned forward, began explaining what he expected of us as students, as men. He could only bring 7 out of 10 to this Bootcamp. If we wanted a 10 out of 10 experience, we were responsible for our week-end, for our success, for our fate. The words Jeffy spoke were like elec-trons charging a capacitor. I felt like that green dude from *Street Fighter* who shoots electricity. I felt prepared for unbridled glory.

"There's a cougarish two set behind us," Jeffy whispered. I was al-ready standing by the time he said to get up and approach.

Leering over the women and interrupting their conversation, I intro-duced myself. One giggled, shook my hand and told me her name. When I turned to the other, offering my hand, all I got in return was a scowl as my hand hung, unshook.

"Soooo . . . , " I continued, turning to the warm girl, and began spit-ting nonsense. She giggled and matched my masculine nonsense with her feminine nonsense. It was on. However, the nonglorious, scowling friend kept interjecting with comments intended to offend and deter me. But it all seemed vaguely humorous and irrelevant. All that mattered was the moment and the feeling. The dawn of nimbus.

"How do you two know each other?" I asked out of habit.

"Friends," my warm, nonsensical feminine girl perked. "How do you know those guys?" she parroted, pointing to our table, shimmering in the glory of Jeffy and my recently knighted brothers in arms.

When I recited the answer Jeffy wanted us to tell when asked this question, Bootcamp would get kicked up a gear.

"Actually, this is a bachelor party. Our friend Jeff is the groom-to-be and we're hunting for his wife. Tonight. At the bar. Once we find her, we're all flying to Vegas so they can get married, then divorced. This is all so Jeff can change his Facebook status to 'divorced.'"

Quick Zack Morris time-out. I am going to interrupt this epic Boot-camp retelling to call attention to the absolute absurdity of the above paragraph. I hope the utter ridiculousness of employing one of the most sanctimonious and costly social institutions to authenticate the frivolity of a "relationship status" on a social networking internet site deviates enough from the average reader's reality that you LOL'd or, at the very least, WTF'd at the aforementioned response.

Well, this was not the case for San Franciscan drunk ex-strippers.

Suddenly the previously cold girl came alive and leaned over the table, touching my arm.

"Wait, you guys are having a bachelor party? Do you guys have strippers?"

"Ehhh . . . no. Well, I mean maybe, if Jeff ends up meeting one at the bar and marrying her . . ."

"I don't have my heels with me, but I have my iPod!" cold woman exclaimed. "I used to strip . . . I'll give you guys a discount!"

"Umm . . . yeah, I think we're all set."

"No! You guys need a stripper! I will work your friend sooo hard!"

"Hmmmm . . . interesting. Well, maybe we can all meet up at the club later or—"

"No!" ex-stripper informed me. "We're not meeting at the club! Wait, do you guys have a hotel room? We can do it there. It'll only take a half hour!"

"Yeah, I should probably get back to my friends . . ."

"Wait," my warm girl chimed in. "I'LL meet you guys at the club. Give me your number!"

"Okay," I said. I programmed my number into her phone and walked back to our table.

Smiling, Jeff congratulated me on a solid open. Not wanting to wreck the moment, I neglected to tell him about the whole stripper thing, figuring it was irrelevant.

Jeff got back to detailing how the night would unfold. After about ten minutes, I felt a sharp tap on my shoulder.

"I want to see ROB." I heard my name spoken with unswerving certainty by the venomous lips of an ex-stripper.

"Ummm . . . okay," I said, getting up as if in reaction. Like Tyler said in *Blueprint*, the weight of a hot girl's beliefs can seem very heavy.

Hilariously, as she led me like a prisoner back to her table, I heard Jeffy cackle and shout: "Pft! See, if she tried that shit on me, I would've been like, NO!"

The ex-stripper sat me in a chair and leaned forward like an interrogator with a spotlight in my face.

"Why don't you have a stripper?"

"Ehhh . . ."

"You guys need a stripper. I'm going to strip for you. I'm even going to give you a discount."

I felt the statements cut through me like gamma rays. She seemed so sure of what she was saying. She seemed so determined to melt me into a puddle of man-mush. This was a woman used to getting her way, used to destroying chodey men. My nimbus wasn't yet strong enough to repel her, I could only repeat: "You should really talk to Jeff."

"Why should I talk to Jeff?" she snorted.

"Because . . . he makes the decisions."

A smile crept over her face. In the candlelight, she looked like an evil temptress, like a sexy comic book villainess who delightedly minces men to their death.

"Yes," she cooed, "I'll talk to JEFF." She spoke his name with oozing contempt. "You just watch! I'll work your friend JEFF." At that, she stood up and pranced over to our table.

"Which one's JEFF?" she demanded.

Jeffy, slumped in the leather armchair, halfheartedly raised his hand.

"SO!" the ex-stripper boomed. "It's your bachelor party? You're look-ing to have some FUN?"

"If by 'fun,'" Jeffy grinned, "you mean 'fucking sluts in the ass,' then yes."

The room exploded. The stripper hit Jeff with congruence test after shit test after chode destroyer and Jeff just kept coming back with bet-ter and better responses. In the course of five minutes, I watched Jeff push her off his lap, stick his hands down her pants (asking if her pock-ets were "girl pockets"), rub his face in her tits and ask "Mommy?," tell her he was going to "purchase for her one fine bottle of red wine, and, perhaps some cheese," all while not flinching a bit and completely owning the frame. I saw mastery firsthand. I saw sex-worthiness. And it looked glorious.

Eventually we left the lounge, finishing the seminar portion in a hotel room, and then hit the club.

Even though Jeff said just to be friendly, I was ready to explode in the club. I promised myself when I walked through the door, I'd hit the first set in sight like a fucking jackhammer.

The door opened . . . and . . . there were only three dudes at the bar and a table with (what we'd later find out were) two transsexuals. Non-glory times.

I ordered a beer and talked to Jeff as more people wandered in. At the time, my thought cycle kept repeating: You're on Bootcamp > You should be in set > You're choding just talking to Jeff. However, in retro-spect, relaxing and settling into the environment calmed my nerves, and, by talking to Jeff, I tuned in to his rhythm and presence, which dialed up my nimbus to state deluxe.

After about twenty minutes, Jeff looked at me, smiling. "Look. There's a table of people in the back," he pointed. "Just roll up, be friendly, try to start the party, and I'll come wing you in a minute."

"Yes!" I clapped my hands. "Awesome!" I spun and did a strut across the club.

If I could distill and bottle what I experienced for the ten seconds I moved across the club, I'd have the elusive magic bullet elixir that could get anyone laid. Literally, my skin was surging with electric current; my eyes could silence throbbing music and freeze motion; my voice boomed from a drum in my stomach; the most powerful and primitive aphrodisiac radiated from every pore: NIMBUS. I was no longer under a jurisdic-tion dictated by the laws of science: my steps were light and ethereal, exempt from the tax of gravity; my brain rearranged the chemistry of my neurotransmitters so that every signaling molecule sang a war anthem of triumph; my biological body transcended its cells and organs and bones to become pure energy, a cloud of party.

I thought I had felt "the nimbus" before. I thought the on nights where everything out of my mouth was gold or I picked up some bitchy model or got a thirty-second tonguedown were "nimbus nights." When I tried to explain this to Jeffy later, he perfectly articulated true nimbus, clarify-ing: "It's like someone who snorts coke. No one who snorts coke for the first time says, 'Hmmmm, I think I may be high.' No! that motherfucker KNOWS he's high cause he's like wooooooooooooooooooooooooooooo ooo!!!!!!!!!"

To get all nerd and analytical about it, I realized nimbus (for me) is three equal parts: 1) the woooo, 2) core confidence, and 3) 100 percent belief.

Back in New York, I had the woooo, I'd cultivated the core confidence, but my belief still wasn't 100 percent. Perhaps I'd thought it was 100 percent, but I realized, as I walked across that club, that 100 percent belief is walking up to a large seated mixed set knowing they were either going to have to accept me as their leader or *physically relocate their party.* There was no way I was going to slink away a chodey failure in front of Jeffy.

Closing in, I started clapping my hands. A toothy smile exploded on my face. I walked up to the group and shouted, "AWESOME!"

Everyone stopped and looked at me, amazed. Nimbus doesn't put people in spectator mode; it puts them in freeze frame. I repeated "Aweeeeeeeeeeeeeeeeeeeee-someeeeeeeeeeeee" until the hottest girl in the group jumped up and shrieked.

She ran up to me like a starstruck groupie. She was hot: blonde, skinny, huge tits, sparkly evening gown deluxe.

"Are you gay?" she chirped, "Are you gay?"

"Am . . . I . . . gay?" I repeated in mockery. "Worst. Pickup line. Ever. Get over here." Boom. Claw. Actually, no. To label the clamp I put on this chickity's shoulder a "claw" is utterly misleading. The nimbus upgraded the civilian's claw to the Embrace of Destiny, to the Midas Touch of Fuck.

I walked her away from her friends, talking simply for the sake of feeling the crackling energy of my voice. I paraded her to the dance floor. Pelvic grind times. I asked her name. She responded, "Does it even matter?" We start making out. Boner-inducing tonguedown (or, according to the Jeffy Kiss Scale, a "Stage 3").

As we're making out, I hear Jeffy cackling. I see him trying to snap a picture. In between makeouts, my girl is whispering erotic nothings into my ear. For the first time, I start thinking logically: Do I pull and leave Bootcamp after two approaches or do I throw away a perfectly good bang session.

My girl swivels to her knees and bites my dick over my jeans. I'm shocked, a little embarrassed and completely turned on. She wants to leave. I tell her I need to spend time with Jeff. But it's me and her tonight. I'll find her later. She asks me again if I'm sure I'm not gay. I'm sure. I'll find her later. Me and her. Tonight. We go our separate ways.

When I return to Jeffy, he says, "Oh man. That's like when you're playing pool and you're breaking, and you accidentally hit the eight ball in. Nice."

While I was dancing and making out, I didn't realize the club had filled up. Cuties were swarming everywhere. I don't even remember how many girls I opened, but I do remember how many blew me out: zero. At one point, I realized I lost one of my peacocky silver rings and was opening girls with "Find my ring for me." They obeyed, getting on their hands and knees, but the ring was lost. Oh well, I guess it's symbolic in a way.

I moved through the crowd like a trail of ignited gasoline. Whatever I did, wherever I went a party ensued. I wasn't even opening anymore; I was PARTY STARTING. It was like the instant I faced a group of girls, they magnetized to me—even before I spoke. One particular highlight was a group of Polish girls who flocked me. As I was speaking to them, these chodes kept piping in stupid comments as the girls blocked them out. I figured they were just linger chodes and continued to make the girls shriek and giggle for my own amusement and fun. When I turned to talk to Jeffy, one of the guys tapped me. With his shoulders slouched and a sad look on his face, he mumbled, "Hey man . . . I just want to let you know . . . those are our . . . our girlfriends." If a white flag of defeat could make noise, this is what it would sound like.

"No problem, dude," I boomed, backslapping him as I surveyed the room. I noticed a chode grinding my girl (blonde evening gown) from behind. I walked toward them with the same impulse I felt as a kid when I played Super Mario and I'd get star power. Sometimes, even if I was past one of those annoying duck guys, I'd still turn Mario around and run him into the duck for the simple reason that I could and it's funny. I decided to ruin this chode's little grindfest for the simple reason that I could and it seemed funny.

Without saying a word, I walked up to my girl, smiled and commenced tonguedown. Instant chode vaporization. We reconvened with inappropriate and salacious acts on the dance floor. Biting and hair pulling deluxe. Genital stimulation times. A boner for me and a doggy dinner bowl for the lady.

I didn't know what to do, so I went to look for Jeffy. I felt someone grab me from behind and say, "Look. One takeaway, you're fine. Two takeaways, you're pushing it. Three takeaways and you're done. This is the second takeaway you've done with this chick. One more and it's over."

I turned around and saw a concerned Jeffy. He continued, "You have to pull this girl. Now."

"But . . . , " I stammered. "But . . . Bootcamp just started. I don't want to leave yet. Can I pull her and come back?"

"I didn't say you had to leave. I said you have to pull her."

"How . . . am I . . . going to pull her . . . but not leave . . ."

I realized the answer simultaneously as Jeffy said, "Bathroom." He seemed to notice my concern and assured me, "If we get kicked out, we'll go somewhere else. Take her to the upstairs bathroom where no one will see. Do it! PULL!"

I've just recently got used to same-night lays and feeling comfortable pulling girls out of clubs, so pulling a chick into a bathroom was not only out of my comfort zone, it was out of my reality. But this is why I came to Bootcamp. This is why I was born with a dick.

"Come on," I said, grabbing my girl by the hand. "I want to show you something upstairs."

"I can't," my girl said, "I don't want to leave my friends."

"Yeah," I said then initiated a passionate tonguedown. "This is really important. We have to see this magical upstairs area. It transcends glorious . . . COME!" Hard hand pull and she's giggling and walking up the stairs with me.

When we get up stairs, I walk past the bar toward the hallway with the bathrooms and say, "Oh wow, we gotta check this out. Interesting . . ."

"Wait, this is just the—" Boom. Push her against the wall, hardcore tonguedown. I pull back, checking for compliance. She's smiling seductively.

"Come," I say and try to pull her into the men's room.

"Nooooooooooooooooo," she laughs. "I'm not going in the men's room with you!"

"Yeah." I kiss her. "Okay."

We do inappropriate and salacious acts outside the bathroom for about ten minutes. She does her little swivel down cock-bite move again. Delicious. As I go to lick her neck, I notice a shimmering silhouette standing crossed-armed in the door frame. Rays of holy light are shinning from his short, golden beard and mullet. It's Jeff. I know what I have to do.

"Come," pull toward bathroom.

"Noooooo."

"Okay," more inappropriate and salacious acts.

Five minutes later: "Come," pull toward bathroom.

"Noooooo."

"Okay," more inappropriate and salacious acts.

Ten minutes later: "Come," pull toward bathroom.

BOOM. Pull to the bathroom. Lock the stall. Glorious, X-rated times. We finish up. She leaves shortly after.

I find Jeff and inform him he's now "27 for 36." After a laugh and gentleman's high-five, he sends me upstairs for more glory.

I bust into the first set I see—two girls—and immediately throw them both in freeze frame. One of the girls actually says, "WOW! You make a GREAT first impression!" (total chodette compliment). As I'm booming self-amusement and spitting nonsense, some chode scampers up and says, "Ohhhh . . . look out for this guy. He's a PLAYA. Aren't you the guy who was just hooking up with some girl IN THE BATHROOM???"

Back in New York, I might've ignored this dude or used some elaborate "alpha" tactic, but, to be honest, it just seemed vaguely funny and distant to me. My response was simply, "Hahahahahahahahahahaha . . . Yeah, that was totally me. Anyway . . ."

Before I could start talking, the guy started in with the logical questions again: "Why were you doing that? Why do you bring girls in the bathroom? Where are you from that you think this is okay? Who are you here with? Why don't you go find them and leave us alone? This is a private party. Why don't you leave. We don't like playas."

Again, it reminded me of that Edward Norton monologue from *Fight Club* where he talks about everything seeming distant with the volume turned down after you've experienced fight club. The same holds true with nimbus: the guy was awkward and embarrassing but seemed small and completely nonthreatening. So I laughed again, "Hahahahahaha-haha . . . dude, you're funny, man. I want to bring you back to New York with me. I'll pack you in my suitcase."

"Oh, you're from New York? The city or New York state? Why did you come to San Francisco? What are you doing here? What—"

"Ah dude," I blurted. "You're like Inspector Gadget with the questions! Just chill out, this is the club! HAVE FUN!"

Eventually the guy chodes off into the night. I talk to some more babes and find Jeffy. Time to venue-change. Time to shift into full creep-mode.

Out on the street Jeffy gives us new objectives. He grabs me and says, "You're going to push it in this club. You don't give a fuck and it's palpable. I can smell it on you. We're gonna do some gangster shit. You open, you isolate as soon as possible, and you go for the makeout." Full nimbus!

When we get inside, I open some throwaway sets before finding a girl who interests me: A tan cutie who probably works as an accountant or in a similar office-related capacity. She's yapping with some rotund fatty. Time for glory.

"AWESOME!" I say, getting the girl's attention. "Aweeeeeee-somm-mmme!!!" (My contribution to "the community" will be my "Awesome Plowing" opener. It involves screaming "AWESOME" to reflect your inner-awesome state.)

My tan cutie responds with "AWESOME!!!!!" Yeah! It's on. I drop my Midas Touch of Fuck on her and tell Fatty that Tan Cutie's my new San Fransisco girlfriend. Fatty is flabbergasted. Jeffy comes in to wing me. I pull Tan Cutie away and parade her around the venue. Fatty is still flabbergasted. Some chode tries to pull Tan Cutie away from me. But the Midas Touch of Fuck is too strong. Chode removes his hand like it's been seared on a hot stove.

I take Tan Cutie to what Jeffy told us is "the makeout spot." I go for the tonguedown. Tan Cutie scolds me: "You don't try to kiss a girl after knowing her for five minutes!"

My reply was simple: "Yes you do."

She laughs and says, "Wow! You're very aggressive . . . and I like it!" That confirmed and articulated everything I've learned over the course of the evening.

"Cool." I smile, go for the tonguedown again and get it. We start moving into a Stage 3 tonguedown. Boners away!

Suddenly a hotel chode rolls up and scolds us. He tells us we can't do that and we can't linger in "the makeout spot." We find a bedlike thing in the lobby and have a lovestruck conversation. We call each other on our cell phones and talk. We figure out the names we will give our children. I go for the makeout, but she turns her head. Hotel chode made her uncomfortable. I plow, go for the makeout a second time.

"Why are you so impatient," Tan Cutie inquires. "I'm going to fuck you later. Just wait, I'm going to jump you once we're alone."

Epiphany-town. I've never had a girl so matter-of-factly tell me "We're having sex." It was almost as if she was annoyed she had to state it out loud, as if this was all implicit and understood by both of us. This is what sex-worthiness looks like. It looks glorious.

Then disaster strikes. Suddenly Fatty from Hell appears in all her rotund misery.

"Your friend Jeff is a liar," she informs me. "I don't like him."

I laugh because this so hilariously laughable.

"I'm a total bitch," she continues. "And I don't like you either. I'm also a cockblock."

I laugh, but I also sort of want to punch this girl in the face. As if she senses this, she pulls a wad of gum from her mouth and hovers it over my cowboy boots. She starts laughing and says she's going to squish it on my leather boots.

"What the fuck is your problem?" I yell. "Why the fuck are you acting like this?"

"I'm a total bitch," she repeats. I realize, even based on this short interaction, this girl has cracked my top ten list of the Most Miserable and Abominable People I've Ever Met.

I try to ignore her as if she were an annoying male but she keeps grabbing my girl and saying dumb shit like reminding her she's driving her home tonight so she can't go home with me. Then the two of them start doing weird secret girl hand motions, so I get up to leave. Fuck this shit. My girl grabs me and apologizes, asks me to hold on a second. A second becomes five minutes. I'm sitting there like a tool.

Finally I've had enough: "Look. Come to my hotel room now. Or I'm going to find my friends."

"Maybe," my Tan Cutie says with a coy smile.

"Cut the maybe bullshit. Yes or no."

"NOOOOOOOOOOOOOOOOO!!!!!!!" Fatty screams. I've had enough; I tell Tan Cutie it was a pleasure meeting her. Maybe I'll text her later. I have to physically restrain myself from slugging Fatty.

The rest of the night featured more tonguedowns and glory, but nothing very educational so not worth mentioning. Ultimately, we ended up at a diner to debrief and end the most insanely awesome night of my life."

—Rob O., New York

"During debrief, I filled out an instructor evaluation form. One question: 'What could the instructor have done to make the program better? Even if you loved it, what could have made it MORE awesome?'

"I have no clue. Maybe if they taught me to fly like Superman. It was easily the best time I have ever had. EVER. Best weekend of my life. Glory times are there to be had. You just have to step up and make it happen.

"Should you take a Bootcamp? Is this a serious question? Don't be a moron."

—Mark N., Seattle

"This by far was the BEST weekend of my life. Several of my wings have taken Bootcamp with Jeffy and seeing them before and then after they've taken a Bootcamp—seriously, afterwards they were like new people. I can say the same for myself; I've got the BELIEF when I walk up to chicks.

"I would highly recommend Bootcamp to anyone and seriously my biggest regret is not taking one earlier as I feel that my improvement would have been even more DRASTIC and probably have shaved some time to reaching the level that I want to reach. Jeffy's given me pretty much all the tools to make my game disturbing."

—K.A., New Jersey

"I've been in the field for about 15 months and using multiple outlets to try and get this area handled. Jeffy's Bootcamp in San Francisco was definitely not the first investment that I made in my journey to get good . . . but it was probably the most worthwhile. The adventure was amazing. I flew across the country and met a great girl who I spent a night with. I felt a new sense of motivation, and thought about how I was going to get this down solid and then GO ON A TEAR. I could travel the world meeting people and doing this . . . I have no reason to not OWN this.

"Reflecting on the weekend, I realize how much my reality has been blown open. The experience would've read like a fairy tale to me a year ago. School's out, bitches, it's time to step up and do this."

—Van S., New York

"The true value of this program is seeing it done live. After seeing it done live a few times I truly realized, 'Hey I could do this.' Then I did it in the field with instant feedback from the coaches.

"I had listened to a bunch of tapes so I felt like I had a base level of understanding. This workshop went WAY beyond that into exact step by step specifics for every phase of a pick up. I'm in my midthirties, going bald and have glasses yet the second night of the Bootcamp I had an 8.5 hitting on me after using some of the methods and material I had just learned."

—Mike T., San Francisco

"The RSD Bootcamp with Jeffy was an incredible, life changing experience which made me realize that intense, focused effort really does produce results. Jeff and Brendan proceeded to blow my mind and change my entire paradigm in terms of how I view the game. All of the key concepts in game are covered in great detail and there is a good balance between theory and fieldwork. The instructors are genuinely interested in everyone's progress, pay close attention to students, and provide both encouragement and valuable feedback which helps you get to the next level as quickly and effortlessly as possible.

"Jeffy's experience teaching Bootcamp for over six years shows—he hones into your problem areas and helps you make the adjustments necessary to propel your game further in three days than you might in six months or a year of going out by yourself. These guys love what they do and it shows. Jeffy could give any of the big motivational gurus a real run for their money—I walk away inspired and determined to change my life."

—Max, New York

"My brain felt like it was on speed the entire weekend. That's how intense the Bootcamp was. If you haven't taken a Bootcamp, I seriously suggest you do. It is an incredible experience . . . it was a fun experience. It taught me that pickup is not something you do, but something you are. All in all, the Bootcamp was crazy, and spending a weekend 'sarging' with Jeff was awesome."

—Romein R., Arizona

"I'm no longer plugged into the social Matrix. I had to just let go. They pushed me past my breaking point. Opened my eyes. Though I still have much more to improve . . . I can't wait. Three years ago I was in my little 20,000 people Missouri town. Sulking over my girlfriend who had dumped me. Now look at me, pimping hos in NYC with some of the coolest guys I've ever met. So I say this to anyone who wants to listen: You want to change your life? You feel like something's missing? Like you have no purpose? Do something about it!!! Take an RSD Bootcamp!!! It's way more than just pickup."

—Joshua M., New York

"Ten months post-Bootcamp: I have gone out five times in the last nine weeks and have gotten laid each time. These are all same night pulls. Last night's girl was a 6 foot, 22 year old Swedish nanny. Hmmmmm good.

   "Can I connect the dots for a moment here? Jeffy seriously helped. There were others, but he was instrumental. If you are thinking about it, then do it."

—Tom, San Francisco

ABOUT THE AUTHOR

Jeff Allen has been employed as an Executive Coach with Real Social Dynamics since 2003. During that time, he has conducted life-changing Bootcamps practically every weekend in cities all over the world, taking clients "in the field" to receive live, firsthand instruction on meeting and attracting women. At the time of this writing, it is likely that he has administered more live programs of this type than literally anyone else on the planet. He possesses an extreme passion for teaching and this is reflected in the dramatic, lasting results enjoyed by his students. In 2007, he recorded *The Jeffy Show,* a six-hour DVD program. He is a regular contributor to the Real Social Dynamics online forum and writes weekly articles for the free RSD newsletter e-course. He continues to travel extensively, conducting seminars and Bootcamps.

He lives in San Francisco, California.

Printed in the United States
By Bookmasters